Thomas Hutchinson

Two Years in Peru

With Exploration of its Antiquities

Thomas Hutchinson

Two Years in Peru
With Exploration of its Antiquities

ISBN/EAN: 9783741183577

Manufactured in Europe, USA, Canada, Australia, Japa

Cover: Foto ©Andreas Hilbeck / pixelio.de

Manufactured and distributed by brebook publishing software (www.brebook.com)

Thomas Hutchinson

Two Years in Peru

TWO YEARS IN PERU,

WITH

EXPLORATION OF ITS ANTIQUITIES.

BY

THOMAS J. HUTCHINSON, F.R.G.S., F.R.S.L., M.A.I.

VICE-PRESIDENT D'HONNEUR DE L'INSTITUT D'AFRIQUE, PARIS;
FOREIGN ASSOCIATE OF THE PALÆONTOLOGICAL SOCIETY OF BUENOS AYRES;
ONE OF THE ORGANISATION MEMBERS OF THE SOCIETY OF FINE ARTS IN PERU;
AUTHOR OF "IMPRESSIONS OF WESTERN AFRICA,"
"THE PARANA AND SOUTH AMERICAN RECOLLECTIONS," &c., &c., &c.

WITH MAP BY DANIEL BARRERA, AND NUMEROUS ILLUSTRATIONS.

IN TWO VOLUMES.
VOL. I.

London:
SAMPSON LOW, MARSTON, LOW, & SEARLE,
CROWN BUILDINGS, 188, FLEET STREET.
1873.

TO HIS EXCELLENCY

SENOR DON MANUEL PARDO,

PRESIDENT OF THE REPUBLIC OF PERU,

THE ADVOCATE OF PROGRESS,—SCIENTIFIC, INDUSTRIAL, AND COMMERCIAL,—

AS WELL AS THE INAUGURATOR OF A NEW ERA IN THE GOVERNMENT OF HIS COUNTRY,

THESE PAGES ARE RESPECTFULLY DEDICATED,

BY HIS OBEDIENT, HUMBLE SERVANT,

THE AUTHOR.

PREFACE.

So many works have been written and published about Peru—from the MSS. of the lawyer Polo de Ondegardo, A.D. 1550, and the fabulous trumpeting in the Commentaries of Garcilasso Inca de la Vega, A.D. 1609, down to the "goody-goody" pages of Dr. Baxley, in 1865—that another may be considered a superfluity.

But Peru has still, within her territory, a mine of archæological lore, as inexhaustible as her treasures of silver and gold. Every one, therefore, who can add his share to the general stock, helps, as Mr. Gladstone happily expresses it, "to piece together, as children do with a pattern map, the fragmentary annals of the past," and needs no excuse for presenting his mite to the public.

Such an immense amount of error, and exaggeration has been pressed into nearly every volume on Peru which I have read, that I find it difficult to guess, where imagination ends, and reality begins. The whole aim and end of the early Spanish writers seem to have been to puff the Incas as so many "inimitable Crichtons"—to represent them as grand, and perfect in everything —in the discipline of their government, their laws, hospitality, arts, and unlimited treasures of gold, as well as silver. I do not insinuate they did this to attribute more glory to the few hundred soldiers under Pizarro, who subdued the Inca empire. But in doing it, they tried to wipe out all knowledge of the tribes, who occupied Peru previous to the Inca period. So that it is chiefly from what we see of their architecture, and their fine arts, that we have any knowledge of these prehistoric people, nearly all of whose works are erroneously credited to the Incas. All these golden treasures from Chan-Chan, wrought by the Chimoos; the exquisitely dyed cloth from the burying-ground at Huacho; the great forts erected behind the modern Trujillo, as well as those at Chatuna, near San José,—at Parmmunca,—in the

Huatica valley, within a few miles of Lima,—at Pacha-Cámac, Cañete, and several other places— are set down by every one to the credit of the Incas. Whilst the latter had no more to do with them, except in hastening their destruction, than any of my readers has had to do with the building of ancient and historic Troy.

It may be scarcely necessary for me to state that, when I first went to Peru in April, 1871, I was in the Inca groove, like most people who take an interest in Peruvian literature. But as soon as I examined,—inquired,—observed,—by travelling along the coast from Arica to San José—a seaboard of beyond a thousand and ten miles— interior farther than Arequipa,—to Ica,—through the Jejetepeque valley,—and up to Maçhucana, I felt convinced that the relics of art and architecture, between the first line of Cordilleras and the Pacific, belong to a time far and away before that of the Incas. Moreover, there appears to me no evidence of the Incas having ever done anything in the parts just named, but to destroy and blot out. The reputed Temples of the Sun, behind Trujillo and at Pacha-Cámac—both visited by me—I believe to be mythical as to accredited character; and the fortress at Paramunca (in the absence of further proof than the *ipse dixit* of Garcilasso de la Vega, or Dr. Mariano Edward Rivero) I cannot consider as ever having been built to celebrate the Inca's victory over the King of the Chimoos, but to have been erected and garrisoned by the Chimoos themselves. An accurate examination of the large forts, as well as the colossal huacas—rivals with the pyramids of Egypt—in the neighbourhood of Lima, confirms me more and more in these points of faith. But every reader will, of course, claim the privilege to judge for himself, from the facts that I place before him.

I therefore confine myself, as much as possible, in the following pages to what came under my own personal observation;—rigidly avoiding that tendency to gasconade, and magnify, which the proximity of the towering Andes seems to communicate, by endemic sympathy, to all those who come within the influence of their shadows.

For the indefatigable aid, and assistance, in my explorations, rendered by my young friend Mr. J. B. Steer, who, as a naturalist, was travelling for the University of Michigan—and a proud Alma Mater it should be too if it have many sons such as he! —I cannot find words to express my thanks. He accompanied me through the Huatica valley, as well as amongst the ruins about Chosica, and at Pacha-Cámac,—doing such work with the pick-axe and spade as only a man of iron constitution, and with sympathies in the task, could do.

To Doctor Don Antonio Raimondi, of Lima—one of the most eminent scientists in Peru—I am deeply indebted, for the loan of numerous works of reference, and objects of Art from the Museum of the Facultad de Medicina, as from his own private collection. For a like obligation, I return my thanks to Senor Don Miceno Espantoso, one of the directors of the National Bank of Peru.

The excellent photographs, taken especially for this work, by Mr. V. L. Richardson, of Lima, will speak for themselves. The same may be said of the pencil sketches,—chiefly of ruins in the Huatica valley,—by a young artist, native of Bolivia, Senor Don José Maria Zaballa. And lastly, the etchings of Pacha-Cámac, by Mr. John Schumaker, of Valparaiso, must not be forgotten.

There are two coincidences in this work on which I desire to remark here. The first refers to the fact of having introduced amongst the chapters about Calláo, considerable extracts of my reports on its trade—that for 1870-71, as well as that for 1872—although these were published amongst the Commercial Reports from her Majesty's Consuls, received at the Foreign Office, and presented by command of the Queen to both Houses of Parliament. I have made this transfer as well,—because they are the first Consular Reports on the subject of trade in Calláo, that were published up to the time of their appearance in the respective dates named,—as that I hope to introduce the features of Peruvian commerce to a wider circle of readers, than is generally supposed to be conversant with the literature of Blue Books.

By the second I have to explain, that some articles from my pen, inserted in the *Calláo and Lima Gazette*, as well as in the *South Pacific Times*, during my residence in Peru, have been introduced into the parts of this work, to which they correspond. Of these newspapers—so useful to the English-speaking community, as to the interests of Peru (at home and abroad)—the latter-named supplanted the former; and both were established by Mr. Lawton during my residence in Calláo. But all the extracts taken therefrom (except where quoted in the usual orthodox mode, with inverted commas), are limited to my own contributions, and in every article, where needed, are abridged or corrected.

To conclude. Peru, under the administration of her citizen President, has entered on a new era. The coming to power of a man so enlightened as Don Manuel Pardo, and the annihilation of the military despotism, which has hitherto kept the Republic in the background, are hopeful presages. With these we have the daily-increasing commercial spirit, chiefly called into life by the Pacific Steam Navigation Company's able, and indefatigable manager, Mr. George Petrie. Through the inexhaustible energy and enterprise of Mr. Henry Meiggs, Peru has a greater length of railways than any other South American Republic, or even than Brazil. She has reformed municipalities,—made grants for bringing out schoolmasters from Europe,—is putting forth educational and scientific schemes,—proposes outlay for immigration purposes,—and through Congress, as well as her Executive, is presenting to the world the *tout-ensemble* of a regenerating progress,—needing only the security of permanent tranquillity to make her hold a primary position amongst the nations of the world.

London, November 1st, 1873.

CONTENTS OF VOL. I.

CHAPTER I.

Outward from Liverpool.—Unusual smoothness of the Irish Channel and Bay of Biscay.—To Bordeaux, Lisbon, and Rio de Janeiro.—Passing the Rio de la Plata, and entering the Straits of Magellan.—La Colonia.—Patagonians and Fuegians.—Peculiarities of scenery passed through.—Colonia or Punta Arenas.—Murder of British sailors.—Missionary enterprise at Tierra del Fuego.—Admiral Fitzroy's description of the natives.—Gold at Colonia.—Civilization of boots.—Beauty of mountains and of glaciers.—Ancient explorers.—Loss of prehistoric Indian titles.—*Reductio ad absurdum* of Darby Cave .... 1—15

CHAPTER II.

Misnomer of Pacific.—Geographical extent of Chile.—Chiloe and adjoining Archipelagos.—Valdivia and Lord Cochrane's bravery.—Coronel and the coal mines at Lota.—The Arauco country and the Araucanian tribes.—Arrival at Valparaiso.—Its bombardment by the Spanish squadron in 1860.—Earthquakes in Valparaiso.—Cleanliness of the city.—The Resguardo, Exchange, and tramway.—Foreigners' club-house and market-place.—Drive to the railway station.—The Estero de las Delicias.—Excellent arrangements of this station.—Scarcity of water in Valparaiso.—Waterworks established by Mr. William Wheelwright.—Railway traffic trebled since 1855.—First triumph of Mr. Henry Meiggs . 16—31

CHAPTER III

Trip to Santiago, the capital.—Stations of Quilpué, Limache, and Quillota.—Ormskirk and Shrewsbury reminiscences.—The Maipú bridge and tunnel.—Entrance to Santiago.—The Southern railroad and hills.—Poplar-trees everywhere.—Square squares.—The Alameda.—Zoological Gardens.—The Museum and its fluffy birds.—Cathedral and arcades.—Burning of Jesuits' Church in 1863.—Monument.—Burning of theatre.—Atrocious insult to Charles Dickens.—Foundation of Santiago in A.D. 1541.—The Mapoche Indians destroy it.—What they left behind.—Connexion of Earl Dundonald with Chile.—Bravery of his eldest son.—Attempted assassination of Lady Cochrane.—Seizing treasure of San Martin's.—Reinstatement in his former honours by Queen Victoria . . . . 32—45

CHAPTER IV

From Valparaiso northwards.—Chilian labourers.—Approaching Peruvian boundary line.—Mr. Squier's description of its peculiar physique.—Explanation by Señor Raimondy of rain never falling on the coast of Peru.—Trade of Iquique.—Exports therefrom.—Tarapaca province.—Railways from Iquique to Noria.—New export law of saltpetre.—Arica and its last earthquake.—Consul Nugent's account of the catastrophe.—Wave fifty feet high.—Corresponding earthquakes elsewhere.—The dead forced out of their graves.—Ships driven on shore.—Relief to the sufferers.—Tacna railway.—Ilo and Moquegua railway . . . . 46—67

CHAPTER V

Towards Cuzco.—Grandeur of its edifices.—General Miller's description.—Stories about gold.—Ancient roads mentioned by Prescott.—Modern railroads made by Mr. Henry Meiggs.—From Mollendo to Arequipa.—Lively night at hotel in Mollendo.—Concession for the Arequipa railroad.—From Ensenada onwards.—Steep gorge.—Pampa of Cachenda.—

Large amount of rolling-stock.—Valley of Tambo and station.
—Quebrada of Cahuntula.—Serpentine curves.—Station of
Vitor.—La Joya.—Sand-heaps.—Huasamayo.—Onishuarani.
—Watering-place of Arequipa.—Tingo.—Sachaka . 68—85

CHAPTER VI.

At Arequipa.—Excellence of its station arrangements.—Hotels of
Arequipa.—The Soroche and Surumpi.—Rarefied atmosphere.
—Earthquaky look of Arequipa.—Appearance of cathedral.—
Number of monasteries.—Heavy rains here.—The Misti volcano.—The Sillar trachyte.—Celebrated men of Arequipa.—
Derivation of its name.—Story of first settlement.—Railways
of Mr. Henry Meiggs.—Reflections on their success.—From
Arequipa on the road to Puno.—Mineral wells of Yura.—
Station of Quisco or Aguas Calientes.—Hospital here.—
Magnetic stone at Cacchipastana .... 86—100

CHAPTER VII.

Return from Arequipa.—From Mollendo northwards.—Islay.—
Exports thence.—The Chincha people.—The Chincha Islands.
—Idols found here at depths of thirty-five feet, and sixty-two
feet under guano.—Guesses at the antiquity of these.—Royal
emblems from under the guano.—First discovery of guano on
the Chincha Islands.—Pisco railway.—Pisco town.—Monotony of railroad to Ica.—Peruvian sandwich.—Burial-mounds
at Ica.—Urn with disarticulated skeleton.—Foundation of
Ica.—Aqueducts of the aborigines, falsely attributed to Incas.
Garcilasso de la Vega.—First coast invasion of the Incas made
in the valley of Ica.—Silver work of art from Ica. 101—127

CHAPTER VIII.

The valley of Chincha.—Tambo de Mora and Cañete.—Cerro
de Anil roadstead.—Chuquimancu sugar estates in Cañete
valley.—Necessity of exploring the ruins about here.—Creation of Society of Fine Arts by President Pardo.—Exhuming

xviii   CONTENTS.

skulls from the Cerro del Oro.—Particulars of things got out.
—Bocina, or shell-trumpet.—Ride through the Cañete valley.
—Chinese labourers here.—Their joss-houses.—Prescott's
opinion of Garcilasso de la Vega.—Progress of the invading
Incas through Cañete valley.—Huarcu and Runahuanac.—
Reputed Inca fortress at Hervay.—Olives from Seville.—
Vessels of Pacific Steamship Company.—Limits of Callao
jurisdiction . . . . 128—146

CHAPTER IX.

Inca progress to Pacha-Cámac and Rimac.—Account of it by
Garcilasso de la Vega.—Cuys Mancu, or Hatun Apu, Lord
of Pacha-Cámac, and valleys adjacent.—Temples of Pacha-
Cámac, and Delphic Oracle of the Rimac.—Message sent to
Cuys Mancu.—Machiavellianism of the Incas.—Craft of
Cupac Yupanqui.—Treaty of the Incas with the Yunca chiefs.
—Conditions of same.—Unconditional surrender of Cuys
Mancu.—The Devil coming to have a finger in the pie.—
Cieza de Leon.—Author's visit to Pacha-Cámac.—Cyclopean
work.—Mr. Steer's tracking.—Evidence of niches for idols, as
of sacrificial fires, in supposed Temple of the Sun.—Skulls
with sutures in the frontal bones.—General conglomeration
of ruins.—Unsatisfactory results.—What Stevenson says of
Pacha-Cámac.—Wonderful messengers . . 147—176

CHAPTER X.

Callao Bay.—Earl Dundonald and the island of San Lorenzo.—
Cutting out of the "Esmeralda."—The concrete works of
Mr. Hodges.—Pacific Steam Navigation Company.—First
appearance of steamboat on the Pacific.—Earliest report of
Pacific Steam Navigation Company in 1843.—Hardihood of
directors.—Present status of Company.—Organization in
Callao.—Programme of sailings.—Large trade created by it.—
Additional steam lines.—Floating-dock of Callao.—Original
establishment.—Utility to Pacific shipping.—Muelle y Dar-
sena (mole and dock); great work of Brassey and Co.—Callao

trade for 1872.—Imports and exports.—Guano existing in deposits.—Amount of supply for future.—No fear of Government securities.—New discoveries of nitrates and of silver mines.—Immense increase of Custom-house receipts.—Port dues . . . . 177—218

CHAPTER XI.

The "Painter" at Callao.—Its different appearances.—Analysis of water during its existence.—Extent of "Painter" on the whole coast of Peru.—Author's observations of appearances of water.—Frezier's writings about Callao.—Earthquake of 1740. —Number of convents and of chapels.—Dreadful effects of earthquake.—On shore at Callao.—Lima and Callao railroad. Club at Callao.—The royal fort.—Its great size and extent.— Fight for independence.—Bombardment of Callao by Spanish fleet in 1866.—The native hospital in Callao.—Revenue of Beneficencia Society.—Hospital tax on shipping.—Silver in Peru.—Misfortunes of 1868.—Parish of Santa Rosa.—La Punta . . . . 219—240

CHAPTER XII.

Hygiene of Callao.—Mr. Paz Soldan's calculations of increase of population.—Mortality at the native hospital.—Excess of deaths over births in the town.—Census of population.— Chinese immigration.—Mortality of Chinese immigrants in the middle passage during the last decade.—Mortality of same in 1871 and 1872.—Law of Congress prohibiting Chinese immigration in 1856.—Its reauthorization by Congress in 1861.—Particulars of contracts.—Mission of Peruvian embassy to China.—Existing convention between Peru and Portugal, touching emigration from Macao.—Coolie immigration to the West Indies.—Sir G. Young's paper on the subject.—Difference of mortality in Guiana and Callao.— Speculators in the Chinese immigration.—National Company of Navigation.—Its intended extensive monopoly.—Decree revoking the concession.—New bill for import duties.— Monopoly of nitrate of soda.—Guano from Mejillones.— General resumé of railroads in Peru.—Drainage of Callao by Mr. Clarke . . . . 241—269

CHAPTER XIII.

From Callao through the Huatica valley.—Bella Vista.—
Viceroy's palace.—Custom-house stores.—Spasmodic efforts to
make suburban residences.—Ruins of old city of Huatica.—
Ruins of castles, temples, and fortresses.—Señor Centoni's
pamphlet about water-supply.—Tracking the Panilo burial-
mound (huaca) by Mr. Steer.—Measurements converging to
multiples of 12.—Extraordinary dimensions.—Made up of
small sun-dried bricks.—Masses dislodged by earthquake.—No
notice of these things by Rivero.—Huaca de la Campana
(Marengo or Arambulo).—Legend about this mound.—Characteristic features of architecture.—Filled up with earth.—
Fortress entitled San Miguel.—Adjacent temple.—Wedge-
shaped walls.—Fortresses to protect old city and burial-ground.
—Ancient temple of Delphic Omelo Rimac . . 270—286

CHAPTER XIV.

Fortresses near Señor Osma's quinta.—Fortress of Garmendi.—
Village of Magdalena.—Ruins of temple in four groups.—
All filled up with clay.—Relics of Rimac temple.—Immense
extent of enclosure.—Turkey-buzzards amongst the ruins.—
Country residence of Viceroy here.—Railroad from Lima to
Magdalena.—Iconoclastic barbarity.—Bad roads.—Warra-
cocheo Castle.—Chacra of Conde de San Isidro.—Painting of
San Isidro.—Winged Seraph at the plough.—Burial-mound
of Pan de Azucar.—Partial exploration of it.—Articles found.
—Senor Raimondy's opinion.—Measurement of this huaca.—
Burial-mound of Juliana (Ocharán).—Enormous structure.—
Multiples of 12 repeated.—Enclosure of half a million square
yards, or 117 acres.—Mr. Steer's calculations.—Adobes forming
the mound.—Cave of hermit burned by the Inquisition in
1673.—Mira Flores.—Chorillos.—The friar's leap.—The hereditary donkeys—Central part of Chorillos . . 287—303

CHAPTER XV.

Lima.—The "City of the Kings."—Number of authors who have
described it.—Foundation by Francisco Pizarro, the conqueror.

—Its former wealth.—Streets paved with blocks of silver.—
Confounding calculations.—Knocking down of the old walls.
—Boulevards made by Mr. Henry Meiggs.—Want of fire-
places in Peruvian houses.—Principal plaza and cathedral of
Lima.—Body of Pizarro in the vaults.—Doubts of its genuine-
ness.—Place of assassination of Pizarro.—Palace of the
Executive.—Plaza de la Independencia.—Bolivar's statue.—
Chambers of senators and deputies.—House of the Inquisition.
—University of San Marcos.—Foundation in A.D. 1576.—
Mint in Lima.—Large number of chapels.—English kings
doing duty for Incas.—Penitentiary.—Public buildings of
Lima.—Its bad hygiene.—Dr. Baxley's opinions of the im-
morality of Lima.—Author's contradiction of it.—Saya y
Manta.—Literary ladies in Lima . . . 304—330

CHAPTER XVI.

Exhibition Palace at Lima.—Inaugurated in President Balta's
time of office.—Delays in opening.—Doctor Fuentes, the
presiding genius.—Situation of the Palace.—Description of
contents, and of adjacent grounds.—Lack of archæological
subjects exhibited.—Mummies at Exhibition.—Magnificent
painting by Peruvian artist, Monteros, of the waking of
Atahualpa.—Death of the artist of yellow fever in 1868.
—Luis Medina's statues of Indian man and woman.—
Excellence of execution.—Mosaic tables from Ecuador.—
Wonderful clock by Major Don Pedro Ruiz.—Condors in
the garden.—Huacas or burial-mounds outside the walls.—
Obscure antiquity side by side with modern civilization.—
View of Callao from top of the Palace.—Absence of President
Balta from the opening ceremony.—Political storms fore-
shadowed . . . . 331—343

ILLUSTRATIONS TO VOL. I.

	PAGE
Portrait of President Pardo	*Frontispiece*
Map of Peru	—
Straits of Magellan	12
View of Crooked Reach in passing through Straits	14
Valparaiso after Spanish Bombardment of 1866	25
Resguardo at the Mole, Valparaiso	27
Plaza where Statue of Earl Dundonald is erected	28
Macqui Bridge on Valparaiso and Santiago Railway	33
Outside View of Santiago City	34
Burning of Jesuit Church in Santiago	38
Monument of the same	39
Arica the day before Earthquake of 1868	64
Arica the day after ditto	66
Barricade in Arequipa during Siege of 1867	86
Arequipa after Earthquake of 1868	90
Stone Idol from under Guano at Chincha Islands	104
Wooden Idol from do. do.	105
Another of same do. do.	106
Regal Emblems from under Guano	107
Mummy from Pisco	113
Silver Badge from Ica	126
Terra-Cotta Mask from Cañete	133
Bosina (Trumpet-shell), front view	134
The same, back view	135
Wooden Idol from Burial Mound at Cañete	139
Prehistoric Crockeryware from ditto	144
General View of Pacha-Cámac	157
Ruins of reputed Temple of Sun	159
Articles excavated at Pacha-Cámac	160

ILLUSTRATIONS.

	PAGE
View on East Side of Ruins at Pacha-Cámac	161
Same on West Side of ditto	163
Plan of Calláo Bay	218
Plan of Calláo Town and Neighbourhood	220
Calláo before the Earthquake of 1746	227
In Front of Entrance to Royal Fortress in Calláo	233
Plan of Huatica Valley	271
Ruined Walls of Ancient Huatica City	273
West View of Pando Huaca	274
East View of same	276
View of Brick-work on top of Pando Huaca	279
Part of Pando Huaca disturbed by Earthquake	280
Ruins of Arambolu Fortress	283
Sketch of same taken on the summit	284
Ruins of small Fort close to San Miguel	284
Ruins of Temple in the vicinity of San Miguel	285
Ruins of Fortress adjacent to Senor Osma's Quinta	288
Ruins of another of the same kind	289
Part of Double Wall enclosing Temple of Rimac	290
Portion of Ruins of Temple of Rimac	292
Small Fortress to left of Rimac Temple	293
Sugar-loaf Huaca at Condo de San Isidro	294
Burial Mound of Juliana (Ocharan)	296
Sketch on top of Burial Mound (do.)	299
Cave of Hermit burned by Inquisition in 1673	299
Malecon (or Promenade) at Chorillos	302
Cathedral of Lima	308
Front of Pizarro's Palace	311
Statue of Bolivar	315
Bridge of Lima	320
Penitentiary of Lima	322
Dress of Lima Ladies (Saya y Manta)	326
The same (Tapada)	327
Principal Entrance to Lima Crystal Palace	332
Exhibition Palace and Grounds	334
Mummies at the Exhibition	336
Gypsum Statue of Indian Woman	337
The same of Indian Man	339

TWO YEARS IN PERU.

CHAPTER I.

Outward from Liverpool.—Unusual smoothness of the Irish Channel, and Bay of Biscay.—To Bordeaux, Lisbon, and Rio de Janeiro.—Passing the Rio de la Plata, and entering the Straits of Magellan.—Patagonians and Fuegians.—Peculiarities of scenery passed through.—La Colonia or Punta Arenas.—Murder of British Sailors.—Missionary enterprise at Tierra del Fuego.—Admiral Fitzroy's description of the Natives.—Gold at Colonia.—Civilization of boots.—Beauty of mountains and of glaciers.—Ancient Explorers.—Loss of pre-historic Indian titles.—*Reductio ad absurdum* of Darby Cove.

OUTWARD bound from Liverpool on the 1st of March, 1871, in that fast and commodious vessel, the Pacific Steam Navigation Company's fine steamer "Cordillera," it was very difficult to realize, during the few early days of our voyage, that we were speeding through the generally-troubled waters of the Irish Channel, and across the dread Bay of Biscay.

All my previous passages of nineteen (to and from England in relation with Western Africa and South America) had been made in these latitudes, under the accompaniments (in a greater or less degree) of equinoctial gales, head-winds, and stormy seas, with their invariable sequence to me of sea-sickness. The smooth ocean, therefore, seemed now to be quite another element. How some of the new hands doubted on the morning of the third day, when, anchor being cast for a few hours in the river Garonne, six miles below Pauillac, to communicate with Bordeaux, as they talked over Dickens's graphic account of sea-sickness in his "American Notes." And the majority came to the conclusion that, if the account of Boz referred to any state of affairs in *that* Atlantic, of which we had had three days' trial, his description was only as much of a romance as any of the marvels of Baron Munchausen, or the extravaganzas of Lilliput. Such a condition, they said, as was described of the "head-wind,"[1] under which the novelist suffered, was simply a physical impossibility in the unruffled water, over which they had just passed from Liverpool.

From the Garonne to Lisbon we touch at the Spanish port of Santander—a wild-looking region, with the hills of Bilbao to the north, and those of Asturias to the south—whilst, as if in punishment of premature presumption, the "Cordillera" had twenty-four hours of regular Atlantic acrobatting between Santander and Lisbon: so much so, indeed, that not a few of the doubters felt disposed to believe in Dickens after all.

[1] "American Notes," Philadelphia Edition, p. 20.

The Pacific Company's steamers call at Santander—chiefly for the purpose of bringing out Basque, Italian, and French emigrants to the River Plate. From Lisbon, too, they carry no small contingencies of the Latin elements in the same direction.

The journey to equatorial latitudes, with its trade-winds, tornadoes, and flying fish; its phosphorescence of the sea by night, with general monotony during the day; the effect of the sun's great heat as well as extent of water, bounded by the bright blue sky; and the small speck of our steamer in such an immensity; have been so often described as not to need being repeated. The magnificent bay of Rio de Janeiro, the next place of stoppage, is familiar to all travellers in the South Atlantic. Lower down, too, in the Rio de la Plata territories,* the run of enthusiastic "gentle shepherds" and aspiring colonists has, for some years, made the Platine countries a beaten track. But when we pass the La Plata, with its broad embouchure of 300 miles across, and approach the Patagonian region,—the mysterious vicinity of Tierra del Fuego, as well as that caldron of the mariner, the terrible Cape Horn, one can scarcely help feeling that he is entering a part of the world which, to no small portion of mankind, is still a *terra incognita*.

* *Vide* Author's two works, "Buenos Ayres," &c., and "The Parana," published by E. Stanford, 6, Charing Cross, London.

When my colleague, Captain Burton, was at my house in Rosario, *en route* to Paraguay, during the year 1868, and spoke of his recent return from the West Coast of South America, he observed that "the beauty and grandeur of the Straits of Magellan were worth being shipwrecked to enjoy, if no other means of seeing them could be had recourse to." The character which all the neighbourhood bears for cold, comfortless, rugged nature, made me rather doubtful of sympathy in such an idea. But *nous verrons*.

From Monte Video downwards, the steamer's track is out of sight of land, except of a long, low bank in the province of Buenos Ayres, about 215 miles from the mouth of the Rio de la Plata, styled Mogola Spit. In four days after our starting from the capital of the Republic of Uruguay, we arrive at the entrance to the Straits of Magellan. Here we are met by the usual kind of stormy weather and huge seas, believed by many to be hereditary to Cape Horn and its surroundings,—by floating seaweed, and flying albatrosses. Here, too, we have an illustration of the grand scale on which everything of the physical world is formed on these American continents; for the entrance has more of the appearance of a large gulf, than what we are accustomed to associate with a Strait or narrow passage.

As the sun rises on the morning of the 2nd of April, the extended coast-line to the north and west of Cape Virgins is of a bright yellow hue, though bare of trees or vegetation of any kind. When we go in,—leaving Dungeness Spit to the right, and in sight of Cliff Hill, with Mount Dinero in the background,—the extent of the entrance strikes me as more palpable. For the low land to the left, laid down in the chart as Cape Espiritu Santo, or Cape Holy Ghost, appears in the early haze of day to be at least from thirty to forty miles away. But our affable second mate, Mr. Brigstock, always ready to do any calculations or find out any information for me, proves by the map that only seventeen miles and a half intervene between Dungeness Spit, and Cape Holy Ghost,—whilst from the former to Catherine Point we have merely fourteen miles and a half.

Passing Possession Bay, in which we overtake, and leave behind, a Russian war-frigate, with an admiral's pennant at her main, the "Cordillera" enters the first narrows, which constitute a channel of eighteen miles and a half in length, and at part of it only two miles in breadth from shore to shore. Then through a large water-space, called (on the right as we go along) Saint Iago Bay and Gregory Bay—on the left Philip Bay. Hence we got into the second narrows, a length of thirteen miles, and a breadth of four miles at the most contracted part from shore to shore.

From the entrance of the straits up to this on either side no sign of tree, or shrub, or life, human or animal, is visible anywhere. Save a few seagulls that only add to the utter desolation of solitude on all that extent of the coast.

Cropping up to the right, to the left, and in front, as we go along, are rocky prominences of different shapes and sizes, at times having the semblance of islands; but as we approach, the greater number of them are found connected with the *terra firma* either of the Fuegian, or Patagonian shore. For they form the projecting spurs of that great chain of volcanic wonders, which ranges from Tierra del Fuego, through the Cordilloras and Andes of South and Central America, and on beyond the Rocky Mountains, in the United States.

It was night when we arrived at Punto de Arenas, or Sandy Point, on the Patagonian shore, a distance of 125 miles from the entrance. This is a place of call for the mail steamers of the Pacific Navigation Steamship Company, on their way to and from Liverpool, and the West Coast, as high up as Callao. It is likewise a penal colony of the Chilian Government, and its whole population numbers only 850.

As our time of stopping here was very short, I did not care to go on shore, and a photograph of the place, which I subsequently procured at Valparaiso, did not cause me to feel that I had lost much in the way of sight-seeing by not visiting this dreary spot.

The Governor, Senor Don Oscar Viel, a Frenchman, whose father served under Napoleon at Waterloo, came on board, and from him I picked up a few items of information about the place. Coal has been found here, and the mine is being worked, but not, I believe, with much success as yet; chiefly because the article realized up to the present is of a rather inferior quality. Quite close to the small compound or canton is a little river, called the Arroyo de las Minas, from which gold can be gathered, as Mr. Viel informs me, "in any quantities." But unfortunately the people are too lazy, and indolent to take the trouble of searching for it, unless when the impulse or necessity for supply comes on them. As illustrative of their idleness, the Governor told me that recently he had offered to some men in the place a dollar each man (or 4s. 2d.) for a few hours' work to put coals on board a ship, but they declined to take, or rather refused to work for it. Yet within the last year 18,000 dollars' worth of gold was sent from this to England.

The jurisdiction of Sandy Point settlement, which is called the Colony, extends along the whole shore of the Patagonian side of the Straits from the Atlantic to the Pacific, and that includes a length of 312 miles.

The Governor informed me that there was an English Bishop residing at Navarin, one of the Tierra del Fuego islands—the most southern of the lot—and that he communicates from time to time, by means of a small craft at his disposal, with the Falkland Islands. I am rather inclined to think he must refer to Bishop Stanley, whose head-quarters are at the Falkland Islands, but who may now and then visit Navarin.

Every one knows of the missionary enterprise to Tierra del Fuego, undertaken by Captain Allen Gardiner in 1850, and of the horrible sufferings of the party he left there, who died of starvation in 1851. Yet another expedition of the same kind was got up in 1854, which sailed from Bristol under command of Captain Parker Snow. This latter had to be abandoned, after many attempts to form a mission here. Indeed, it is very difficult to hope for success of missionary efforts amongst such people as the Fuegians are described by Admiral Fitzroy in his volume of the "'Beagle's' Adventures round the World." "The Tekeeneca," he says, "natives of the south-eastern portion of Tierra del Fuego, are low in stature, ill-looking, and badly proportioned. Their colour is of very old mahogany, or rather between copper and bronze. The trunk of the body is large in proportion to their cramped and crooked limbs; their rough, coarse, and extremely dirty black hair half hides, yet heightens, a villanous expression of the worst description of savage features. The Yakanny-Kurmy, natives of the north-eastern portion of Tierra del Fuego, resemble the Patagonians* in colour, stature, and (except in boots) in clothing. They seem now to be in the condition in which the Patagonians must have been before they had horses. With their dogs, with bows and arrows, balls (bolas), slings, lances, and clubs, they kill huanacos, ostriches, birds, and seals."

That they are getting up a taste for boots may be inferred from what they did to the legs of an unfortunate master-mariner a few weeks before our passage through, and which was thus related to me by the Governor. At the time, the English schooner "Propontis" was at anchor in the bay after returning from the scene of disaster, and without her luckless captain.

It appears that the master of the "Propontis" had his vessel anchored close to the Patagonian shore, near Cape Gallant, when some of the Fuegian Indians in their canoes came off, and were climbing up the ship's side without any previous parley. They were driven off with poles and hatchets, and, strange to say, retreated to the Patagonian beach. Stranger still, and with a sort of perverse fatuity, next morning the captain went ashore with two of his crew and a boy,—all unarmed,—to get water; landing at the distance of

* Of the Tchuelches, or true Patagonians, the reader may see a memoir of mine about them read at the Ethnological Society, London, Professor Huxley in the chair, in the year 1868, and published in vol. vii. of "Transactions," p. 313.

only a few hundred yards from where the Fuegians disembarked. Some days passed; none of the party returned; and the boat had likewise disappeared from the part of the beach to which it had been attached. The mate went in search, when he found, not very far from where they had landed, the four bodies murdered, and dreadfully disfigured; the unfortunate captain with his skull stove in as if from a club,—a deep wound in his side, from which had come out his life-blood, and his legs cut off. This last was supposed by the mate to be accounted for by the fact, that he was the only one of the party who wore sea-boots.

We were under way again at eleven p.m., and steamed along the channel at half-speed. It was bright moonlight; and, indeed, under no other circumstances could such a tortuous navigation be effected during the night.

At six o'clock next morning we entered English Reach, and passed close to where the hapless master of the "Propontis" had been murdered. Here, and for a considerable distance forward, the channel is not more than from three quarters of a mile to a mile across. But it seems to me doubtful whether I should write of the mountain scenery around as beautiful and picturesque, or as savagely wild in the desolation of its aspect. Now we have all the hills in the background, covered with snow to their peaks, whilst those near to the sea are clothed with stunted brushwood down to the water's edge; ravines, valleys, cliffs, glaciers, boulders, as well as islands, creeks, and bays on both sides. Whilst the rising sun makes the snow-capped mountains, in many places, appear as if they were decked out with shining laminæ of silver and gold. The beauty and variety of colours, caused by the refraction of the sun's rays on the snow, combined with the varying shade from cloud, and rock, and tree, together with the sombreness of ravines, where the dark green of brushwood muffled the solar light, was pretty in the extreme. Many of the mountain-tops, away in the distance, glistened as if they were fretted with diamonds, whilst the sun was rising a little higher. Passing by Whale Creek we saw the effect last mentioned in its most perfect beauty.

A little farther on there appeared, at the southern side, in a small bay, a column of smoke, indicative of a fire being lighted up. This was on the Fuegian shore; but no sign of humanity was anywhere. As we proceed, the black heads of seals occasionally pop over the water, whilst now and then one or two of the paddle-wheel ducks are seen at a distance.

Around the upper end of English Reach, there appears in front, and as if blocking up our passage, a mountain mass of snow-capped pinnacles of various heights, on which the sun shone with a resplendent glare. This is where we enter Crooked

Reach (in which glaciers abound), by proceeding up the passage to the left of the mountain just

VIEW OF MOUNTAINS AND GLACIERS IN MAGELLAN STRAITS.

mentioned; whereas the channel to the right, though to our view backed by a lofty Cordillera, leads up to what is represented on the chart as a large bay, called Otway Cave, in the Patagonian territory. It is such a short reach, that, at the distance of a few hundred yards ahead, we can see no channel; and, looking back to the same distance, we seem equally land-locked behind. There is little or no snow on the hills that skirt the water, whilst those in the interior, to the very farthest range behind, are covered to their summits.

All through Long Reach, by Swallow Bay, Condesa Bay, Stewart Bay, and past Cape Notch, the mountain scenery is the same as that represented in the illustration of Crooked Reach. An excellent panorama of the journey through Magellan was done by Commander Rennedy, R.N., of H.M.S. "Reindeer," which has been photographed by Mr. Richardson of Lima.

At the end of the Reach last mentioned we turn to the left, past the entrance to the Gulf of Xaultegua, and on the left of that by which we are proceeding we skirt by what is called the Cordova Channel, which leads out at the southern end of Desolation Island* into the Pacific Ocean. On the same side of this passage is a large island, called Santa Ives, island of Sarmiento. Between Swallow Bay and Cape Notch, on the Tierra del Fuego side, are more glaciers, the dark blue, solid glitter of which has little of attraction in them. On the right-hand side of our passage here is another collection of pinnacles, to which I am told is given the name of Westminster Hall. Coming within view of Cape Pilar, in its gigantic haycock form, we see before us the Pacific Ocean; and, though much gratified at having, during some portion of my life, been able to make a transit through these Straits, I am not at all disposed to agree with Captain Burton, that there

* On this island the Pacific Navigation Company's steamer "Santiago" was wrecked in 1870.

is anything in the whole voyage, which would compensate for the inevitable discomfort, and annoyance of being shipwrecked there.

Although many a famous sea-captain has won laurels in this desolate region, since the bold Spanish navigator, Fernando Magalhaens discovered the passage in A.D. 1519, none could have had the difficulties to contend with that he encountered. The whole voyage through brings to mind memories, not only of him, but of his successors in the exploration—of Frezier, of Captain Basil Hall, Sir Francis Drake, Admiral Fitzroy, and Professor Darwin. The names of bays, points, islets, anchorages, and other topographical bearings are nearly all given by the early explorers—of Saints by the Spaniards—of more practical nomenclature by the English. But of the old pre-historic titles few are preserved. We have, however, the gulf of Xaultegua at the northern end of Long Reach, —the bay of Apuilqua, not far from Cape Ildefonso—the port of Cuaviguilga, contiguous to the latter, and the harbour of Pachachuilga to the westward of Echenique Point. To one who thinks as I do, that these old Indian names (although in cases unintelligible as to their philology) have a grand Homeric ring in their pronunciation, it may seem but a step from the sublime to the ridiculous to go from Pachachuilga as we do, through the port of Churruca to the sheltered anchorage in Darby Cove. What a pity there was not some other

Continued from A.

Continued from B.

inlet thereabouts discovered, to which the title of Joan Creek could have been given!

I was very much disappointed, as we approached the end of the Straits, at not having seen any of the Fuegians. From what I had been told by our purser, M. Ditchfield, who had often come across them, I cannot doubt their being the veriest of savages. They wear no clothing except a bit of seal-skin on the back; they live in caves and under rocks, subsisting chiefly on sholl-fish; but, when driven to famine condition, they eat their old women. They have canoes made of rushes matted together, and lined with seal-skins. Always with a fire in the canoe, the women do the paddling after the fashion of New Zealanders; their paddles are only like slices of wood. No estimate can be made of the population of Tierra del Fuego; it is guessed at 2000, but this can only be a random calculation.

Tierra del Fuego is a large archipelago, consisting of several islands, on some of which, as those of Sarmiento and Mount Darwin, are mountains of from 6000 to 8000 feet high, covered with perpetual snow.

CHAPTER II.

Misnomer of Pacific.—Geographical extent of Chili.—Chiloé and adjoining Archipelagos.—Valdivia and Lord Cochrane's bravery.—Coronel and the coal-mines at Lota.—The Arauco country and the Araucanian tribes.—Arrival at Valparaiso.—Its bombardment by the Spanish squadron in 1866.—Earthquakes in Valparaiso.—Cleanliness of the city.—The Resguardo, Exchange, and Tramway.—Foreigners' Clubhouse and Market-place.—Drive to the Railway Station.—The Fatero de las Delicias.—Excellent arrangements of this Station.—Scarcity of Water in Valparaiso.—Waterworks established by Mr. William Wheelwright.—Railway traffic trebled since 1855.—First triumph of Mr. Henry Meiggs.

ROUNDING Cape Pilar, and coming out into the ocean, I was at once impressed with the idea of this having a *lucus a non lucendo* style of name, in being called the "Pacific." It was blowing a gale worthy of the Bay of Biscay in its equinoctial mood; the sea was rough and the ship was rolling; whilst rain fell as I never saw it fall before, except on the West Coast of Africa. Not very long after going out we met the Pacific Navigation Company's steamer "Patagones," bound to Liverpool, but we only lowered our flags to each other, as the weather was too distressingly bad to stop for any other exchange of courtesies.

CHAP. II.] DARING PLAN OF EARL DUNDONALD. 17

Now we are speeding along by the southern part of Chile. This Republic has a coast extent on the Pacific of more than 700 leagues, or beyond 2000 miles. It is said to contain within its territory thirty volcanoes, none of which are permanent, but all having from time to time their episodes of eruption.

To day (April 6th) we are steaming past Chiloë, one of an archipelago of islands. There is no inconsiderable traffic between it and Valparaiso. On looking at the map I find that, since our exit from the Straits, we have passed other archipelagos, as those of the Madre de Dios, the Taytao archipelago, and the Chonos. Somewhat north of Chiloë we skirt the colony of Valdivia, where there is a large settlement of prosperous Germans.

This last-named place has, however, historic reminiscences connected with it, which no English writer should pass by unnoticed. For it was the scene of one of the most gallant exploits of a noble Englishman, whose name must ever have an imperishable halo around it on the shores of the Pacific—I mean the brave Cochrane, Earl of Dundonald.

Early in 1820,[1] and whilst fighting for the Independence of Chile, Cochrane conceived the daring plan of carrying Valdivia by storm—the place at the time being a strong Spanish garri-

[1] See "Chambers' Miscellany," vol. iii.

son. Circumstances beyond his own control had checked him at Calláo (of which I shall speak hereafter), and he now resolved on something completely in his own style. "Cool calculation," he said to General Miller, "would make it appear that the attempt to take Valdivia is madness. This is one reason why the Spaniards will hardly believe us in earnest, even when we commence; and you will see that a bold onset and a little perseverance afterwards will give a complete triumph; for operations unexpected by the enemy are, when well executed, almost certain to succeed, whatever may be the odds; and success will preserve the enterprise from the imputation of rashness." The result proved that these tactics were right. He had with him only a frigate, a schooner, and a brig. On the way down from Valparaiso he narrowly escaped shipwreck in the frigate, and only kept the vessel afloat by continual pumping—Cochrane repairing the pumps with his own hands.

Valdivia, a noble harbour, was defended by a chain of nine Spanish forts; each fort had a ditch and rampart, and the whole mounted 118 guns, manned by 1600 troops. This was, indeed, a formidable place to attack with three small ships. The forts were, however, much isolated, with very indifferent passages between them. Cochrane, therefore, planned with Miller to attack them singly, which was done with astonishing success. In truth, the Spaniards were so dismayed at the audacity of the attempt on the night of the 3rd of February, that they failed to make due resistance. Fort after fort fell to the invaders; and on the 5th, Valdivia, with the whole of the forts, surrendered to Cochrane. Large quantities of stores were captured, as well as much treasure.*

Pursuing our voyage, on the 7th of April we entered the harbour of Coronel (or the Colonel), in the Bay of Arauco, where there are coal-mines in full work. At each side of the bay in Coronel, which is almost land-locked, except from the narrow entrance at the south, the coal-mining industry is carried on with much vigour. The mines on the right-hand side, in the district of Lota, as we enter, produce from four mines 100,000 to 120,000 tons in the year. Those to the left, in the locale which is entitled Puchoco, realize 80,000 tons per annum from three mines. At Lota, mining operations were initiated in 1850, whilst at Puchoco they were not begun until 1859. There is a small town of Coronel at the Lota side, with about 3000 inhabitants. I was only for a short time on shore here, mounting up to the top

* Up to Valdivia on the Chilian side, and to Point Rosa not far below Bahia Blanca, on the Atlantic, the Chilians claim territory for the Colony,—bounded on the north by the Rio Negro, and on the south by the Straits of Magellan. This, however, is not acceded to by the Argentine Republic, for to the south of Rio Negro is the Welsh colony of Chupat, under the protection of the Buenos Ayres Government.

of a hill, overlooking the sea at the Puchoco establishment.

The country interior to this Bay of Arauco [1] is inhabited by the Araucanian Indians, whose possessions, not yet completely submitted to the authorities of the Chilian Republic, are bounded on the north by the line of fortifications of the river Malleco, the Andes to Angol, at the foot of the central range of Nahuelbuta, and towards the centre and west of that range by the new military establishments of Puren, Cañete, and Lebu; on the east by the Cordillera of the Andes; on the west by the Pacific, near to which have been founded a series of small towns all along the coast. It is finally bounded on the south by a line drawn from the *morro* (bluff) Bonifacio, at the entrance to Port Corral, in the province of Valdivia, which follows a north-easterly direction as far as the river Mehuin, and from thence in a south-easterly direction as far as the right bank of the river Callo-Calle, where it joins the Malilhue, a little to the east of the mission of Quinchilca. It continues from thence along that river to the Andes. Its northern limit is therefore situated to the south of the first line in lat. 37° 51', and its southern in lat. 39° 40'.

Fort Purco is situated to the south of the first

[1] From a pamphlet on the Araucanian territory, published in 1870, by Messrs. Cox and Taylor, of Valparaiso, "On the Araucanian Indians."

line, in lat. 38° 10', whilst the second valley of the river Cruces is occupied by civilized people as far as the village of San José, which is located in lat. 39° 28'.

The configuration of this vast territory bears a very marked analogy to the rest of the Republic. The two natural barriers which enclose it to the east and to the west—the Andes and the sea—give to it the form of a long and narrow strip, or rather that of a great parallelogram, very regular in its form.

The Araucanians consist of six different tribes—

1st. The Arribanos, or Muluches, who inhabit the slopes of the Andes, and are more ferocious than the rest of the Indians. These are the gentry who make inroads into the Argentine Republic, from the estançias of which they sweep countless herds of cattle.

2nd. The Abajinos, who inhabit the eastern slopes of the Nahuechuta range of Andes, and who are of the same *Arcades ambos* pattern as the Arribanos.

3rd. The Costinos or Luvquenches, who are found in the proximity of the Coast from Lebu southwards. These are spoken of as being very quiet people, on account of the moral force, in a physical point of view, of the various military establishments in the shape of forts, that exist to keep them in awe.

4th. The Huilliches, to the south of the Cantin.

5th. The Huilliches to the south of the Tolten. Yet it puzzles me to understand why people of the same name should be divided into two different tribes from the accidental division of a river.

Both of these last-named are agriculturists, and breed cattle—both have blacksmiths and silversmiths amongst them, and both manufacture ponchos. Further, I am told that "these tribes, from the circumstance perhaps of their inhabiting the most central part of the territory, are the most independent of all the Araucanians. It is, however, generally believed that, if colonial settlements were founded in their vicinity, it would be a comparatively easy task to bring them completely under the influences of civilization,"—a conclusion with which I regret that I cannot agree.

There is a 6th tribe, the Pehuenches, who inhabit the plains situated in the interior of the Andes, and the slopes of the Cordillera. All the tribes inhabiting the Araucania territory would seem to be of one race. They are of moderate stature, robust and well formed, agile in their movements, of a dark copper colour, and slight beards. Amongst the Maquga Boren, and others, are often found examples of extraordinary height, of fair complexion, light-coloured eyes, and such characteristics, indicating that they owe their origin to a different race from the Araucanians.

Like all the Indian nomadic tribes, their government consists of settlements, to which the Spaniards give the title of *Reduciones*. At the head of each of these is a Caçique, or chief. Under this chief is a lot of *Moçetones*, or warriors, who in times of peace attend to the practical business of agriculture, as well as to looking after the flocks and herds. Several *Caçicazos* (chieftainships united under one common head) constitute what is called a Butalmapu. But the authority of a chief of a Butalmapu is limited to the most important matters in connexion with war and its prosecution, by and with the advice and consent of the rest of the Caçiques met in *parlamento*. There is no regular order of hereditary succession amongst them, their election to posts of confidence being chiefly a matter of personal prestige.

The population of the Araucanian territory must be a matter of the wildest guess-work. I therefore decline to take the estimates from the number of lances that are accredited to each district.

Of the superstitions of these Indians, or of their religious belief, we know nothing, except that they are in the habit of consulting Machis, or wise men, to ascertain the cause of death of any one. And as death is always attributed by these sages to sorcery (Dano), it is enough to bear in mind the similarity in idea to what we know of the Egbo practices amongst the West Africans.[1]

[1] *Vide* Author's "Impressions of Western Africa." Longmans, London, 1858.

From Coronel (whence to Valparaiso there is an electric telegraph) we skirt by Concepcion, and a number of smaller ports—without touching at any of them—and in less than thirty-six hours find ourselves rounding the sharp-pointed jutting rocks that form the western boundary of the Bay of Valparaiso.

On entering the harbour it is very difficult for the stranger to conceive any aptitude in the derivation of its name—from the Spanish, *Va* (go), *al* (to), *Paraiso* (Paradise); unless indeed the frequency of earthquakes in the time of its early foundation—a frequency continuing to the present day—made its first inhabitants hopeful of getting up every morning in that heavenly Paradise where "the wicked cease from troubling, and the weary are at rest."

For here, as well as farther north in Peru, the *temblór*, or *terra-mota*, is an hereditary institution. In 1822 the town was nearly destroyed by one of these convulsions; and only a fortnight before our arrival, in the second week of April, 1871, the whole country round, from Valparaiso to Santiago, and as far south as Talca, was shaken,—to the cracking of walls, the throwing of people out of their beds, the breaking of bottles by tumbling them off the shelves, the frightening of population (chiefly the female part) into the open air, and the general appalling terror which such an occurrence engenders. A gentleman who was staying at an hotel in Santiago during the last earthquake, and whom I met here, told me that his chief idea, when roused out of sleep by the commotion, was that of somebody knocking at all the doors of the hotel. Not far from the house whereat I was temporarily stopping, the cornice of a store, which was in course of construction, had fallen down on the heads of a boy and a girl who were passing by, but who fortunately received only a trifling shock. Valparaiso is built at the base and on the side of a hill, overtopped by rugged sierras, without the shadow of vegetation. The houses above the level ground are scattered far and wide, here and there in groups, now and then in isolated dwellings.[5]

The most important topic discussed with refer-

VALPARAISO AFTER DESTRUCTION OF THE CUSTOM-HOUSE BY SPANISH BOMBARDMENT IN 1866.

[5] Twice this year (1873) Valparaiso has been twisted about—

once to Valparaiso for many years after the event
was the bombardment of the city by a Spanish
squadron under Admiral Nunez on the 31st of
March, 1866. The provoking cause of this was
said by the Spaniards to be, that the Chilian
Government had allowed Peruvian men-of-war to
be supplied with coals at the time that Peru
was in a quarrel with Spain. Some insults to
Spaniards in other parts of the world, and still
unatoned for, were likewise brought forward as
an urging cause. Valparaiso was not only perfectly unprotected, unfortified, and therefore
undefended at the time of the assault, but contained a far greater amount of foreign property
than it did of native. The fact of its bombardment under these circumstances, therefore, excited
general indignation. The Custom-house was demolished, and more than three millions' worth of
property, belonging to foreigners, was destroyed on
the occasion.

When you land at the Mole at Valparaiso, you
pass under the archway of the Resguardo or
Customs guard-house,—and, crossing into a square,
turn round to observe that the back of this
building is the Exchange. Then, proceeding
onwards, no one can fail to be struck with
the extreme cleanliness of the streets, and the

its last shock in June, amongst other peculiarities, whirling round,
on the pedestal, the statue of Earl Dundonald put up in the
previous month of February.

CHAP. II.] CLEANLINESS OF VALPARAISO. 27

excellent style of the pavement. These two are
effected by the untiring energy and activity of

RESGUARDO, OR CUSTOMS GUARD-HOUSE, VALPARAISO.

the Intendente, Senor Don Francisco Echaurren
Hindorro, Governor of the Province, and President
of the Municipality. All through the line of
street along which the tramway runs—the whole
length of the town from the Custom-house stores,
still unfinished in their revival, to the Santiago
railway station—it is the same.

Valparaiso appears like the inner or middle
layer of a sandwich—the sea on one side and the
cliffs on the other. It is, in fact, a miniature
representation of the Chilian Republic, which a
glance at the map will show any of my readers
seems but as a slice of the great South American
Continent. It may be said to have only one principal street, the southern part of which begins near

the market-place, and stretches along northward to the railway station. This is about a mile and

PLAZA OF VALPARAISO, WHEREIN EARL DUNDONALD'S STATUE HAS BEEN RECENTLY ERECTED.

a half in length, and can be done on a tramway for five cents.

As you travel along this street you see overhead, and as if ready to topple down on you, several house groups on the tops of sierras, with *quebradas* (or ravines) intervening. The sensation of looking at these, whilst remembering the possibility of an earthquake at any moment, is far from comforting to a nervous person. On one of these sierras several English merchants have their private residences. The general appearance of the shops and stores, particularly of the French and English, would do credit to any city in the world.

Water is very scarce in Valparaiso, the only certain supply being that obtained in the waterworks, and chiefly resulting from rainfalls. These were constructed many years ago by that indefatigable friend of South America, Mr. William Wheelwright, whose labours in the Argentine Republic, on the other side of the Andes, are too well known to need recapitulation. All through the main street there are many wells, but those are of salt water, and chiefly used by the firemen (of whom there are several excellent companies here) to extinguish conflagrations.

There is a foreigners' club in the city, many of its members being English. They have recently erected an excellent and commodious, as well as very handsome, club-house. Not far from the club-house is a rather small market-place, enclosed and roofed over. On the front gate is an inscription in Latin: "Domini est terra et plenitudo ejus."[*] It was erected in 1863.

Making a trip in the tramway carriage to have a look at the railway station, the cleanliness is still palpable everywhere. From street to street at the crossings there are wooden culverts, beneath which the water flows (when it is there to flow), without offending sense of sight or smell. As you come to the end of the main street, Calle

[*] "The earth is the Lord's, and the fulness thereof."

Victoria, you cross a bridge, and then turn at a right angle to the left down to the railway station. This bridge traverses a large river-bed, now dry and empty, but quite as large as the Corral bed in Madeira, before it debouches into the sea at Funchal. Here it is called the "Estero de las Delicias," or the Salt Marsh of Delights—although it is difficult for a stranger to understand the applicability of the title. Hence to its mouth, which abuts into the sea about a quarter of a mile lower down, and quite close to the station, we pass by a number of small bridges, leading over to the tramway track from the streets of the northern end of the town. These bridges are distant only about 50 to 100 yards from each other. Only a few of them are wide enough to admit any traffic except that of foot passengers. The whole course of this Arroyo, or river-bed, hereabouts is walled in with substantial masonry, to prevent the overflow which would naturally result after a great rainfall in the sierras.

The railway station is very substantial in its arrangements, although its space is rather limited, owing to the intruding of a perpendicular cliff, nearly two hundred feet high. It is excellently arranged in its ticket department, engine sheds, workshops, and goods stores, under the superintendence of Mr. Martin.' Since its first

' I regret to record that Mr. Martin died a few months after my arrival at Callao, and subsequent to my having known him here.

opening in 1855, it has more than trebled its receipts in cargo as well as in passenger traffic.

This railway was constructed under a contract between the Government of Chile and Mr. Henry Meiggs, now the famous railway king of Peru, and was one of his first great triumphs on the shores of the Southern Pacific. I use the word "triumph" advisedly, because Mr. Meiggs accomplished what has been rarely done in Spanish South America, namely, completed the work a considerable time before the period prescribed by contract had arrived.

CHAPTER III.

Trip to Santiago, the Capital.—Stations of Quilpue, Limache, and Quillota.—Ormskirk and Shrewsbury reminiscences.—The Maqui Bridge and Tunnel.—Entrance to Santiago.—The Southern Railroad and Baths.—Poplar-trees everywhere.—Square Squares.—The Alemada.—Zoological Gardens.—The Museum and its Fluffy Birds.—Cathedral and Arcades.—Burning of Jesuits' Church in 1863.—Monument.—Burning of Theatre.—Atrocious insult to Charles Dickens.—Foundation of Santiago in A.D. 1541.—The Mapocho Indians destroy it.—What they left behind.—Connexion of Earl Dundonald with Chile.—Bravery of his eldest son.—Attempted Assassination of Lady Cochrane.—Seizing Treasure of San Martin's.—Reinstatement in his former honours by Queen Victoria.

As the "Cordillera" had to remain for a week at Valparaiso, I took advantage of the occasion, and ran up to have a look at Santiago, the capital of Chile. The distance set down on the railway time-tables is 114¾ miles.

So soon as we get outside of the town, we find ourselves at once amongst the Cordilleras, which are here, as well as elsewhere, the spurs of the Andes. The morning being very clear, we had a view of the snow-capped Aconcagua, reputed to be the highest of the Andean chain. At the station of Quilpue, twelve miles from the starting-point,

LOWER BRIDGE ON VIADUCT AND REFUGE PLACE.

little boys and girls came up to the carriages with uncorked bottles of *Chicha*,[1] and holding glasses in their hands, offered the beverage for sale. When we stop at the stations of Limache and Quillota—the first being twenty-six, and the second thirty-four miles from Valparaiso—again the carriages are stormed with vendors of pears, apples, grapes, tuna, and chirimoya; the last-named being considered the unrivalled fruit of the Pacific. I know I shall be held as deficient in taste, for confessing it is a fruit that I never could esteem. But these little incidents, in the far-off country of Chile, brought me back in fancy to the gingerbread of Ormskirk, and the cakes of Shrewsbury.

From Llallai station to Montenegro, a distance of fifteen miles, we have a very steep gradient. Thence we skirt along the valley of Tabon,—rush round a precipice, over the Macqui bridge,—and into a tunnel, amongst a class of scenery, the wildness and majesty of which are very impressive.

From the tunnel to Santiago there is not much time to observe anything, as we are in an express train, and arrive in the city after a run of four hours and a half. The station has a double terminus; one being that into which we have just entered, the other belonging to a line

[1] The Chicha sold here is made from grapes; that of Peru is manufactured from Indian corn.

which goes south as far as Curico, on the road to Concepcion. The distance from Santiago to Curico is about the same as from the first-named to Valparaiso—say from 114 to 115 miles.

Down the road of Curico are to be found some of the baths for which Chile is famous, as well as a variety of magnificent scenery. Of the latter I saw beautiful photographs in Valparaiso. The baths of Cauquenes are said to resemble those of Harrogate. But there are others, as Colina, Apoquinda, and Chillian, the constituent peculiarities whereof I am ignorant.

Entering Santiago by railway to the station,

VIEW OF SANTIAGO FROM OUTSIDE.

you pass on each side a row of tall poplar-trees.

From this to the city, along the Alemada, you have two more rows of poplar-trees; and if you drive either to the Campo del Marte, or to the Zoological Gardens, you find poplar trees everywhere,—symbolical of two lines of soldiers in a state of permanent, and perpetual drill. The unbending uprightness of the poplar-trees, with the squareness of all the street blocks, makes one feel the city of Santiago to be exceedingly prim; for it is, as Dickens said of Philadelphia, "distractingly regular."

The Alemada, however, by which we go down to the city, would be very pleasant for a morning promenade if we could get rid of the perpendicular and quadrilateral ideas, which thrust themselves upon us everywhere. Standing at either end of this, and in the middle of the space between the two rows of trees, I see nothing but two parallel lines of poplars, in front of me— parallel ranges of houses—parallel azequias or water-courses, and parallel rails for a tramway. At the end no more is visible than a patch of sky, which forbids my attempting its mathematical measurement. Still, if I walk outside the line of trees, crossing the azequias and the tramway, at every 150 yards, or at the end of every cuadra, I come to the opening of another line of squares, stretching away too far for me to guess their extent, but having a poplar-tree or two at the extreme end, as if they were notes of admiration against the distant mountains, and the bright blue sky. Trying to escape from the school trammels, which all these appearances stir up, and ejaculating, "From ghostly poplar-trees, and square cuadradas, good Lord, deliver us!" I speed over the orthodox pavement, to enjoy my walk in the fresh air, and on the clean roads of the Alemada.

The Alemada is as wide, from houses to houses across, as is Sackville Street in Dublin, and whilst strolling along I can have a drink of milk from one of the many cows, that are tied up to trees in my pathway. These have been brought here for the constitutional morning tiffin of the debilitated, or the phthisical. There are several statues in this Alemada; amongst them a bronze one, in which General San Martin is mounted on a charger, pawing the air in an impracticable manner. Some few kiosks are about, dedicated to the sale of sandias (water-melons), grapes, and other fruit; and after about half an hour of rambling, I pass by the beautiful and princely quinta of Mr. Henry Meiggs, to which the title of palace would not be misapplied.

I paid a visit to the Zoological and Botanical Gardens, in both of which the poplar-tree was again too intrusive to allow me to relish anything. The Zoological collection consisted of three monkeys on one side, a sneaking jaguar of diminutive size on the other, and, not far from this, a miserable Jemmy-Dismal looking baboon.

The National Museum is in the square behind

the Cathedral; and one can scarcely help feeling the mustiness of the place to be hovering about him as he enters it. It was originally organized by the Jesuits, who here, at the present time, are only known as the Padres Francescs, or French priests. I enter through a gateway, large enough for a mail-coach to pass in; and on either side of the vestibule is a door with the word "Libreria" (Library) painted atop. These two doors are locked, and no one to be found to open them. Locked, too, is the entrance of the Museum up a flight of steps in front, after crossing over about twelve yards of a Patio. In the corridor I got a peep through a dirty window at some small stuffed birds, that appeared as fluffy and dusty, as if they had been so many cock-sparrows, in Charterhouse Square, during the fire of London in 1667.

The principal plaza of Santiago, where the Cathedral stands, is very pretty, and is rendered doubly agreeable in hot weather by having two fountains, which throw jets of water in columns of spray to the height of more than thirty feet. Of course it is the usual square—square; but the angularity of it is very much rubbed off by a circular flower parterre, protected with iron railings. From this plaza to the adjoining street runs off an arcade, crossed in its centre by another, and both covered over with glass. These are fitted up in so very much of a French style, that when they are brilliantly lighted at night with gas, one might, without much stretch of fancy, consider himself in the *passage* of the Palais Royal at Paris.

Not far from the Cathedral was, at the time of my visit, an empty space, where once stood the Jesuits' Church. In this were burnt nearly two thousand of the fair sex of Santiago, of all ranks and ages, on the night of 8th December, 1863.

BURNING OF JESUITS' CHURCH, IN SANTIAGO, DECEMBER, 1863.

They were present on that evening at the ceremonies dedicated to the Immaculate Conception of the Blessed Virgin, when some of the church ornaments took fire, and the conflagration spread with a rapidity that it was impossible to suppress. Women, naturally frightened at such an occurrence, rushed tumultuously to the doorways—of which the two that had been open were soon blocked up by the falling down of the crowd, in their impetuosity to get out.

MONUMENT TO 2000 LADIES WHO PERISHED IN THE FIRE, DECEMBER, 1863.

Those coming after, trampling on the fallen, were, by their very helplessness from terror, mingled up with the struggling mass; and still they came, and still the blocking up grew more impossible for relief; whilst the shrieks of the living and the groans of the dying made the scene to be most appalling. No help could be given from outside, and they nearly all perished miserably in the flames. The only relic of the sad catastrophe is a monument which has been erected near the spot, and beneath which the charred remains taken out were interred.

When the ruins were searched, nothing but portions of bodies in the condition of cinders was discovered; and it was melancholy, for several weeks, to hear of persons in the city every day becoming conscious of having lost personal friends or relatives. The monument says, "2000 victims, more or less."

Not far from this is the site of a theatre, where another tragedy had nearly taken place last year (1870), when the building was burnt to the ground, in about an hour after a numerous attendance at one of Carlotta Patti's concerts had left the theatre, and gone home.

Santiago is almost as remarkable for the cleanliness of its streets as Valparaiso; and I regretted very much not being able to pass more than one day here, as I wished to see it thoroughly.

Whilst waiting at the railway station till the train was ready, by which I purposed returning to Valparaiso, the name of "Carlos Dickens," yelled out by a news-boy, who had a bundle of books and newspapers in his arm, attracted my attention.

On my calling the youth, to see what works of the immortal spirit of Gad's Hill he had to dispose of, he handed me a volume in yellow paper binding, whilst again screaming out the title, "Los Bandidos de Londres, por Carlos Dickens!" ("The Bandits of London, by Charles Dickens.") I almost flung the book at him, and must confess that I, never in my life, so much thirsted to have the liberty to do anything, as to give that young whelp a whaling on the spot. Here I was obliged to content myself with preaching to him a strong reprimand, in his native dialect, for the infamy of selling such trash under the name of Dickens. How my sentiments were appreciated by the listeners may be inferred from the fact, that whilst I was lecturing the vagabond, a Chilian, who was going by the same train, came up and purchased it. So I had nothing to do but walk to the other end of the platform in disgust, and to make up my mind not to travel in the same carriage with the man who had patronized such an imposture.

The city of Santiago dates its foundation from A.D. 1541, when Señor Don Pedro de Valdivia wrote to King Charles V. of Spain that he "had populated, in the valley called Mapocho, the city of Santiago of the new extremity," on the 24th of February, 1541, constituting a Cabildo,—establishing courts of justice,—and giving it a name in honour of the apostle who was most popular amongst the Spanish adventurers of the period.

It was first peopled with about 200 colonists;

but six months had not passed away before the
adjoining Indians, of the Mapocho tribe, made an
assault on it, killing many of the settlers, and burning nearly all the houses that had been built up to
that time. These latter were made of straw, and
therefore were easily consumed. With them were
likewise destroyed by the fire all the provisions
they contained, leaving, as Valdivia reported,
"only the rags of the regimental clothing, the
fire-arms which they had on their shoulders, a
pair of young pigs, one guinea-pig, one hen, one
rooster, and no more than two breakfasts of
wheat."

But the city was soon rebuilt, and established
itself as the centre of the colony, taking precedence over the other cities that followed its
foundation.

Coming back to Valparaiso, the journey is all
down an incline, although nothing like such a
steep gradient as is the railway of San Paulo from
Rio de Janeiro. Yet between Montenegro and
Llallai, the rate at which the train went was
terrific.

The express of the morning stops at Llallai for
breakfast; and here again we have a repetition of
the Ormskirk and Shrewsbury remembrancers, in
the excellent sponge-cakes that were hawked about
at the station. At Quilloto the fruit is very
excellent, and very cheap.

I cannot leave Chile without once more recalling to mind what this Republic owes to the memory of our illustrious countryman, Lord Cochrane, Earl of Dundonald, whose prowess was one of the chief causes in enabling this people to shake off the Spanish dynasty, and establish their independence. From the memoir that I have already quoted I find that he passed four years in the service of Chile,—years of indomitable activity, and of brilliant enterprise. On one occasion, as he was about sailing from Valparaiso—whereat I am now reading of it—to commence operations against the Spaniards, he received an unexpected volunteer in the person of his eldest son[a]—a child of five years old, who had escaped from his mother's watchfulness, and appeared, mounted on the shoulders of a lieutenant, waving his little cap, and shouting, "Viva la Patria!" Nothing would satisfy him but to accompany his father, which, no doubt with considerable reluctance, he was permitted to do; and we shall hear more of him again at Callao.

Whilst Cochrane was carrying on his operations up and down the coast—capturing treasures belonging to the Spaniards on board of their ships of war, as well as intercepting treasure-trains inland—Lady Cochrane, who had taken up her abode in a villa outside of Valparaiso, was attacked one night by a Spaniard, who threatened her with instant death unless she revealed the secret orders,

[a] The present Earl Dundonald.

which had been given to her husband by the
Government. This she heroically refused to do.
She was then stabbed with a stiletto, and her
life was saved only by the prompt attendance of
servants, who secured the would-be assassin.

It appears, further, that the ending of Lord
Cochrane's career in Chile was not such as his
extraordinary services entitled him to, or as his
high and generous spirit had anticipated. He
was surrounded by men, who looked rather to
their own interests than to the welfare of their
country. General San Martin contrived to make
himself Dictator, as well as President, of Peru, and
then disavowed all obligations to Cochrane, without whose aid, I have no hesitation in saying,
he never could have assumed such a position.
Cochrane's seamen and marines were at this time
almost reduced to want, so that, nearly maddened by what was going on around him, he seized
a treasure-ship belonging to the Government
of San Martin, with nearly three hundred thousand dollars on board, and paid his poor fellows
their wages out of it, as well as supplied them
with necessaries. He kept a strict account of
these transactions to render to the Chilian
Government; but, tired out, and almost unrewarded for his exertions, Lord Cochrane quitted
the service of Chile in 1823.

Indeed, this grand old Englishman might, at that
period of his life, have lost all faith in the world,

when it is known that upon false charges[*] he was expelled from the House of Commons, his name rubbed out of the Navy List, and the Order of the Bath taken from him by his own Government, previous to his leaving England for service in Chile. It is a comfort, not only to his descendants, but to all lovers of justice and truth, to know, that the undeserved accusations which clouded his fair fame in his early manhood were triumphantly rebutted, and, thirty-nine years afterwards, he was reinstated in all his honours, as well as appointed by Her Most Gracious Majesty the Queen to command the West-India squadron.

Since the period of my visit to Valparaiso— indeed, on the 12th of February in this year, 1873 —a statue has been erected (with all the pomp and ceremony which such an occasion merited) to Lord Cochrane. It is situated in the plaza behind the Resguardo, and in front of the Exchange,—near to the Intendencia and Corporation House—the first of which is not the least noticeable of the pretty buildings in Valparaiso.

[*] Every one is cognizant of the fact, that these charges were connected with what is called the Stock Exchange Fraud of 1814, and in which he was made to appear a *particeps criminis* by the author of the fraud, a Captain de Bourg or Berrenger.

CHAPTER IV.

From Valparaiso northwards.—Chilian labourers.—Approaching Peruvian boundary-line.—Mr. Squier's description of its peculiar physique.—Explanation by Senor Raimondy of rain never falling on the coast of Peru.—Trade of Iquique.—Exports therefrom.—Tarapaca province.—Railways from Iquique to Noria.—New export law of Saltpetre.—Arica and its last earthquake.—Consul Nugent's account of the catastrophe.—Wave fifty feet high.—Corresponding earthquakes elsewhere.—The dead forced out of their graves.—Ships driven on shore.—Relief to the sufferers.—Tacna railway.—Ilo and Moquega railway.

Our steamer, when leaving Valparaiso to proceed northwards, had on board, besides the few passengers now remaining from Liverpool, over 200 Chilian labourers, to be landed at Mollendo, the seaport of the Arequipa railroad. They did not add much to the comfort of our deck-walking; but they were inevitable, so it was of no use to grumble about them. These were hired in Valparaiso by the agent of Mr. Henry Meiggs.

From Valparaiso we go along without touching at any other port of note in Chile. Indeed, the only two places to be called at in this northern passage (as far as the boundary-line at Chimba Bay between Chile and the little promontory of Bolivia, which runs out there) are Coquimbo and Caldera. Both of these are famous for their mineral productions; and the latter is noticeable as being the port at which Mr. William Wheelwright's line of Central Argentine Railway, surveyed by Mr. Campbell in A.D. 1852, was to make its exit, after crossing the San Francisco pass and through Copiapo, to the coast. After passing the Chilian boundary we go by Mejillones and the small port of Cobija in Bolivia. Then by the river Loa, which is the boundary-line separating Peru from Bolivia on the coast. In the neighbourhood of Mejillones here are the Caracoles silver-mines. These, at the time of our visit, were being negotiated by their owner, the Baron de la Rivière, who was a fellow-passenger with us on board the "Cordillera" from Monte Video.

As we enter Peruvian waters, I am reminded of what is said by the eminent North American archæologist, Mr. Squier :[1]—

"No portion of the globe has bolder or more marked geographical or topographical features than Peru. In no part of the world does Nature assume grander, more imposing, or more varied forms. Along the Pacific coast is a belt of desert, intersected here and there by narrow valleys of wonderful fertility, or relieved near the mountains by oases not less fertile. Succeeding this belt inland is the declivity of the Cordillera, notched

[1] "Observations on the Geography and Archæology of Peru." By E. G. Squier, M.A., F.S.A., late Commissioner of the United States in Peru. (A Paper read before the American Geographical Society, February, 1870, p. 4.) London: Trübner and Co., 1870.

by gorges, through which flow streams of varying size, fed by melting snows, or the rains that fall for part of the year in the interior. On the coast, except as a remarkable meteorological phenomenon, rain never falls—a fact bearing in a marked manner on the aboriginal architecture of that region. Ascending the escarpment of mountains we find a grand, elevated ridge or mountain billow, bristling with snowy and volcanic peaks, and often spreading out on broken, cold, and arid plains; or Punas (deserts), with little of life to relieve their forbidding monotony. This broad and frozen belt, called the El Despoplado (the unpeopled), varying from 14,000 to 18,000 feet in height, is succeeded, in the south of Peru and Bolivia, by the great terrestrial basin of Lakes Titicaca and Aullagas, which is shut in completely by the Andes and the Cordillera. Above, or to the northward of this, the two ranges separate again, forming the vast Andean plateau, the Thibet of America, deeply grooved by streams, which all find their way eastward into the Amazon."

The fact stated by Mr. Squier, that "rain never falls on the coast," was not interrupted by any variety of the phenomenon during my residence of two years at Lima and Callao.' As I have seen no explanation of its *rationale* with which I can agree

---

* In Mr. Markham's translation of the Travels of Piedra de Cieza de Leon, this is also explained by an extract from Captain Maury's "Physical Geography of the Sea." *Vide* Op. cit. p. 216.

so well as that given by Senor Don Antonio Raimondy in his little pamphlet on the province of Loreto. I therefore introduce it here.[1] After replying to some of what he considers erroneous ideas on this matter, he continues :—

"In my opinion, the direction of the wind is one of the principal causes of the non-falling of rain on the coast; but it is not the only one, because in this cause is likewise much concerned the formation of the ground over which it passes. To form a clear idea of these phenomena are only necessary very simple notions on meteorology. Therefore, searching the cause from its origin, I should observe, that the sea is the principal fountain source of the watery vapours spread about in the atmosphere. These evaporating from the surface are raised to a point where, the temperature being lower, they reunite, combine, and are condensed, becoming visible in the shape of clouds. The watery vapours through the atmosphere, whether invisible, or condensed under the form of clouds, must necessarily remain immovable, without the aid of winds produced by the inequality of temperature of different localities. Consequently, the winds are the medium by which watery vapours are transported to the interior of continents. A wind will therefore be more charged with watery vapour, the greater that may be the superficies of sea over

[1] "Apuntes sobre la Provincia Litoral de Loreto," p. 6.

which it has passed. But in order that a wind which comes from the sea should transport to the interior a large quantity of watery vapours, it is necessary that it should have a direction almost perpendicular to the earth. Casting an eye-glance over the map, and taking in the shape of South America with that of its coasts, it may be seen that the general form of that continent is triangular, and that at the west side it runs with very little difference from south to north. Now, if we observe the most general direction of winds that prevail on the west coast of America, it may be observed that they are almost invariably from south to north. So that the winds follow in a parallel the line of the coast. Consequently the south wind, which is charged with watery vapours from passing over a certain superficies of the sea, does nothing more than skirt the coast, without penetrating to the interior of the land. Moreover, the watery vapours, transported by the winds to the lofty and snowy regions of the Cordilleras through the lower temperature of these parts, become condensed, fall in rains, and give origin to the little rivulets which, by their union, form rivers. But these watery vapours, for the reasons before expressed, not being abundant, cannot by their condensation give origin to large streams; and we can therefore easily conceive the lack of large currents of water on the western side of the Cordillera."

Mr. Raimondy further explains how the physical formation of the continent tends to the passage of the larger quantity of wind, with its moist vapour, on account of the angularity of South America to the eastern sides; thus accounting for the heavy rains, which go to form the Amazon, the Orinoco, the Parana, and the Paraguay rivers.[*] The immense extent of sand stretching along the coast of Peru, in some places from fifteen to twenty leagues in breadth, has likewise to do with the absence of rain, because, being a good conductor of caloric, the sand, acted upon by the sun, evaporates a current of warm air, which prevents the watery vapours already spoken of from becoming condensed. In winter time, the atmosphere being, of course, colder, and the sand being a better conductor of heat than the water of the sea, becomes colder than the latter: so that its low temperature causes the condensation from which we have these fogs, so general in winter time, on the coast of Peru. These are said to be the same reasons to account for the non-falling of rain in Egypt, and the east coast of Africa.

Travelling as we are along the coast of Peru, from south to north, and wishing to visit every place of importance, I was very sorry that we did not touch at Iquique—a port which is becoming every day of more importance to British, and

[*] This is, in fact, the explanation that is given by Professor Maury, as mentioned at page 48 previous.

general commercial interests, from the extending export of its mineral salines. Iquique* suffered much by the earthquake of 1868. Of its products I copy here an extract taken from my last Report on the Trade of Callao, published in the Foreign Office Blue Book of Consular Reports for 1873:—

The reports of the exports of nitrate from Iquique show a marked increase during the last two years. For the month of July I append the following table, which indicates an increase for the same month, compared with the corresponding month in the year 1870, of 861,812 quintals:—

To—	1870.	1871.	1872.
	Quintals.	Quintals.	Quintals.
England	340,672	449,966	260,385
France	187,438	24,443	29,000
Germany	104,929	95,211	202,917
Holland	23,438	38,267	16,540
Belgium	12,200	—	—
Spain	40,643	—	—
Portugal	—	22,001	—
Italy	—	—	9,500
Order	712,675	1,022,964	1,697,168
United States	246,546	182,955	311,193
California	15,160	14,687	7,659
Chile and Coast	2,454	8,999	4,919
West Indies	—	—	18,681
Total	1,696,155	1,859,493	2,557,967

The exports of nitrate for the month of June,

* For information about the archæology of Iquique and the province of Tarapaca in which it is situated, see Bollaert's "Antiquities of Peru."

1872, amounted to 384,437 quintals against 307,240 in the same month last year.

The following is a comparative statement of the exports of nitrate from Iquique for the first six months in the years 1870, 1871, and 1872, respectively. The increase is prodigious, being 805,624 quintals over the corresponding period of 1870, and 678,658 over the same month in 1871:—

To—	1870.	1871.	1872.
	Quintals.	Quintals.	Quintals.
England	299,663	382,698	200,385
France	168,172	24,443	20,000
Germany	90,586	67,822	202,917
Holland	23,438	21,267	16,540
Belgium	12,200	—	—
Spain	40,643	—	—
Portugal	—	22,001	—
Italy	—	—	9,500
To Order	565,240	854,637	1,423,434
United States	199,550	154,492	240,107
California	15,160	8,082	7,658
Chile and the Coast	1,254	7,440	4,318
West Indies	—	—	18,681
Total	1,415,916	1,542,882	2,221,540

At the beginning of this current month (August, 1872), the prices quoted were dol. 2·55 Chile currency in Valparaiso, but they have since then somewhat declined.

The following represents the total exports of the years indicated up to the 30th of November, 1872; as before, the numerals being quintals, or 100 lbs. weights:—

To—	1870.	1871.	1872.
	Quintals.	Quintals.	Quintals.
England	528,379	661,166	393,700
France	227,115	53,043	92,895
Germany	111,929	180,888	217,917
Holland	23,438	47,537	16,540
Belgium	12,200	—	—
Spain	40,643	14,256	6,000
Portugal	—	22,001	—
Italy	—	—	9,500
To various Orders	1,367,857	1,891,382	2,794,930
United States	411,498	298,214	397,452
California	15,160	22,187	17,071
Chili and elsewhere	—	—	8,280
The Pacific Coast	4,321	12,189	29,567
Total	2,742,631	3,202,964	3,983,798

Writing of this place Mr. Markham* says :—
"While the desolate Chinchas pour millions into the Treasury, the pampa of Tamarugal, in the Tarapaca province, contributes its nitrate of soda (salitre) and borate of lime to swell the riches of this favoured land. It is calculated that the nitrate of soda grounds in this district cover fifty square leagues, and, allowing one hundred pounds weight of nitrate for each square yard, this will give 63,000,000 tons, which, at *the present rate of consumption,* will last for 1393 years. In 1860 the export of nitrate of soda from the port of Iquique amounted to 1,370,248 cwts., and a good deal of borax is also exported, though its shipment is prohibited by the Government."

* "Travels in Peru and India," c. xviii. p. 306. Murray, London, 1862.

Although it is given in a note that these calculations are founded on data from "Bollaert's Account of Tarapaca," it will be seen how erroneous must have been deductions based on "the present rate of consumption" as it existed twelve years ago when we contrast the 1,370,248 quintals of the whole year 1860 with 3,983,798 quintals for eleven months of 1872.

The railways of Peru—the most extensive system of railways in South America—may be said to commence here. From Iquique to the interior nitrate-producing localities of Noria, and La Carolina, as well as from the neighbouring port of Pisagua to the saltpetre places of Sal de Obispo and Zapiga, railway trains have been plying for the last few years. The line from Iquique to La Noria goes through a length of only thirty-five miles. But it is a dreadful ascent and descent—a sandy, salty country to visit,—I am told,—without a drop of water to be found anywhere, except what is distilled from the sea.

This railway from Pisagua was contracted for by Messrs. Don Ramon Montero, and Brothers, of Lima, by sanction of special laws passed on the 8th of November, 1864, and the 15th of January, 1869. That from Iquique to Noria was established by a Supreme Decree of the 18th of November, 1856. The original contract with the Government bears date Lima, 1st of November, 1860, on the part of Messrs. Don Jose Maria Costa and Don

Frederick Pezet, under the rubric of Minister Morales. It has the exclusive monopoly for twenty-five years, and is allowed to extend branches over the whole department of Tarapaca.

Since the accession of President Pardo to the head of the Government, the following law in reference to this place was sanctioned by Congress in the month of January last. It met with considerable opposition, but was carried by fifty-six affirmative votes against twenty-three in the negative:—

"Art. 1st. Saltpetre is a monopoly in the Republic.

"Art. 2nd. The State will pay on delivery, and in cash, 2 soles 40 cents for each quintal of saltpetre, whose grade is not less than 95 per cent., placed alongside the launches in Iquique, or in any of the ports or bays which may be qualified in the province of Tarapaca. Should the State be able to sell the saltpetre at a higher rate than 3 soles 10 cents per quintal, the price of 2 soles 40 cents will be augmented by half the excess.

"Art. 3rd. The Government will take as a base the production of saltpetre in the year 1872, and the producing power of the manufactories on which money has already been laid out, and will make the necessary regulations to establish the monopoly and sale of saltpetre.

"Art. 4. The adjudication of saltpetre grounds is prohibited in every part of the Republic.

"Art. 5. The exportation of the earth from which

the saltpetre is extracted is hereby totally prohibited.

"Art. 6. The exportation of saltpetre which has not been bought from the State is prohibited, and all which it may be sought to export in infringement of this clause will be confiscated.

"Art. 7. The Government will inform the next Congress of the results of the monopoly, and are prohibited from making any agreement which may compromise for more than two years the interests attached to it. Every contract, whatever may be its nature or form, which is binding on the State for more than that time, is null and of no legal effect.

"Transitory Article. This law will come into operation two months after its promulgation, from which date all the saltpetre that may be exported from the Republic will be subject to its regulations."

It was, however, confirmed by a subsequent law of July last. The argument in its favour, besides the inevitable necessity of covering the deficit of the last Government, is that nitrate of soda at present competes in European markets with guano, and that it is therefore the interest of the State to be enabled to regulate and take advantage of this rivalry. Time only will be able to solve the soundness of this opinion. The last law is published in the *Official Gazette*, and runs thus:—

"Art. 1st.—The Monopoly of Saltpetre will begin to have effect on the 1st day of September next :"

"Art. 2nd.—From that day the Monopoly Department shall pay 2 soles and 40 cents for every quintal of saltpetre in sack, and placed alongside of the launch at Iquique, Pisagua, Mejillones, Junin, Patillos, or Mollo, if its quality proved by proper essay be that of 95 per cent. :

"Art. 3rd.—If its quality be less than 95 per cent., the price of 2 soles and 40 cents shall be reduced in the following proportions :

"In 1 per cent. if the quality is 94 per cent.

    In 4 per cent. if it come to 93 per cent.
    In 8 per cent. if it come to 92 per cent.
    In 13 per cent. if it come to 91 per cent.
    In 19 per cent. if it come to 90 per cent.

"For intermediate fractions a proportionate allowance shall be made. Saltpetre being less than 90 per cent. in quality shall not be received, nor that which has 6 per cent. or more of dampness.

"Art. 4th.—If the quality reaches 96 per cent. the Department shall pay 2 soles and 47½ cents per

---

¹ We can scarcely wonder that President Pardo initiated his rule with such edicts, when we know of the impecuniosity of the Treasury at the period of his coming into power. But no stronger evidence of his governing with the country, as well as for the country, need be adduced than the fact that these are now about to be repealed, and an export duty put on in their place.

quintal. If the quality should be above 90 per cent. and the saltpetre should not contain more than 1 per cent. of salt, the Department shall pay 2 soles and 60 cents per quintal.

"Art. 5th.—The quantity of saltpetre that the Monopoly Department shall buy during the year beginning the 1st September, 1873, and ending on the 31st August, 1874, is fixed at 4,500,000 quintals.

"Art. 6th.—To establish the proportion that belongs to each producer in the total of saltpetre that the Department may buy yearly, the Prefect of Tarapaca will appoint a commission, composed of five producers, which commission will draw up and present, within twenty days after nomination, a statement of the producing power of each office interested, and will fix the per centum that may of right fall to the lot of each producer, in the quantity that the State may buy annually.

"Art. 7th.—If the persons named by the Prefect should not accept the charge to make up the first Commission, or should fail to fulfil it, the Prefect shall officially and definitely fix the proportion that may respectively belong to each producer.

"Art. 8th.—While some producers may be unable to furnish their respective quotas, on account of the machinery in their respective offices not being in working condition, the others shall have the right to furnish the deficit, so that the State may always buy 375,000 quintals per month.

"Art. 9th.—During the first six months the Department shall not receive more than 375,000 quintals in each month; after the first six months producers may furnish more or less than 375,000 quintals every month; but in such manner that the total amount may not exceed 4,500,000 quintals per annum.

"Art. 10th.—The selling price of saltpetre that may be disposed of by Government in the first quarter, that is, during the months of September, October, and November next, shall be at S. 2.65 cts. per quintal, being 95 per cent. in quality, and the better or inferior qualities in proportion, that is with an addition of 25 cents upon the price at which it is bought. For the second quarter the addition shall be of 35 cents upon said price. The price that is to guide the sales of the Monopoly will be announced to the public sixty days at least before its operation, and under all circumstances it will be higher than that named for the second quarter.

"Art. 11th.—Producers may export the quantity of saltpetre that may fall to their quota without delivering it to the Monopoly Department; but in this case they shall pay the difference between S. 2.40 cts. and the prices fixed for the sales of the Monopoly with a deduction of 10 cents per quintal, that is, 15 cents difference in the first quarter and

25 in the second. This exportation shall be made under the supervision of the Monopoly.

"The producers that may desire to exercise this right will communicate their wishes to the Monopoly on the 15th of August for those who may deliver in September; on the 15th of September for those who may deliver in October, and so on successively. The producers that do not give notice in time shall be obliged to deliver to the Monopoly their respective quotas to the month for which the notice should have been given.

"The ships that may be loading saltpetre on the 31st August next shall be allowed to complete their cargo in the succeeding days, the parties interested paying for each quintal embarked after the 1st of September, the 15 cents spoken of in the 11th article, and without subjecting to the regulations of the Monopoly all the saltpetre that may have been previously embarked.

"The Minister of State in the Department of Finances and Commerce is charged with the fulfilment of this Decree.

"Given at the Government Palace in Lima, on the 12th day of July, 1873.

"Manuel Pardo.
"Jose Maria de la Jara."

Arica, the first port of Peru at which we touch, and where I find myself this morning (the 19th of April, 1871), has a most desolate aspect from the steamer's deck. This, however, is trifling compared to what it presents when we go ashore. Being situated in a corner bight of the continent, it suffered in a strongly-marked manner from the earthquake of 1868; because the volcanic wave coming from the north, and that from the south, meeting here, as it were, in a sort of confluence, swept everything up the valley before them. One of the chief sufferers was my colleague, Consul G. H. Nugent, who lost 60,000 dollars' worth by the swoop of the wave, and who with his wife and children had a narrow escape of their lives. His description of it, published in the *Panama Star and Herald* of September, 1868, is so graphic that I cannot avoid making a few extracts:—" I had hardly time," he writes, "to get my wife and children into the street when the whole of the walls of my house fell. 'Fell' is hardly the word, for they were blown out as if they had been spat at me. At the same time the earth opened probably two or three inches, and belched out dust, accompanied with a terrible stench as of powder. The air became darkened, and I could not see my wife, who was within two feet of me with the children. If this had lasted any time, so to speak, we must have been suffocated; but in about a couple of minutes it cleared off. Collecting my household together, we started for the hills. How we passed through falling houses, when we saw men struck down—some stone dead, others

maimed—is to me a mystery; but a merciful
Providence was over us. We wended our sad way
as well as we could towards the hills, with the
earth shaking, making us stagger like drunken
people, when a great cry went up to heaven
from all the town, 'The sea has retired!' I
hurried on, but before I got to the outskirts I
looked back, and saw all the vessels in the bay
carried out irresistibly to sea, probably with a
speed of ten miles an hour. In a few minutes the
great outer current stopped; then arose a mighty
wave—I should judge about fifty feet high—which
swept in with a resistless rush, carrying everything with it in its awful majesty. It brought
back all of the shipping, some of the latter turning
in circles, but the whole speeding on to an inevitable doom. Meanwhile, the wave had passed
in, crushed the mole into atoms, swallowed up my
office as a bit in its giant mouth, gulped down the
Custom-house, and, rushing along the same street,
carried everything before it in its irresistible force.
The whole of these things were done quicker than
the changes in a Christmas pantomime."

In the same short space of time the Peruvian
war-steamer "America" lost about eighty-five
hands. The United States steamer "Wateree"
escaped with the loss of one life. Having a
small draft of water, she was carried bodily on the
top of the sea, and landed about a quarter of a mile
in-shore of the railway track, distant at the spot

more than a quarter of a mile from the sea. The
"Fridoma," United States store-ship, was bottom
upwards. Every soul on board perished except
the captain, surgeon, and paymaster, who were
fortunately on shore at the moment. An American
barque, laden with guano, was swallowed up along
with all her crew, and not a vestige left to tell of
her fate. "For nearly two days," adds Mr.
Nugent, "we lay on the hills, without covering
and without food (his wife, himself, and seven
children), in a constant state of alarm, as the
shocks of earthquake were for some days incessant."

I must confess that this is not a very comforting
style of thing, to be made acquainted with, on
first landing in a country that may be one's home
for an indefinite number of years.

This earthquake was sensibly felt along the
whole coast, although at no place were its devastations so palpable as at Arica. Iquique suffered
very much, so also did Mejillones, Pisagua, Ilo,
and Chala, as well as nearly all the other towns of
the coast. It went inland to Tacna, interior to
Arica, and northward to Arequipa, the second
city in the Republic. It likewise proceeded farther north, beyond Callao and Lima, at both of
which places it was sensibly felt, although with
comparatively little damage.

One of the most remarkable incidents of this
earthquake was the heaving up, in some place not

ARICA, THE DAY BEFORE THE EARTHQUAKE OF 1868.

very far from Arica, of a number of bodies, buried in the usual style of interment along this coast—namely, the squatting posture, in which the legs are flexed on the pelvis, and the knees bent in to the chin. They were covered, as usual, with cloth, and padded with cotton flock. They had, as elsewhere, one-half of a bivalve, about the ordinary size of an oyster, attached to the palm of each hand. The usual style of funereal accessories in heads of Indian corn, beans, fishing-nets, needles for making the same, and bits of cloth, were likewise thrown up. From some of the skulls the eyes had been extracted and fishes' eyes put in their place. Of those latter—the eyes of the cuttle-fish—a number were given to me by Mr. Bracey R. Wilson, our vice-consul at Callao, who had been many years resident at Arica, and was intimate with all its bearings. This putting of the fish-eyes into the orbits, from which their original eye-balls had been extracted, may perhaps be considered as a symbol of their fish worship.

As soon as it was possible to be despatched, after the earthquake, the United States war-steamer "Powhattan" went from Callao to Arica, being the bearer from the Peruvian Government of funds and stores to relieve the sufferers. Mr. Henry Meiggs and Mr. Calderon of Lima each contributed 50,000 soles (10,000*l*.) in behalf of the families left destitute by the terrible calamity.

From Arica to Tacna, a distance of sixty miles to the interior, there is also a railway. Our short stay here did not allow me time to visit the latter city, and unfortunately I had no opportunity afterwards. The concession for this railway was made out when General Senor Don Jose Rufino Echenique was President in 1851. The first contractor was Mr. Joseph Hegan, of London, by agreement of 28th September, 1853, and he transferred its privileges to a company, under the title of "Railway Company of Arica to Tacna," on the 23rd May, 1857. In November, 1864, and in January, 1869, proposals were made by Messrs. Dockendorf, as well as several other persons of Lima, for extension of the Tacna line to the frontiers of Bolivia; but this was never carried into effect.

Many likewise were the propositions for the line from the port of Ilo to Moquegua. This was, however, granted to Deves Brothers and Company, of Paris, on the 10th of December, 1870, under the condition of concluding the work in two years and a half, and for the cost of 6,700,000 soles in bonds at par. In six months after, or on the 14th of January, 1871, Deves Brothers made over, as they were authorized to do by the 29th clause of the contract, the affair to Mr. Henry Meiggs, who with his accustomed energy had the line finished and in the hands of the Government in less than two years after transfer of the concession.

Moquegua is said to be a great wine-producing

ARICA, THE DAY AFTER THE EARTHQUAKE OF 1868.

country, but I can say nothing about it, as I never was there.

Not very far from Ilo we stop at the port of Mollendo, and from this is to be the direct route to Cuzco.

CHAPTER V.

Towards Cuzco.—Grandeur of its edifices.—General Miller's description.—Stories about gold.—Ancient roads mentioned by Prescott.—Modern railroads made by Mr. Henry Meiggs.—From Mollendo to Arequipa.—Lively night at hotel in Mollendo.—Concession for the Arequipa railroad.—From Ensenada onwards.—Steep gorge.—Pampa of Cachenda.—Large amount of rolling stock.—Valley of Tambo and station.—Quebrada of Cabuintala.—Serpentine curves.—Station of Vitor.—La Joya.—Sand-heaps.—Husamayo.—Onishuarani.—Watering-place of Arequipa.—Tingo—Sakacha.

Cuzco! What varied impressions, to be sure, are revived in the minds of every one interested in this part of the world, merely by the name of this grand old Peruvian city! How Prescott[1] tells us that "it stood in a beautiful valley on an elevated region of the plateau, which among the Alps would have been buried in eternal snows, but which, within the tropics, enjoyed a genial and salubrious temperature." How "towards the north it was defended by a lofty eminence, a spur of the great Cordillera, and the city was traversed by a river, or rather a small stream, over which bridges of timber, covered with heavy slabs of stone, furnished an easy communication with the op-

---

[1] "History of the Conquest of Peru," p. 6.

posite banks." How, "although the streets were
long and narrow, the houses low, and those of
the poorer sort built of clay and reeds," it was
still "the royal residence, and was adorned with
the ample dwellings of the great nobility." How
amongst its great buildings stood a strong fortress,
the remains of which at the present day, by their
vast size, excite the admiration of the traveller,
as we are told in the "Memoirs of General
Miller." [1]

On the side facing the city this fortress was
defended by a wall of great thickness, and three
hundred feet long. It consisted of three towers,
one of which was appropriated to the Inca, and
was garnished with the sumptuous decorations
befitting a royal residence. Twenty thousand men
are said to have been employed on this structure,
and fifty years occupied in building it.

One of the other grand edifices that ornamented
Cuzco was the Great Temple of the Sun—"the
pride of the capital and the wonder of the empire"
—which was designated *Corieancha*, or the "Place
of Gold." Well it must have merited the name,
too, from Prescott's description.[2] The interior of
the temple was the most worthy of admiration;
it was literally a mine of gold. On the western
wall was emblazoned a representation of the Deity,
consisting of a human countenance looking forth
from amidst innumerable rays of light, which

[1] Vol. ii. p. 223. [2] Op. cit. p. 41.

emanated from it in every direction, in the same manner as the sun is often personified with us. The figure was engraved on a massive plate of gold of enormous dimensions, thickly powdered with emeralds and precious stones. It was so situated in front of the great eastern portal, that the rays of the morning sun fell directly upon it at its rising, lighting up the whole apartment with an effulgence that seemed more than natural, and which was reflected back from the golden ornaments with which the walls and ceiling were everywhere incrusted. Gold, in the figurative language of the people, was "the tears wept by the sun;" and every part of the interior of the temple glowed with burnished plates and studs of the precious metal. The cornices which surrounded the walls of the sanctuary were of the same costly material, and a broad belt or frieze of gold let into the stonework encompassed the whole exterior of the edifice.

The sentiment of pleasant, though painful, veneration is absorbed in the contemplation of all these records of ancient history. Can these relations be entitled "History," or are they to be believed as all belonging solely to the Inca period, when we find, on examining, that nearly all the history of pre-historic times in Peru has been destroyed by these very Incas, of whom we can moreover learn nothing but from their Spanish conquerors, whose boast it was to have subdued them? We must, however, try to fancy ourselves amongst this galaxy of grandeur—in this city beloved of the Sun—where his worship was maintained in its splendour, "where every fountain, pathway, and wall," says an ancient chronicler, "was regarded as a holy mystery; where, besides the great temple, there was a large number of inferior temples in the city and its environs, amounting to three or four hundred—where one of the principal of these religious houses was the Convent of the Sun—this one at Cuzco, consisting wholly of maidens of the royal blood, who amounted, it is said, to no less than 1500."

But gone now to the "tomb of the Capulets" —if the Capulets ever had a home in Peru—are all these things of grandeur. No more can we have the gorgeous spectacle held in presence of the Incas in lighting up the sacred fire of Raymi. Destroyed, too, are the four roads[1] that diverged from Cuzco, the capital or navel of the ancient Peruvian monarchy. "One of these roads," we are told by Prescott, "passed over the grand plateau, and the other along the lowlands on the borders of the ocean. It was conducted over sierras, across rivers by suspension bridges, up

[1] These roads are first described by Pedro de Cieza de Leon. He gives no account of how they got over the rocky bluffs on the sea-coast, though describing their style amongst the valleys and sandy deserts. *Vide* Mr. Markham's translation of Pedro de Cieza de Leon's Travels, page 219. Garcilasso de la Vega takes description of these roads from Don Pedro.

and down precipices by stairways, through ravines filled up with solid masonry. The length of the road, of which scattered fragments only remain, is variously estimated at from fifteen hundred to two thousand miles; its breadth scarcely exceeded twenty feet. It was built of heavy flags of freestone, and in some parts covered with a bituminous cement, which time has made harder than the stone itself."[3]

Although I am the last person to throw any doubt on descriptions of things and places which I have not seen, and whilst I entertain the most profound faith in the celebrated Baron Von Humboldt, who says that "the roads of the Incas were amongst the most useful and stupendous works ever executed by man," still I must confess myself as puzzled to understand how "only scattered fragments of these roads remain" at the present epoch when they were done of materials which "time has made harder than the stone itself." More especially when I know the enormously conservative faculties of the Peruvian climate, and when I have searched at every place I visited from Arica to San José, a coast distance of more than a thousand miles, without ever being able to find out one single yard of such a road as that described by Prescott through "the level country between the Andes and the Ocean."[4] That no such level country exists, except in

[3] Op. cit. c. ii. p. 28.   [4] Op. cit. c. xi. p. 28.

patches of small valleys, may be seen from what I have already quoted from Professor Forbes.¹ Besides, all the roads in the valleys show unmistakable evidences of their having been done by the people who were there long before the Incas came,—the Chinchas at Canete, the Yuncas at Rimac, and the Chimoos in their valleys from Supé up to Sechura. Much of these latter roads bear signs of the physical variations made in a country so subject to earthquakes as Peru.

But whosoever desires to go to Cuzco now-a-days, must journey by railway; and in case the incredulous foreigner should doubt the possibility of a railway to Cuzco—in the centre of Peru—across these Andean masses, some of which are above 18,000 feet high, and over them one would imagine that only the Condor could traverse—let him come with me to the place at which we are now, the port of Mollendo near Islay, in latitude 17° 5' south. There he will find a railway going at present to Quisco, and since January, 1871, to Arequipa,² which in another year will reach to Puno, and in two years after that from Puno to Cuzco—a total distance of 547 miles from the coast of the Pacific.

I believe that, except Mr. Markham, Mr. Pentland, and a few others, there are many persons

¹ Chap. iv. p. 47.
² This was written more than a year ago—so that it is probable the track is at present not far from Puno.

(like myself, previous to my visit in March of last year) who only know of Arequipa as a city of Peru, very high up in the Andes, yet with three towering mountains overshadowing it,— namely, Misti to the right, Pichu Pichu to the left, and Charcani between, each of these being 18,000 feet above the level of the sea. I had likewise heard of its being a remarkable "head centre" in regard to the matters of earthquakes below and earthquakes above; or, to speak less figuratively, of volcanic shakings and of political revolutions. The first named are said to be most frequent in their occurrence from September to December, and the chronicles tell us, this city has been almost entirely destroyed in each of fourteen different earthquakes. The earliest of these is recorded as having occurred on the 2nd of January, 1582, and the last on August 16, 1868. So extensive were the ravages done by that of 1582, that the Vicunas and Huanacos came down from the mountains, mingling themselves, as if for protection, with the inhabitants in the streets.

The Misti was a volcano in the memory of some of the old writers, but at what period its fire-vomiting ceased I could not ascertain.*

* Pedro de Ciaza de Leon writes of this volcano, " which some fear will burst forth, and do mischief."—Mr. Markham's translation, Op. cit. p. 266. He commits an error, however, in saying it is " fourteen leagues from the sea," for it is more than three times that distance.

Several attempts, I am told, have been made to reach the summit, but they were all unsuccessful from the fact of the rarefied atmosphere having brought on *soroche*, or congestion of the lungs, and *surumpi*, or difficulty of vision. These causes, at all events, acted upon Senor Valdez de Velasco and Doctor Suero, as well as on Senor Hænckc, the German Naturalist, and Mr. Pentland. The last-named gentleman got nearer to the top than any of the others.

The Misti at its summit is 20,300 English feet above the level of the sea: but I must not plunge *in medias res*, or aspire to the top of this mountain before starting from Mollendo.

The roadstead of Mollendo, at the time of my visit, was so covered with sea-foam, on our approaching the beach, as to suggest the idea of its having been the birthplace of Venus—mentioned in the heathen mythology to have been born in this element. It is a very open and exposed roadstead, being often for weeks together impracticable of communication to or from the vessels in the harbour.

Landing on an iron molo and crossing the rails, I passed up to the town, which has all the appearance of freshness in its dwelling-houses as of solidity in the buildings. Amongst these the chiefest are the stores of the railway station.[1] A

[1] The note of introduction, whereof I was the bearer, to Mr. E. C. Dubois, the excellent managing superintendent of this rail-

few years ago Mollendo was a barren, and uninhabited rock, and although the barrenness is not much improved upon, it has a sufficiently numerous population. That it is keeping up with the necessities of its progress is evident from the fact that it has four hotels—one of which is an *Hôtel de Paris*—a custom-house, and a post-office. Of the accommodation at the hotels I can say nothing, as I did not enter them; but a fellow-traveller of mine to Aroquipa next morning assured me that he had spent a night in one, under circumstances that he had never endured before at an hotel in any part of the world. He was in bed for six hours, and that period he described as—

> "One of sleeping,
> Two of scratching,
> Three of hunting,
> None of catching."

Besides the institutions before mentioned, I find here a theatrical company, holding performances on a temporary stage, fitted up in the yard of the railway premises. On the wall adjacent to the post-office, and on a bill nearly as large as that about a Drury Lane pantomime posted up near Temple Bar, the theatre-loving people of Mollendo were told that the play of that night was to be "La Mujer de un Artista" ("The Wife of an Artist"), with other contingencies.

_{way, procured me the luxury of hospitality in his comfortable dwelling, for which I shall feel ever grateful.}

Alongside of the residence of Mr. Dubois is a pretty little chapel, erected by Mr. Meiggs for the use of the workmen here; and from the front of this house is an extensive view of the Pacific. At this time there were thirteen vessels at anchor in the roads, amongst which were some with materials for fifteen locomotives on board.

The first concession by the Government of Peru for the railway by which I am about to travel was from Islay to Arequipa, by a decree of Congress on the 2nd of October, 1860. To this, on the 28th of January, in the year 1863, a guarantee of 7 per cent. on the same was added, also by Congress. It was made over to Mr. Patrick Gibson, merchant, of Islay.

By the survey of the engineers, Messrs. Blume and Echegarray, as likewise by a recommendation of Senor M. F. Paz-Soldan,[1] the line of road was changed from Islay to Mejias, which is quite close to Mollendo. Then a project came to the Government from Mr. Paz-Soldan, dated April 20th, 1863, recommending that the concession be made anew to Mr. Gibson. The line was again surveyed by Mr. Oswald Younghusband, civil engineer, whose report is dated Lima, 20th of April, 1864. On this was founded the decree, which under the rubric of Senor Zegarra, Minister of the Interior, and under date May 28th, 1864, proposes to lay the

[1] At the period holding the post of Director-General of Public Works.

affair before Congress, as there was a difference
in the first proposal of the contractors (Soles
17,929,924 32 centimes) and the last (Soles
15,000,000), either of which exceeded that
primarily laid before the Government.

The Congress then, on the 18th of November,
1864, sanctioned the concession so as not to
exceed 15,000,000 of soles, with the interest of
7 per cent., General Juan Antonio Pezet being at
the time President of the Republic. The proposal
of Mr. Patrick Gibson, now joined with a Mr.
Joseph Pickering, was accepted on the 12th of
June, 1864.

But Messrs. Gibson and Pickering carried the
matter no farther; for it appears that in September,
1864, or seven years after starting the first idea of
this railroad, five proposals were sent in. First
from Mr. Edward Harmsen, of Lima; second from
Mr. Robert H. Beddy; third from Mr. Benjamin
E. Bates; fourth from John Dockendorff and Co.;
and fifth from Mr. Henry Meiggs. Bates offered
to take the contract for seven millions of soles;
Dockendorff and Meiggs each proposed twelve
millions. Harmsen projected the formation of a
company, in which the Government was to take the
initiative by issuing four millions of soles in bonds
as representing so many shares, with an interest
of 7 per cent., and an amortization of 4 per cent.
per annum; whilst Beddy followed in the same
track as Harmsen, with the little difference of eight

millions of soles instead of four. This is all stated in a report by Paz-Soldan, but he makes no recommendation in favour of any of the new proposals; the former one of Gibson and Pickering having been declared invalid from their not "coming up to time." Mr. Henry Meiggs sent in his proposal on the 31st of March, 1868, one of not the least important items of which was, that he compromised himself to pay a fine of 20,000 soles or 5000*l.* for each month exceeding the term of three years within which he engaged to finish the work. That he accomplished it in time may be guessed from the fact that the railway was finished to Arequipa, and opened on the 1st of January, 1871, or two years and nine months after signing the contract, instead of three years.

The train started from Mollendo—to the best of my recollection at eight o'clock—its first thirteen miles to the station at Ensenada being southward along the coast and parallel with the sea. About four miles at the Mollendo side of Ensenada we halt inside of Mejia point, where there are a few dirty-looking tents of filthy canvas for houses. This is said to be a bathing-place. Between it and Ensenada is a playa, or level ground, called Chulu, where a hacienda (farm-house) formerly stood, occupying both sides of the track as we go along. The farm just alluded to was represented to me as destroyed by the volcanic wave of 1868—part, no doubt, of that which swept over Arica in the same year. At this place we observe an extensive space of clover, with horses feeding on it, and a number of trees.

At the station of Ensenada is a reservoir capable of containing 10,000 gallons of water, which is brought by an azequia, or watercourse, from some quebrada (ravine) high up in the country. Hence water has to be carried to the stations —at Mollendo, thirteen miles behind, to Tambo, six miles in advance, and to Cachenda, fifteen miles farther on. To Mollendo is supplied the quantity of 12,000 gallons per day. The portion of line from Arequipa to Cachenda is furnished with water from the former place.

The expense of water, therefore, on this line at the period of which I write must have been an enormous outlay, as the locomotives with tanks were daily employed in conveying it to the different points. Just then, however, an aqueduct from the river Chile[1] was being constructed for Mr. Meiggs by Messrs. Hart Brothers, of Lima. It was to conduct water along the whole course of the line. Besides the two locomotives employed in the water transport, with two more—one up and one down daily—on the passenger traffic, there are five engaged in carrying material, or plant, for the road being laid down to Puno en route to Cuzco.

From Ensenada commences the three per cent. grade. At Tambo, distant from Ensenada only

[1] "Chile" in the Quichua language signifies "a rounded stone."

six miles, we find ourselves on a level plateau, where there is a large collection of stores, engine houses, and machine shops, with a few improvised stalls by the natives, offering plantains and bananas for sale. These are brought from the valley of Tambo, a fertile part of the province, the green fields of which can be seen low down, about a mile or so behind the railway station, and on the right-hand side as we go up. That valley extends for a long distance to the interior—Mr. East, the superintendent of locomotives, tells me forty miles. There is a very neat-looking little hotel close to the station, with bright flowers and creeping plants, that mount up to a lattice-work over the doorway, having bananas growing in front. From this station, at half-past five o'clock every morning, an engine starts with plant and material for the Puno road from Arequipa. The whole of the railway accessories at this place have quite an air of comfortable freshness about them, in strong contrast with the sandy soil around, and the dark brown spurs of the Cordilleras in the far distance.

From Tambo to Cachendo, fifteen miles distant, we go through the "Quebrada de Cahuintala." The journey here is a sort of turning, and tacking on almost parallel tracks, but still mounting up at a grade of four per cent. in a series of serpentine curves. We pass a tank for holding water near where the Posco station is to be, and after a sweep round a hill here, we get out into a bit

of level ground. Then another curve to turn
the hill of Posco; and still we go on, gradually
creeping up, winding about, and seeming as if
retrograding in the same direction, till, looking out
of the carriage window down into a gorge, we see,
at several hundred feet below us, the trackway on
which we have passed some minutes previously.

At the Cachenda station, thirty-four miles from
Mollendo, we come on what is called the Pampa
of Cachenda. And here I get the first sensation
of sharpness in the air, from its being so rarefied
owing to our lofty position. There is nothing at
Cachenda but a neat wooden station-house with
a zinc roof, and an excellent as well as spacious
platform. A water-tank likewise. But on whatever
side you look you can see nothing except
sand-plains, bounded on all sides by the Cordilleras.

The Pampa of Cachenda extends for many
leagues farther on. To any one who has travelled,
as I have, for thousands of miles over the grass-
grown Pampas of the Argentine Republic—particularly
that part of it in Buenos Ayres and in the
Gran Chaco, at the eastern side of the Andes—the
term Pampas here seems an anomaly. For we
have nothing but a plain of brown and red sand,
shut in on every side by dark and lofty mountains;
whilst the Pampas of Buenos Ayres, covered
with grass for several thousand square
leagues, have no apparent limit but the horizon.
The ground, as we proceed, is dotted with large

clumps of cinder rock, resembling basalt, which fell here, no doubt, from some volcanic shower of the early ages. In some parts are boulders of gypsum; whilst several of the far-off sand-hills present the appearance of snow. But this, I am told, is some kind of alkaline pearlash.

Not the least curious features of these plains are the Médanos, or large mounds of fine sand, of the same class as that with which we are familiar in minute-glasses. These are most frequently seen in the form of a horse-shoe, with the convex part facing the S.W. or the point from which the wind nearly always comes, and the concave side inwards towards the land. I have subsequently seen them, not so much in the vallies that I visited along the sea side, as at a considerable distance inland.

At La Joya station, half-way to Arequipa, we stop for breakfast, and here we meet the down-train for Mollondo. From Cachenda, the previous station mentioned, to La Joya, we have five miles. At La Joya there is not much to be seen, and not much desire to look for anything, except one's breakfast on the table, for which the sharp air has long ago given us an appetite. Twenty-two miles beyond La Joya we stop at the station of Vitor, where commences the Huasa-mayo district of Sierras. Here the lights, and shades on the distant hills are charming in the extreme. From Vitor to Onishuarani we go through the same style of scenery for eight miles.

At part of the route we turn round a sharp cliff, and, looking down, can see the river Chile, which flows from Arequipa, trickling through a gorge. The side of the latter is almost perpendicular to a depth of several hundred feet. This river rises amongst the small hills, behind the Misti.

Farther on, and down in the valley, we see glimpses of trees and clover, affording a relief to the eye after so many hours' contemplation of sand, and rock. Contrasting this little "emerald gem" with the brown, bare, volcanic, and barren tract, through which we had been travelling for the last four hours, was very refreshing. From this we had the first view of the Misti, towering up gigantic in the distance, its topmost peak peering through a large cumulus, that enwrapped a considerable share of its upper part.

Leaving Onishuarani we have another run of ten miles to Uchu-Mayo.[*] We are now on almost level ground, the same plateau as the city of Arequipa. After skirting the pretty valley of Congata, at the upper end of which are the thermal waters of Catari, we proceed to the penultimate station of Tingo, six miles beyond Uchu-Mayo, and five miles from Arequipa. A fellow-traveller points out to me the village of Fiavaya—a pic-

---

[*] Uchu-Mayo, in Quichua, signifies "narrow river;" and I am informed the Chile river, in its passage here, bears the same name as the locale through which it flows.

turesque little spot, all of green meadows, and trees interspersed with houses, not far beyond Catari—to which the Arequipenos resort in summer time, as to a Sydenham or Richmond. At Catari there are chalybeate waters. But here at Tingo we have the Buxton of Arequipa. There are two Tingos—the Tingo Grande (Big Tingo), and Tingo Chico (Little Tingo). The latter is famous for its thermal waters.

On the rising ground in front, and to the left as we go along, is a ruined cluster of houses on a hill-top, which is entitled Sachaka. Amongst the most notable of these, damaged by the earthquake of 1868, are the remains of a large church, quite a "Triton amongst the minnows." All the property round here, which is very valuable, belonged to his Grace the Most Reverend Doctor Don José Sebastian Goyanaché, the Archbishop of Lima, who died only very recently from the result of an accident.

CHAPTER VI.

At Arequipa.—Excellence of its station arrangements.—Hotels at Arequipa.—The Soroché and Surumpi.—Rarefied atmosphere.—Earthquaky look of Arequipa.—Appearance of Cathedral.—Number of Monasteries.—Heavy rains here.—The Misti volcano.—The Sillar trachyte.—Celebrated men of Arequipa.—Derivation of its name.—Story of first settlement.—Railways of Mr. Henry Meiggs.—Reflections on their success.—From Arequipa on the road to Puno.—Mineral wells of Yura.—Station of Quisca.—Aguas Calientes.—Hospital here.—Magnetic stone at Cachipcsane.

THE station at Arequipa, with its appurtenances of manager's residence, office, artisans' houses, engine-sheds, goods-stores, and so forth, occupies thirty acres of ground. This includes the station for the Puno line, which is divided from that of Mollendo by a road of ordinary width—both communicating by rails. The manager's (Mr. Dubois) house, when completed, will be, as regards comfort, combined with luxury, a palace in miniature. It has a top-story, open at all sides, which is the perfection of coolness and ventilation, as well as an indescribable kind of architecture. From the basement of the building extends the

BARRICADE IN AREQUIPA DURING SIEGE OF 1857.

CHAP. VI.]   AGREEABLE ATTENTIONS.   87

line of offices for passenger-tickets and of goods-stores alongside the platform. At right angles, is one line of neat cottages for the workmen. Of these there are two other similar lines within the enclosure—one lower, and the other in front of the ticket-office. In fact, everything about here is made on the style of perfect adaptability, which characterizes all the works of Mr. Meiggs done in Peru.[1]

Nearly a mile and a half from the station is the centre of the town, to which I was obliged to walk, with a porter carrying my luggage, as there are no conveyances in Arequipa except horses, and bullock-carts of very antediluvian pattern. At the station I met Mr. William Harrison, managing agent for Messrs. William Gibbs and Co., and, although I brought to him no introduction, was invited to share the hospitality of his house.[2] To tell the truth, the offer was at once accepted, inasmuch as from the general appearance of Arequipa, and from remembrance of what my recent fellow-traveller had experienced on the previous night at Mollendo, I was not at all disposed to venture into an hotel. This, however, I soon learned, in the matter of insectivorous

[1] To Mr. H. J. Bertrand, the station-master (*locum tenens* for Mr. Dubois), I am indebted for the most courteous endeavours to aid me in going about.

[2] I cannot refrain from expressing my grateful remembrance of the attentions received from Mrs. Harrison and her husband during my few days' stay at Arequipa.

Leotarding, was not so much to be dreaded. For, on remarking about what is here patent to every one on a first visit—of the sensible rarefication of the atmosphere—I was told of an important entomological fact, that fleas do not *thrive* in Arequipa. Indeed, they are never *felt* here, although no doubt they migrate in large numbers with passengers from Lima, Valparaiso, Mollendo, and every place abroad. They are supposed to die a short time after their arrival, but whether from *soroche* (congestion of the lungs), or *surumpi* (inflammation of the eyes), I could not ascertain. So that, after my experiences in other parts of South America, I could not help exclaiming, "Happy Arequipenos!"

It may be difficult for many of my readers, as it was for myself, to imagine what the volcanic earthquake could have done in 1868, when I received from Mr. Harrison the photographic sketches in this chapter, illustrating some of the topographical phases of the city after the Prado siege. This may be explained as follows:—It appears that in 1867 General Canseco was proclaimed in Arequipa, with the character of Second Constitutional Vice-President, whilst the people and the army rose up against the Government of General Prado, at the time reigning as Dictator in Lima. Prado came down with his troops, and laid siege to the city, but with such bad results that he was obliged to retreat precipitately for the coast, and return with his steamer. The Government of Prado was concluded in January, 1868. Of his successor, President Balta's fate, I shall write when we come to Lima.

Even independent of this bombardment, the city must always have had more or less of an earthquaky appearance, during the whole of the period intervening between the fourteen earthquakes that occurred from the first, recorded January 2nd, 1582, to the last, of August, 1868, or a space of two hundred and eighty-six years. What it was in pre-historic times (if a city existed in these days) must be left to the imagination. Although nearly four years have passed since their houses tumbled about their ears, many of the inhabitants would seem to take the ruined state of things, as an inevitable and irremediable destiny. Here and there something has been done to repair a church, but, with huge piles of stones put up in many places, as if in preparation for building, no mason-work is going on; whilst people look at you, and at the stones with a sort of a *cui bono?* air, as much as to say, "What is the use of building up, when we don't know the moment it may tumble down again? Our strongest houses, built of freestone, limestone, or Sillar, may rattle about our ears as a house made of a pack of cards will do at a single breath."

I must confess, it appears to me that the sensation of living in a place so subject as Arequipa is

to earthquakes cannot be a very comfortable one.
And this should not be set down to cowardice.
Because from storms, fires, revolutions, or ship-
wrecks you may have means of escape, in the
proportion say of ninety-nine to one of those which
you have from earthquakes.

The Cathedral, which was rebuilt many times
after convulsions, as well as burned in 1844, presents a sad appearance. In no part of South America, through which I have travelled at both sides of
the Andes, have I seen a building of this kind, which,
even in ruins, shows such rare beauty of majestic
simplicity in architecture as this Cathedral. It
occupies the whole northern and most elevated side
of the principal plaza. The towers and roof were
destroyed in 1868, and the whole edifice shaken.
Indeed, at one corner of it there is a rent in the
wall from top to bottom. At the other side of the
street running out of the plaza, opposite the
Cathedral, and towards the left, is the Church of
the Jesuits—the topmost part of the tower whereof
is in a condition of chaotic ruin. The front of
this last-mentioned is a wonderful work of Sillar-
stone carving. There are several large quarries in
the neighbourhood of Arequipa, whence it is transported into town, dressed in square blocks of about
eighteen inches long, a foot broad, and four inches
in thickness. These are carried in leathern or
straw panniers, on the backs of donkeys—a stone
at each side being a load.

ARDBEG: THE MILLS EARTHQUAKE OF 1869.

The houses in Arequipa are generally built with boveda, or arched roofs, and these are done with the Sillar. Heavy rains fall in Arequipa, and the arched roof is believed to resist the earthquake better than a flat one could.

All the churches of San Augustin, San Marco, San Domingo, Santa Rosa, La Merced, and many others, are in conditions of a most distressingly tumble-down appearance. Santa Rosa is, however, being rebuilt, and one or two others, including that of San Francisco, have been perfectly restored; but the larger number of churches as well as houses still exist in the shattered state, in which they were left by the earthquake of August, 1868.

At the corner of nearly every street in Arequipa we find drinking-fountains, from which water can be taken in any quantities by persons who desire it. In nearly all the streets, we see the usual Peruvian institution of *acequias*, or watercourses, running down the centre. And these are presided over by the turkey-buzzards.

There are two hotels in this city, but of their internal *régime* I can say nothing more than that, judging by externals, I should not like being obliged to risk a trial of either.

On the second morning of my stay in Arequipa, I rode out with Mr. Harrison to see the quarries from which the Sillar[a] (trachytic) stone is taken,

[a] "The rocks of this volcanic formation," says Professor David Forbes, in his pamphlet on the "Geology of South America,"

and this locale is styled Chilini. A considerable part of our road, after emerging from the suburbs, was simply a bridle-path, alongside of a medium-sized azequia, on the banks of which grew wild nasturtians, forming a cheerful fringe, of nearly a mile in length, by their bright scarlet blossoms. The quarry is situated a few hundred feet above the level of the town, and there was nothing noticeable in it save the *laissez-aller* mode in which the cutters worked. This was also symbolized by the equally impassive pace of the donkeys, wending towards their destination with the square blocks of Sillar fastened to their sides.

From the position of these quarries, the town looks as if it were in a valley or amphitheatre beneath, and the view beyond is limited, as are all views in this part of the world, by a background of Cordilleras. There is an ice, or rather snow, trade carried on at Arequipa, by men who fetch down the glacier element from Pichu-Pichu.

Besides five nunneries and churches innume-

---

and writing of Arequipa, "are all trachytic, and frequently present a most striking similarity to the domite of Auvergne, being like that composed of quartz, black or brown hexagonal mica, and a weathered-looking felspar. They form some four or six beds, superposed one on another, and of an average thickness of about ten feet each. These are either a white trachytic tuffa, like domite, with abundant embedded fragments of pumice, or a compact trachyte of a reddish or white colour, and similar composition."

rable, there are three monastic establishments in this city. We find also a university here—named after the great Father San Augustin—which my limited stay in Arequipa did not permit me to visit. It is alongside the convent of San Augustin, that, as a religious house, has been suppressed, and is now a college called "Independencia." But the first rank of colleges in Arequipa belongs to that of San Geronimo, which has sent forth to the world many eminent men—not the least among them being Senor Don Jose Gregorio Paz Soldan, and Dr. T. de Paula Gonzalez Vigil, both men of world-wide fame.

Amongst other institutions at Arequipa is a retreat for poor priests,—the Hospital of St. Peter. The general hospital of the town is unfortunately situated in the very centre of the population, at the convent of San Juan de Dios (St. John of God), the religious ladies whereof constitute its nurses. It has usually less than a hundred patients, all of whom are badly attended for want of funds. The Orphan House suffers from the same poverty as the hospital. One of the most melancholy reminiscences connected with the earthquake of 1868 is the fact that, although not more than 200 persons were killed during that frightful catastrophe, the greater number of victims in any one locale was at this hospital.

Crossing the river from one side of the town to the other, there is a bridge of very massive proportions, which, although only about 100 yards in length, with six large arches and a small one, is said to have cost a million of dollars.

Thunderstorms are reported to me to be very violent amongst the Cordilleras of Arequipa. Many of the Indian *arriéros*,[1] as well as their mules, perish by the lightning. The drivers have a superstition that, if there happens to be a white mule amongst the troupe, the lightning will single it out from the lot as its first victim.

I learn from a book about the Arequipa railway[2] that this city was founded by order of Francisco Pizarro, and with solemn proclamation, on the 15th of August, 1540. Its first site was behind Caima—that is, on the right-hand side of the river Chile—but afterwards, and subsequent to one of the earthquakes, it was transferred to its present locale. "The etymology of the name," says the book, "is very uncertain. Amongst other guesses the Padre Calancha believes it to be derived from two Quichua words, *Ari* and *Quepai*, which signify 'Yes, stay here;' because, on the return to Cuzco of the Inca Maita Capac, after having conquered the provinces of Chumbivilcas, Parivacochas, and others, some of his companions, captivated by the beauty of this place, solicited per-

---

[1] Mule-drivers.
[2] Written in Spanish, and without the author's name; published in Lima, at the State printing-office, in 1871, and dedicated to President Balta and Mr. Henry Meiggs.

mission to remain, and the monarch answered them in the words just mentioned "* (upon which I presume to comment).

The Inca who is accredited to have made the first attempt on the coast side was the ninth of his race, Pachacutec. And he, according to Garcilasso de la Vega, crossed over into the valley of Ica, much higher up than Arequipa. Moreover, there was a difference of from A.D. 1126, when Maita Capac came to the throne, and Pachacutec ascended in A.D. 1340. "According to Garcilasso de la Vega, the word Arequipa means 'sounding trumpet,'" says the book before me. "But whichever of these is correct," it continues, "there is one thing certain, that this place was inhabited during the time of the Incas." Of which I can find no other proof or evidence.

I may here take an extract from my notebook made whilst waiting for the train in which

* Pedro de Cieza de Leon devotes only two pages to Arequipa, and says nothing of this legend. This author went to Peru in 1532—the city of Lima was founded in 1535, previous to which time the Spaniards had not come down the coast—Arequipa was founded in 1540, and yet in De Leon's work, published at Seville in 1553, we are informed (page 267, Op. cit. Markham's translation)—" Hubinas, Chiquiguanita, Quimistaga and Collaguas, are villages belonging to this city (Arequipa), which were formerly very populous, and possessed many flocks of sheep. *The civil wars of the Spaniards have now destroyed the greater part, both of the natives and of the sheep.*" This after thirteen years seems doubtful. Of its occupation by the Incas he says nothing.

I was to go on the road towards Puno:—" All these railroads of Mr. Meiggs, taking them in the order of their geographical position—1st, from Ilo to Moquegua; 2nd, from Mollendo to Arequipa, to Puno, and on to Cuzco; 3rd, from Callao over the Andes to Oroya, and thence (as I hope it will extend) to the Uyacali, one of the important sources of the Amazon; 4th, from Chimbote to Huaraz; 5th, from Pacasmayo to Guadaloupe, and to Cajamarca —seem to me but the initiatory steps, or breaking of the ice, into Peru. I do not speak authoritatively—for I hold no claim to be in the confidence of Mr. Meiggs on the subject—but simply from my own observations of such of them as I have visited. The result of these makes me opposed to a belief I often hear expressed,—that the lines in question can never pay, or, in fact, never can be a commercial success. Admitted that they are not likely to do so for some time; but they lead to and connect with lines that must pay, because penetrating through the richest mineral districts in the world. That of the Oroya, after branching off to the silver country of Cerro del Pasco, leads on to the valley of Chanchamoya, with its teeming fertility, and thence to the Amazon; whilst that of Arequipa, before going to Cuzco, branches off from Puno to Lake Titicaca, "one of the richest in natural soil of the valleys of the world."

Emerging with the train from the station at Arequipa in a line at right angles from the road by which we came up from Mollendo, we cross a long bridge, a considerable portion of which may be entitled a viaduct; for only a short fragment of it is required to traverse the Chile river. This bridge is 1580 feet long, and 65 feet high, at the loftiest part of its centre over the water. Soon after crossing, one of my fellow-passengers pointed out to me a place near the Cerro Colorado (Red Hill)—so called, I believe, from its principal stone formation being of a red-coloured trachyte. At this is the position, entitled the " Siete Chumbos " (or Seven Pots of Chicha), from which General Prado bombarded Arequipa in 1867.

The road from Arequipa to the first station at Totoras, a journey of eight leagues, is a series of curvatures and windings about, still ascending, but with no retrograde journey, as we have between Mollendo and Arequipa. At this station and in front, towards the south, we see before us the lofty mountain of Pan de Azucar, or Sugar Loaf, which is behind the Misti, and is calculated as 17,000 feet above the level of the sea.

At the distance of a mile and a half on the north side of this station is the little town of Yura, which has thermal waters. They are chalybeate and sulphurous, having a very extensive reputation. Just about the time of my passing here, a concession had been made to Senor Don Luis Carranza, Don Estanislao Pardo Figares, and Don Leandro Loli, for the construction of a bath establishment at Yurn, and for an exclusive monopoly of the same for several years. There was, however, such an opposition got up against it in Arequipa that the National Government at Lima, under the rubric of the Minister of Finance, Senor Masias, immediately did away with it. One of the arguments against the concession was to the effect, that tradition had recorded these waters having been used for medicinal purposes long anterior to the conquest.

From Totoras to Urajapampa we have a journey of five to six miles,—all the surroundings looking as freshly volcanic as if they were only eruptions of yesterday—basaltic, cindery, ashy, sulphurous, solid lava, copper-coloured, and generally grating to the sight. At the station of Aguas Calientes (Warm Waters), in the valley of Quisco, we are twenty-eight miles from Arequipa, and 3500 feet above that city, as well as a total of more than 10,000 feet above the sea level. The sharpness of the air speaks emphatically of the altitude of the position, and suggests thoughts of *soroche*. There is a small stream of warm water here (whence the name of the place), which has an unvarying temperature of 90° Fahr. Parallel with this, and only a few yards distant, runs a rivulet of cold water from the Sumbay: that I am told is the parent source of the Arequipa river, the Chile.

I visited the hospital with the Padre Augustin Clementin Uriah. This is one of those ambulance hospitals, which Mr. Meiggs has attached to the temporary working-places, or "camps," as they are called, of all his railways. It has accommodation for about fifty patients; but there were no more than thirty in it at the time of my visit,—the chief disease being of the lungs, from which it is not easy to be cured up here in the thin air, more particularly amongst the natives, who do not, in general, attend to the functions of the skin, as an adjuvant to healthy respiration.

The old Padre Augustin is an amateur artist, and showed me some excellent busts, although very small, of Mr. Henry Meiggs and his brother John, which he had chiselled with a penknife out of marble brought from the Guamango department of the valley of Ayacucho. The medical man, Doctor Juan Rafael Sarautz, accompanied me through all the wards, to see the sick. There is a commodious Botica (apothecaries' room) attached, with accommodation for the padre, doctor, and a few male nurses. The whole is constructed of galvanized iron, and can be taken asunder to be removed farther on, as the line progresses to the interior.

Twelve leagues beyond this is the Sumbay camp, where a bridge is to cross the river of that name, with a span of 180 feet, and a height of 120 feet over the water. The only tunnel on this line, as far as Puno, is to be in the Quisco district, and 323 feet long. At Cachipesané, nearly 100 miles interior from where we are now, it appears that a qunutity of magnetic stone exists. Mr. Taylor, one of the engineers, who was a fellow-traveller in my return journey from Quisco, tells me that in the department of Cachepesané the railway line is to run between two lagunas or lakes, at a height of 13,960 feet above the level of the sea. One of these lakes is six miles long and two miles wide. They are sixty miles from Puno, at the Arequipa side.

At Sumbay, on this Puno railroad, and extending six miles from the rails to the south-west, has been discovered this year an extensive tract of coal. The reports of the chemical analysis made on it by Professor Raimondi, of Lima, as well as of the extent of its veins by the engineer, Mr. Alexander Hall, give highly favourable accounts of the excellent quality of the coal. In Lima a company has been formed to work it, under the title of " Industria Carbonifera de Sumbay," with a capital of 2,000,000 soles.

CHAPTER VII.

Return from Arequipa.—From Mollendo northwards.—Islay.—Exports thence.—The Chincha people.—The Chincha Islands.—Idols found here at depths of thirty-five feet, and sixty-two feet under guano.—Guesses at the antiquity of these.—Regal emblems from under the guano.—First discovery of guano on the Chincha Islands.—Pisco railway.—Pisco town.—Monotony of railroad to Ica.—Peruvian Sandwich.—Burial-mounds at Ica.—Urn with dis-articulated skeleton.—Foundation of Ica.—Aqueducts of the aborigines, falsely attributed to Incas.—Garcilasso de la Vega.—First coast invasion of the Incas made in the valley of Ica.—Silver work of art from Ica.

RETURNING to Mollendo, I found the question on the *tapis*—and which I was told had been frequently started of late years—to be that of making a railroad from Islay to La Joya, remembered no doubt by my readers, as the mid-way station between Mollendo, and Arequipa, whereat the passengers stop to breakfast. The advocates for this advance two facts:—the first, that in the port of Islay you generally find quiet waters, and therefore an almost unvarying facility of communicating with the shore, whilst in that of Mollendo the tranquillity of the sea is exceptional. The second is, that from Islay to Arequipa there exists a distance of only seventy-five miles, whilst from Mollendo to the latter there are more than one hundred miles.

Those who support the existing state of things aver that the railway from Mollendo to Arequipa being *un fait accompli*, it would be very ridiculous to do away with it for a railway from Pisco, only ten miles distant on the shore-line. For neither the passenger nor goods traffic could support two lines of railway here.

From Mollendo proceeding northward, the first place sighted is Islay. As we approach, and the steamer's anchor is let down, the appearance of the town from the roadstead is of a large bunch of houses huddled together, without any semblance of street or open space, except the surrounding rocky plateau, to walk upon. High above the houses is the convex, oblong, brown-tiled roof of the church. Islay is said to have about 700 inhabitants. Its chief exports are alpaca, vicuna, and sheep's wool, together with Peruvian bark. Alpaca wool is exported at the rate of sixty to seventy thousand bales per year, each bale from 100 to 120 lbs. in weight. It comes chiefly from Puno, but some of it is likewise brought from Cuzco.

The following data were given to me by Mr. A. Barclay, who is at present her Majesty's Acting Consul at this port:—

EXPORTS FROM ISLAY.

WOOL EXPORTED FROM ISLAY, PERU, IN THE YEARS 1869 AND 1870.

		Bales.	Quintals.	lbs.
1869.	1st class Alpaca	18,431	21,298	58
	2nd class Alpaca	6,177	4,676	65
	Vicuña	80	86	75
	Sheep	28,920	19,567	02
	Total	53,608	45,629	00
1870.	1st class Alpaca	17,754	21,285	21
	2nd class Alpaca	3,504	2,778	50
	Vicuña	95	93	05
	Sheep	22,950	15,489	25
	Total	44,303	39,645	01

Between Mollendo and Islay we pass some rocky islets, on which are slight streaks of guano. On the rocks hereabouts, bounding the coast, is something white, presenting the semblance of hoar frost, but which I am told is pearlash. Past Quilca,[1] twenty-five miles from Mollendo—a small green bight being the only part visible adjoining the shore, and from whence olives, oil, and wine are exported. This place suffered much from the earthquake of 1868. From Quilca, after a voyage of 119 miles, we have a look at Chala—another of these small ports wherent the Pacific Company's steamers call—also producing wine, olives, and wool. Chala has a church with some houses, all of the same colour as the rock

[1] Mr. Markham tells us this was the port of Arequipa till the year 1827, when it was supplanted by Islay. It is mentioned in the same character by Pedro de Cieza de Leon, but the "great rivers" of which he speaks as being here have dried up.—Op. cit. p. 265.

on which they are perched. The population is said to be near 200. About thirty-five miles beyond

STONE IDOL AND WATER-POTS FOUND 62 FEET UNDER GUANO.

Chala we pass Loma, from which the principal exports are cotton and sugar. Then, not much farther on, steaming inside of the Chincha Islands, anchor is cast in the roadstead of Pisco.

Long, long time before the birds and seals began to accumulate guano on these Chincha Islands— indeed, so long that, on looking at the illustrations subjoined, I am almost afraid to guess—the Chincha people must have held sway down here. How many thousand years may have passed—in a case like this it is nonsense to talk of hundreds —since that stone idol was made and worshipped

CHAP. VII.]   ANTIQUITY OF IDOLS.   105

before it got by design or accident in a position that the daily droppings of birds and seals covered it to a depth of sixty-two feet?¹ How many

WOODEN IDOL FOUND AT A DEPTH OF 65 FEET UNDER THE GUANO.

decades have elapsed between this evidence of the stone age, and the period of the wooden idol discovered at a depth of thirty-two feet, or with twenty-seven feet intervening? Let us reflect for

¹ Mr. Bollaert tells us that Dr. Tschudi kept one of the guano birds, the *Lula variegata*, and found its daily weight of excrement to be three and a half to five ounces. This would be an erroneous basis to take for calculation, because Dr. Tschudi's bird, being in confinement, must have left all its deposit in its prison; whereas the guano birds on the Chincha and elsewhere are often on the wing in quest of food, and therefore may be supposed to leave part of their droppings abroad.

a moment. Is there any living, calculating Pedder, who could find out the quantity of birds it would require, in the ordinary action of such cases, to deposit the smaller of these depths—say of twenty-seven feet—about the height of four men and a half, each six feet high? and with this to find out the probable period occupied in such operation? If so, I should like to have it done. And the twenty-seven being doubled, with eight more feet added on, an approximate calculation to be made. "I find myself," observes Mr. Baldwin,[1] "more and more inclined to the opinion that the aboriginal South Americans are the oldest people on the continent; that they are distinct in race, and that the wild Indians of the north came originally from Asia, where the race to which they belong seems still represented by the Koraks and Chookchees found in that part of Asia which extends to Behring's Straits."

All my observations hereabouts,—at Chincha Islands, Pisco, Ica, the Cañete Valley, and subsequently elsewhere,—convince me of the correctness of Mr. Baldwin's opinion in the first sentence stated. The relics of household gods and regal emblems, taken from a depth not known to me, but very, very deep, show there must have been a people in the country, who were driven out either by the Chinchas, or by a

---

[1] "Ancient America." By John D. Baldwin, A.M.

tribe who preceded them. The Chinchas,[1] be it remembered, were anterior to the Yuncas, who

REGAL EMBLEMS AND HOUSEHOLD GODS.[2]

were conquered by the Inca Pachacutec in the fifteenth century. Royalty could have had no

[1] Pedro de Cieza de Leon says, "As to the origin of the Indians of Chincha, they say that, in time past, a quantity of them set out under the banner of a valiant captain of their own tribe, and arrived at this valley of Chincha, where they found many inhabitants, but all of such small stature, that the tallest was barely two cubits high." (Op. cit. p. 260.) Whence they set out we are not told. Don Pedro does not give the same account of the subjugation of these valleys as Garcilasso de la Vega.

[2] One resembling the right-hand emblem is in the Christie Collection presented by Mr. Harris, as from Guanape or Maccabes.

residence on such a small place as this Chincha Island. But no doubt these things were hidden in it, when their proprietors were about to be expelled from their altar firesides by the force of some ruthless invader. The emblems in this case are made of very hard wood. Of the idols, five of the figures are wooden, and the other two of very coarse pottery-ware.

The Chincha Islands, three in number, are esti-

WOODEN IDOL FOUND AT A DEPTH OF 33 FEET UNDER GUANO.

mated in 13° 38′ S. lat. and 79° 13′ W. long. They are nearly front of, and only a distance of ten to twelve miles outside, the open roadstead of Pisco.

From Gore's Liverpool Directory, I find that South American guano was first imported into Liverpool by the brig " Heroine," from Valparaiso, consigned to Messrs. W. J. Myers and Co., and arrived on the 23rd of July, 1836. It was a sample of only thirty bags, and was given away to parties for experiment.

In 1866 there were 351,674 tons of guano exported from the Chincha Islands, of which 74,851 tons were in British ships.

But the regular exportation began only in 1841. It was not until 1853 that the Peruvian Government ordered a survey of the islands, in which they calculated the total amount of guano to exceed twelve millions of tons.[1] It seems almost impossible for the mind to conceive the length of time, and the number of birds required, for such an accumulation.

"The three Chincha Islands," observes Mr. Markham,[2] "in the Bay of Pisco, contained a total of 12,376,100 tons of guano in 1853, and as since that time 2,837,365 tons have been exported up to 1860, there were 9,538,735 tons remaining in 1861. In 1860, as many as 433 vessels, with a tonnage of 348,554, loaded at the Chincha Islands, so that at the above rate the guano will last for twenty-three years—until 1883."

I may here point out a few errors in the fore-

---

[1] "Geography of Peru," p. 47. By M. Felipe Paz Soldan.
[2] "Travels in Peru and India," ch. xviii. p. 306. London: Murray, 1862.

going calculation. In the first place, for corroboration of the paragraph ending at the words "remaining in 1861," the reader is referred to a small pamphlet, with plans, published by the Peruvian Government in 1854. Secondly, that they were founded on mistaken data is proved by the fact that the guano of the Chincha Islands has been exhausted two years ago, or in 1871. So that here is the supply for nine years to be rubbed out. And thirdly, to base a calculation for so many successive years on the status existing at the period of "the above rate," must have been a foregone conclusion (as it has proved) without foundation. Because the increasing knowledge of the utility of guano, joined to the daily progressive commerce on the Pacific, should have been considered, to make an estimate approximating to a less exaggerated result than the foregoing.

Writing further of the guano, Mr. Markham* says, "The Peruvians may consider themselves secure of their strange source of revenue for some twenty years to come." It is very difficult to limit the amount of injury done to the Peruvian Government, as to the Peruvian people, by publication of a statement proved to be so very wide of the mark as this last-mentioned.

Although guano was said to have been discovered only at the period of the small cargo referred to, it appears to have been known to the Peruvians from

* Op. cit. ch. xviii. p. 308.

time immemorial.* Stevenson[10] tells us, "Some small islands at the entrance to the Bay of Pisco are famous for the manure which they produce, and which is embarked and carried to different parts of the coast, and often into the interior, on the backs of mules and llamas. The quantity of this manure is enormous, and its qualities are truly astonishing. Of this I shall have occasion to speak when treating of the cultivation of maize at Chancay."

On one of my visits to Chancay I saw heaps of guano in the neighbourhood of the Captain of the Port's office, where it is stored for use of the agriculturists in the valley.

From the exposed and unruly sea in the roadstead of Pisco we land by means of an iron mole, seven hundred yards in length. This terminates with the Custom-house on one side, and the Captain of the Port's office on the other. From hence there is also a line of rails laid down to the station which is near the port, along with from fifteen to twenty business houses, in the shape of shops, and one hotel. But to go to Pisco proper we have

---

* Garcilasso de la Vega, writing of the guano here, says, "Each island was by the Incas set apart for the use of a particular province" (Op. cit. lib. v. cap. viii.); whence we might infer there were only three provinces in the Inca territory.

[10] "An Historical and Descriptive Narrative of Twenty Years' Residence in South America." By W. B. Stevenson. Three vols. London: Hurst, Robinson, and Co., 1825. Vol i. p. 357.

a drive of about a mile, a considerable part of which is alongside of an ill-flavoured açequia, or watercourse, and past the railway station. The town itself is a melancholy-looking place, although having a very large church in the centre of a very spacious plaza, where the market stands. Pisco was founded probably not long after Pizarro's time; for we find that in A.D. 1640, the then Viceroy, the Marquis of Mansera, raised it to the position of a city, with the additional nomenclature of San Clemente de Mansera. Senor Paz Soldan tells us it was sacked by English pirates in A.D. 1622, and A.D. 1685. Then it stood by the side of the sea; but in the earthquake of 1687 it was destroyed by a great wave; therefore it was subsequently erected where we now find it. So early as 1602 it had a convent of Franciscan Recluses; in 1634 was erected a like building of St. John of God (San Juan de Dios); and the temple of San Ignacio was established by the Jesuits in 1700.

To go to Ica[1] by the railway, we must, however, return to the port. I had the pleasure of being accompanied in my trip on this line by Mr. Grundy, one of the engineers, who superintended the track-laying. It is forty-eight miles from Pisco to Ica.

[1] This word is spelt by Senor Don F. Larrabure y Unanue, an eminent *littérateur* of Lima, as Eeca. Mr. Unanue is a frequent and graceful contributor to that excellent periodical, 'El Correo del Peru.'

CHAP. VII.] LARGE BURYING-MOUNDS. 113

When first projected, hopes were entertained that it would be prolonged to the interior districts of Huanca, Velica, and Ayacucho—the last-named being celebrated as the locale where was fought, on the 9th of December, 1824, one of the most famous battles of the independence period.

Before starting from Pisco,* I may observe that there are several very large burying-mounds, or huacas, not far distant from this town. Others are

MUMMY FROM A HUACA AT PISCO.

likewise to be seen ranging along the coast up by Tambo de Mora to the Canete Valley. But no difference exists in what I have observed of the mum-

---

* Coal has been discovered this year at Paracas, about eight miles to the south of Pisco.

VOL. I. 1

mies taken out here, or of the accompaniments in the graves, from those observed in other places.

The road from Pisco to Ica is one of the most dreary and uninteresting that can be imagined. Rocks and sand are everywhere.

There is scarcely anything worth calling a station along the road—our first stopping-place being at Joanquil, about 15½ miles from Pisco. Here there is a cutting through gypsum, and about half a dozen date-trees away to the right, making a most miserable failure to appear as an oasis in the desert. While the train stops I had the first acquaintance of that most unappetizing condiment, the Peruvian sandwich,[2] sold by the Cholo women at what may be styled the embryo stations. This and chicha (the brew of Indian corn) seem to be the chief things relished by the natives. The sandwich must be a thing most difficult of digestion, unless to a stomach of ostrich organization. It is composed of a little roll of bread half-baked. Cut in two, we have in the centre a slice of pork, a shrimp, an olive, bit of sausage, over all which is poured some oil for sauce, and the article is ready.

After journeying across forty-eight miles of a country, every inch of which was suggestive of the African Sahara, the freshness of the valley of Ica, with its cornfields, trees, and vineyards, was

[2] It is called *Butifárra*, which, I observe in the Dictionary, is the orthodox Spanish word for sausage.

CHAP. VII.]   PERUVIAN CROCKERY-WARE.   115

very pleasant. The town itself is enough to give one the glooms for many years. Every house, as at Arequipa, speaks the word " Earthquake " in all its features. There are a few hotels, not the worst of which is the " Hotel Americano," with the anomaly of being kept by an Italian. About one mile outside the town is the hacienda of Senor Don Enrique Martinez, to whose brother I was introduced at the railway station by Mr. Grundy. To this I made a visit for the purpose of exploring a Huaca.

At the farm of Senor Martinez I found nothing in the shape of building, mound, or other erection. In his yard was a portion of ground elevating gradually to the wall, and in no place rising more than a few feet above the circumjacent soil. In this I was told bodies were buried. But, although there were a few arm-bones lying scattered about, and no inconsiderable quantity of bits of old Peruvian crockery-ware, nothing resulted from a few hours' labour of excavation.

At another burying-ground, however, a mile or so farther on, I had better results. Here I employed, for a dollar, a man who worked some hours in digging, and did it in a style that I never saw surpassed by an English navvy. The result was several dishes of very plain pottery, and some few bodies. All of the latter crumbled into ashes the moment they came into contact with the external air. Here also was taken out of a grave a crock or urn, about two feet high or thereabouts, which contained the whole of the bones of a human being. It came to be rapidly disintegrated on exposure to the air, like those previously disinterred. I did not think of examining whether it was of man or woman. The joints no doubt had been disarticulated, or separated one from the other, before being put into this urn. The last-named likewise contained some burnt cloth, and a quantity of ashes.

The most curious fact connected with this interment of a body in an urn appears that the same practice took place with the Indians at the Bracho' in Santiago del Estero, a province of the Argentine Republic, at the other side of the Andes. These people last-mentioned present a strange feature amongst their Spanish-speaking neighbours, namely, that their idiom is the Quichua, the ancient language of Peru, and that not two out of the whole community can talk a word of Spanish. I sent this urn from Ica to Dr. Barnard Davis; but unfortunately it was broken on the voyage.

The city of Ica was first founded in the year 1563, near Tacaraca, which is four miles to the south-east of the present site. But the terrible earthquake of 1571 obliged the inhabitants to alter

---

* *Vide* Author's "Buenos Ayres and Argentine Gleanings," p. 175. Stanford, London, 1865.

CHAP. VII.] REMAINS OF AQUEDUCTS. 117

the position, and the town built after that is now called the old one (Pueblo viejo). Subsequent earthquakes in 1647 and 1664 gave it other shakings; and another new town was built close to the ancient. It is very difficult, looking at it now, to imagine that there ever could have been anything of new connected with it. The exports from Ica through Pisco are wine, Aguardiente, Italia (a sort of brandy), cotton, and cochinilla. This city is the capital of the province, which contains seven districts, and a reputed population of 14,000 inhabitants.

Paz Soldan, in his "Geography of Peru,"[1] speaking of one of these districts called Nasca, says, "There can be seen in Nasca the remains of the aqueducts of the Incas, that astonish the beholder by the grandeur of their construction. I am sorry not to be able to give an exact description of them. I can only say that they are two walls of rough stone, with flags on top to form the aqueduct, which in parts is so high that one can walk inside without stooping. They are from four to five feet in height, and about three in width. Some of them are narrow. There are so many that it is not possible to count them."

Besides this, Senor Paz Soldan tells us in the next sentence, "At eight leagues from Pisco are the remains of a palace, which in the present

[1] Page 568.

day is called the *Tambo*⁶ *Colorada* (or coloured milk-shop). Said palace was constructed by the Incas, under the reign of Pachacutec, in whose time the conquest of this valley was effected."⁷

To these two statements my subsequent travels oblige me to give a most unqualified denial. For neither the aqueducts nor the palace could have been made by the Incas, who came here, as it will be seen, to destroy everything. On these same matters, Garcilasso de la Vega,⁸ from whom Señor Paz Soldan takes his cue, has written a tissue of—to use the mildest terms—the most meagre of fables.

Before going into Garcilasso's volume I wish to point out that another author, and native like him, descended likewise from Incaito blood, has been recently brought to light,⁹ who records the invasion

---

⁶ The word Tambo is also applied to some towns in the north.

⁷ Pedro de Cieza de Leon says, "In this valley of Ica (he spells it Yca) there were great lords who were much feared and reverenced. The Yncas ordered palaces and other buildings to be made in this valley." It is very curious there is not even a vestige of these Inca palaces, whilst the ruins of the Indians, who preceded them, are about everywhere.

⁸ Commentarios Reales, que tratan de el Origen de los Incas, Reies que fueron del Peru, de su Idolatria, Leies, y Govierno en paz y en guerra, de sus vidas y Conquistas, y de todo lo que fue aquel Imperio, y su Republica, antes que los Espanoles pasaron a el, escritos por el Inca Garcilass de la Vega, Natural de Cuzco, y Capitan de Su Majestad, Madrid, 1609. Of this work a translation into English has been made by Mr. Clements R. Markham, and published by the Hakluyt Society.

⁹ "Narrative of the Rites and Laws of the Yncas." Trans-

of the Incas in the coast valleys as from north to south, whilst the former brings them from south to north. Juan de Santa Cruz Pachacuti-Yamqui Salca Mayhua, whose great, great, grandfathers were amongst the first to embrace the Christianity of Pizarro at Cajamarca, after several pages' profession of his faith, thus writes:—" The Ynca Pachacuti obtained great sums of gold, silver, and *umiña* (emeralds), and he came to an island of the Yuncas, where there were many pearls called *churup mamam*, and many more *umiñas*. Thence he marched to the country of Chimu, where was Chimu Capac, the chief of the Yuncas, who submitted (?) and did all that was required of him. The curaça of Cassamarca, named *Pisar Capac*, did the same. The Ynca then marched along the coast [from Chimoo south] to Rimac Yuncas, where he found many small villages, each with its *huaca* (idol). Here he found *Chuspi-huaca* and *Puma-huaca*, and a great devil called *Aissa-vilca*. He then advanced by Pacha-Cámac to Chincha, where he found another *huaca* and devil. Returning to Pacha-Cámac, he rested there for some days. At that time there was hail and thunder, which terrified the Yuncas. The Ynca did not demand tribute here as he had done in the other provinces." Thus it may be seen, that whilst

lated from the original Spanish MSS., and edited with Notes and Illustrations, by Clements R. Markham, C.B., F.R.S. London, 1873. Printed for the Hakluyt Society. Page 94.

Juan de Santa Cruz traces the Inca progress from north to south, Garcilasso does the reverse—from south to north.

According to Mr. Markham,¹—" Xeres [this was Francis Xeres, Secretary to the conqueror Pizarro] never seems to have heard the word Ynca [so spelt by Mr. Markham in contradistinction to Garcilasso, who has it Inca]. He calls the Ynca Huayna Capac—the father of Atahualpa and Huascar, by the name of 'Old Cuzco' throughout—mistaking the name of the capital city for the name of the sovereign. He also calls Huascar 'Young Cuzco.' Hernando Pizarro (brother of the conqueror) makes the same mistake."

From which it might be inferred that the Incas, or Yncas, were not invented till after the conquest—perhaps when Polo de Ondegardo first wrote of them in 1550.

In the 13th chapter of the 3rd book of the Commentaries, we are told that the Inca Capac Yupanqui, the fifth of his race, conquered many provinces in Cuntisuyu, and after subduing the Quichuas, reduced many valleys on the coast of the sea—that is the Pacific. All the people in these valleys were named Yuncas, which signifies "warm ground." The valleys, so subdued, were called Hacari, Vina, Camana, Caravelli, Picta,

---

¹ "Reports of the Discoveries of Peru." Translated and edited by Clements R. Markham, C.B. London. Printed for the Hakluyt Society, 1872. Page 33.

CHAP. VII.] INVASIONS OF COAST VALLEYS. 121

Quellca, and others. Of these I can find only Acari (no doubt Hacari), Camana, and Quilca—three which are to the north of Islay, between it and Nasca—on the latest map of Peru, published with this book.

The chief invasions of the coast valleys took place under the reign of Pachacutec,[1] the ninth of the Incas, and were chiefly carried on by the Inca's brother, named Capac Yupanqui, and his son and heir, Inca Yupanqui, a lad of only sixteen years old on his first expedition. Pachacutec, with his brother and son, set out from Cuzco with an army of sixty thousand men, one half of which was to remain as a *corps de reserve* at the appointed halting-place, which was Rucana, seen on the map as San Juan de Lucana. Here the Inca stopped with thirty thousand men, whilst the other moiety went on to Nanasca (no doubt the present Nasca). Thence the brother general sent a peaceful kind of message to the rulers of the Ica and Pisco valleys—namely, that he came to put them under the sweet government of the Incas, with the provision that they should give up adoring their heathen gods, and worship the sun, who was the father of Pachacutec.

These people, having found that they could get no succour from the neighbouring tribes of the valley of Chincha, submitted. All the Yuncas

[1] Op. cit. b. vi. ch. xvii. p. 191.

of the coast at the time worshipped the sea and its products—more especially sardines—wherewith they manured their land. This was of course independent of their family idols.

Polo de Ondegardo tells us:[1]—"The Incas were for a long time unable to conquer more than the provinces bordering on Cuzco until the time of Pachacuti Yuca Yupanqui. His father had been defeated by the Chancas and retreated to Cuzco, leaving his troops in a *pucara* (fortress). Then the son formed an army out of the fugitives, and out of the garrison of Cuzco, and out of the men of Cancs and Caneches, and turned back to attack the Chancas. Before he set out, his mother had a dream—that the reason of the victory of the Chancas was that more veneration was shown for the Sun than Pechayachic, who was the universal creator. Henceforward a promise was made, that more sacrifices and prayers should be made to that statue."

This, it may be seen, is diametrically opposed to Garcilasso de la Vega, who makes the Pacha-Cámac,[2] (no doubt, the prototype or *alter et ego* of Pachayachic,) to be worshipped only interiorly, whereas here he is spoken of as regards his statue.

---

[1] "Narrative of the Rites and Laws of the Yucas." Translated from the original Spanish MSS., &c., by Clements R. Markham, C.B., F.R.S. Printed for the Hakluyt Society. London, 1873. Page 154.

[2] *Cámac* means *Creator*, and *Pacha* the *world*.—Cieza de Leon, Op. cit. p. 253.

In the valley of Ica—Garcilasso continues[1]—
"the Incas ennobled themselves by making most
beautiful azequias, or aqueducts, to bring water
from the lofty mountains, on its journey from
east to west. For the small river which ran
through the valley carried very little water in the
winter time, and the residents suffered much from
want of it. But with the help of the azequias,
which were larger than the natural stream, their
crops were plentifully supplied, so that over
after they lived in great abundance and prosperity."[4]

In the next column to this we are told that the
conquering Incas, having gained the allegiance of
the valleys of Ica and Pisco, sent like messages to
the ruler of the Chincha valley—a powerful chief,
who was recommended to give up the idolatry of his
people, and come over to the true faith of the sun
worship. With this was sent the advice, if they did
not do it willingly, to take up arms as soon as they
pleased, for the Incas came to compel them. They
replied to the first message, that they did not want
the Inca for their king, nor the sun for their god;
that they had gods of their own to adore, and a
king to serve; that their chief god was the sea,
of which they had a higher opinion than they
could have of the sun; that the former gave them
fish, whilst the latter scorched up their soil and

---

[1] Op. cit p. 192.
[4] This is copied from Cieza de Leon.

prevented its yielding sufficient fruits; that their land and climate was hot enough without making devotions to the sun, who made it hotter. They wanted no strangers in their land, and there was no necessity for Pachacutec to advise their taking up arms, as they were always prepared to fight in defence of their gods, their liberty, and their country. Their god, they added, was Chincha Camac, who was the creator and supporter of their native place So that the Incas had better return to their own country, and not begin a war with the Lord and King of Chincha, the brave Chuqui-Mancu, who was one of the most powerful of princes.

These Chincha people, Garcilasso confesses, were not the original occupiers of the soil here. For they, according to a tradition of their own, had come from foreign parts, although they knew not whence, and with a captain-general,[1] as religious as he was brave, took possession of this valley by force of arms. War in this case did not require much, as their predecessors—the old story—were a vile, contemptible, and sneaking race. Therefore they were all rooted out without leaving one. Here an inquiry may be suggested: Were the Chinchas, or their predecessors, the builders of these mounds and fortresses in the valley which bears their name?

[1] Likewise copied from Pedro de Cieza de Leon. *Vide* chap. vii. p. 106.

No information on this subject can, at any rate, be gained from Garcilasso; for in the next chapter I feel myself once more puzzled by the author's anachronisms.

We are expected to believe that the Incas, coming down here to make war, carved out, as they must have done in such a short time, and by something of the Jack and the Bean-stalk process, azequias for the Yuncas to bring water from the lofty mountains. In the same page with this we learn that the campaign proceeded with great cruelty and slaughter on both sides, "the Yuncas fighting to defend their country, and the Incas to enlarge their empire, honour, and fame." Now and then the Incas sent messages to the besieged, offering peace and friendship on the old terms, all of which were refused most courageously. The fighting continued for several months, during which the army from Cuzco had to be renewed three different times, 90,000 men being thus required.

But the General Capac Yupanqui tried the plan of starving them out, by laying waste their crops, as well as by besieging them more closely. Moreover, says Garcilasso, "he ordered to have their azequias or aqueducts broken up, so that they could not irrigate their fields; and this was most sensibly felt by the Yuncas, because, as their land is so warm, and the sun burns it up so much, it was indispensable to have it irrigated every three or four days to enable it to give fruit."

Depriving them of water was, of course, successful in bringing the operations to a close—of water brought to their fields by aqueducts, which must have been made by the Yuncas themselves, or their predecessors. For the Incas, never having been in this locale previously, could have nothing to do with the azequias on the seacoast valleys.

Garcilasso denies, what he says some authors state, that this war lasted many years instead of months: but the more I read of his book the less faith have I in it. Especially when he tries to depreciate the Yuncas of Ica, Pisco, and the Chincha valleys as dirty and of idle habits—qualities not at all likely to be held by people who were

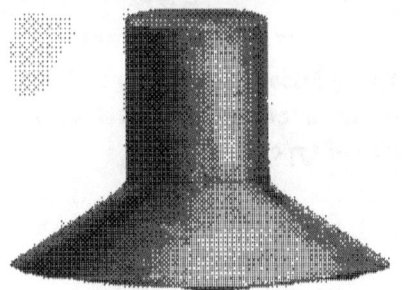

SILVER CYLINDER FROM ICA.

so advanced in the arts, as is shown by the silver cylinder accompanying this. The figure is caused by stamping from behind, and the form of the whole work is exactly similar to one which I hold in my possession, that was taken out of a burial-place at Chan-Chan, the capital of Chimoo, and nearly a thousand miles farther north. This one was got in a burial-place at Ica. It was lent to me, for taking a copy, from the collection

FACE OF PRECIOUS SILVER CYLINDER.

of Senor Don Miceno Espantoso at Lima. In art, therefore, as in craniology, we may recognize a persistence of type.

CHAPTER VIII.

The Valley of Chincha.—Tambo de Mora and Cañete.—Cerro de Azul roadstead.—Chuqui-Mancu.—Sugar estates in Cañete Valley.—Necessity of exploring the ruins about here.—Creation of Society of Fine Arts by President Pardo.—Exhuming skulls from the Cerro del Oro.—Particulars of things got out.—Ikaina, or shell-trumpet.—Ride through the Cañete Valley.—Chinese labourers.—Their joss-houses.—Prescott's opinion of Garcilasso de la Vega.—Progress of the invading Incas through Cañete Valley.—Huarca and Runahuanac.—Reputed Inca fortress at Hervay.—Olives from Seville.—Vessels of Pacific Steamship Company.—Limits of Callao jurisdiction.

STILL I am bound northward from Pisco, past the small rivulets of Pisco and Caucato, beyond which the equally diminutive stream of Chincha empties itself into the sea. From hence, skirting a long stretch of valley by Tambo de Mora, and Chincha Alta, in which I recognize ancient and modern institutions quite close to each other—namely, the grave-mounds and ruins of old forts adjacent to sugar manufactories, with their lofty chimneys, indicating the presence of steam-engines. The best way to get into the Chincha valley, or Cañete (as it is now called, from the extensive plantations of sugar-cane), is to land at Cerro Azul, whence I can get up in a tramway to either of the three haciendas belonging to my very good friend, Mr. Henry Swayne, of Lima.

The province of Cañete is a very important one, as well as very extensive. It is about fifty-seven miles in width, and occupies a shore face to the Pacific of 270 miles, namely, from Tambo de Mora, which is its southern boundary, outside the province of Pisco, to the hacienda of San Pedro, dividing it from the province of Lima, a few miles south of the far-famed Pacha-Cámac. The whole valley is occupied with sugar plantations, and it has often been a wonder to me, that a railway hence to Lima has not been opened, as I believe no better paying railway could be established in Peru. The roadstead of Cerro Azul is one of the most violent on the coast, and sometimes for many days communication cannot be made between the shore and ships, riding at anchor a few hundred yards off.

After what I have submitted of Senor Paz Soldan's dogma about aqueducts and the palace of the Incas at Ica, it may perhaps be unnecessary to state that I cannot agree with him or with Senor Don E. Larraburu y Unanue in reference to the azequias and the old palace here. These are accredited by both gentlemen just named, as well as by Garcilasso de la Vega (from whom, no doubt, they took the idea), to have been works of the Incas. Mr. Soldan speaks of the "Palacio del Inca" (Palace of the Inca) as well as of a fortress in the valley of Limahuaná, one of the districts of Cañete, both of which works he writes of, as done by the Incas. The grand fortress, it appears, was nearly all pulled down in the seventeenth century, by the Viceroy Conde de Monclova, to build up the castle of Callao.

Yet Senor Unanue does not go so far as Mr. Soldan. For though to a certain extent walking in the tracks of Garcilasso de la Vega, he describes the ruins of Canchari, which he suggests was either the residence of some powerful Yunca, or of the King Chuqui-Mancu himself. The description which he gives of it would apply to many such ruins of greater extent, that I have visited only a few miles outside of Limá in the Huatica valley. He then sketches the fortress of Chuqui-Mancu, no doubt the one over the desecration of which Mr. Soldan mourns. This fortress stood not far from the river Cañete, between a chain of small hills, that bounded the valley on the eastern side. The conquest of the brave king who occupied it was not a walk over, like that at Ica and Pisco, as Senor Unanue tells us that bloody battles were fought during eight months, and the army of the Inca had to be renewed four times from Cuzco. Each of these levies consisted of thirty thousand men, so that there was needed a force of one hundred and twenty thousand.[1] The account of the bulwarks resembles exactly a description of the

[1] "Correo del Peru," Nos. 13, 14, and 16, vol. i.

grand ruins of La Campana, and San Miguel in the Huatica valley, of which I shall speak hereafter.

Chuqui-Mancu was called the lord of four valleys—Chillca, Huarcu, Runahuanac, Malla—and his subjugation was a great thing. But I am inclined to believe many readers will agree with me in requiring other evidence than that of Garcilasso de la Vega, to suppose that the so-called monument of Hervae was built in the valley of Huarcu by the Incas to commemorate their great victories here.[1] When Garcilasso de Vega came to look at this place in 1560 (less than two hundred years after it was reported to have been built by order of Pachacutec), it was in a state of deplorable ruin—a thing perfectly impossible after such a short period, in a climate so conservative of everything as Peru. This building is described as having been constructed of the best materials of workmanship. There are many more niches in the walls of it than in either of the other two edifices, and therefore it is more likely to have been a temple for the heathen gods of the Yuncas, than a memorial erected by people, who professed that they came to root out idolatry, and to substitute for it the worship of the Sun. The principal walls were built of *Adobones*, or colossal mud bricks,

[1] Dr. J. Von Tschudi, speaking of Paramanca, a similar edifice to this, but farther up the coast, says, "It was not, however, built as a monument of victory; for such monuments were always erected in Cusco, the capital, and never on the field of battle." (Tschudi's "Travels in Peru," p. 289.)

in the same style as the fort of Chuqui-Mancu. Its walls had been scratched over by some of the conquerors coming here with Pizarro, who apparently had no one to fight against in these valleys, and whose soldiers, probably, were some of the first that dug down into the building under the ridiculous impression that the Incas had hidden treasure here.

All through this valley, over much of which I rode in company with Mr. Martin (the superintendent of Mr. Swayne's hacienda at Quebrada), burial-mounds are passed everywhere. Of such as these Mr. Squier speaks in relation of his exploration in the United States:[*]—"The mounds and their contents, as disclosed by the mattock and the spade, serve more particularly to reflect light upon their customs, and the condition of the arts amongst the natives who built them. Within these mounds we must look for the only authentic remains of their builders. They are the principal depositories of ancient art; they cover the bones of the distinguished dead of remote ages, and hide from the profane gaze of invading races the altars of the ancient people." That the existing Government of Peru is about, even at the eleventh hour, to take these principles into consideration, is shown by the fact that it is keeping pace with the progress of the times. The

[*] "Ancient Monuments of the Mississippi Valley." Published by the Smithsonian Institute, 1847.

CHAP. VIII.]   EXPLORATION OF MOUNDS.   133

first step has been taken by a decree of his Excellency the President, Senor Don Manuel Pardo, issued on the 17th of December last, constituting a Society of Fine Arts (Sociedad de Bellas Artes), one of the objects of which is to have a National Museum in the Exhibition Palace at Lima.

From one of these burial-grounds at Cañete has

TERRA-COTTA MASK FOUND IN A HUACA.

been dug out a mask of terra-cotta, similar to that of which there is a drawing in Mr. Squier's report of his explorations in the State of New York. The latter was discovered some years ago in making excavations for the St. Lawrence canal. The one illustrated here is to be seen in its original amongst the articles, shown at the Exhibition Palace, from the National Museum at Lima.

During my stay at Cañete I rode on another day,

BOSINA, FRONT VIEW.[1]

in company with Mr. Swayne's general superintendent, Mr. William Ronwick, to the top of the hill called the Cerro del Oro. Some people say it

[1] The shell called "Bosina," I am informed by Senor Raimondy, was used as a trumpet by the Indians, to announce the approach of any great man into a town. The title above indicated is given on account of the sound produced by blowing into it having resemblance to the roar of a bull. The tassels on it are of human hair, and the leather strap holding it is of exquisite workmanship. It was lent to me for photographing by Mr. Walter Shaw (Pacific Steam Navigation Company), of Callao, but I learnt subsequently it had been dug up at Cañete.

derives this title from the quantity of gold found here by the Spaniards. That they made extensive excavations is evident from the fact of some thousands of human skulls lying exposed to the sun, mingled with leg, arm, and rib bones, as well as with pieces of cloth, and masses of cotton flock, that enveloped the bodies in their interment. These are all on the side of the hill which faces the south. On the top are very extensive ruins of

BOSINA, BACK VIEW.

houses, consisting of only parts of walls, and in the centre of which appears to have been a large fort. From these graves, too, were taken out several copper and silver pins, of the class with which shawls are fastened, tweezers for pulling out the hair of eyebrows, of the eyelids, and whiskers, as well as silver drinking-cups.

On the day that I went across part of this valley with Mr. Martin, we passed through ruins innumerable—ruins of houses, walls, burying-mounds, and forts. To all of these in Peru the name of Huaca is indiscriminately given. The word Huaca, according to Garcilasso de la Vega, is derived from a verb which signifies "to weep," and therefore appears to me to be applicable only to the mounds, which are known to contain dead bodies. At one part of our journey, after rounding a hill beyond Hualcara—the principal sugar estate of Senor Ramos of Lima—we came to an aqueduct, or azequia, which had half a mile in length of a tunnel, and that was from four to five feet in height. This is reputed to have been constructed by a Spanish padre named Olairda, who wrote a book under the title of "El Evangelio del Triumfo" (the Gospel of Triumph). It runs under the Cerro de Andala, and is a work of pre-eminent utility to the lower grounds. For my part, I am not inclined to believe it was done by other persons than the original holders of the soil here, unless better testimony than the *ipse dixit* of any man can be given to me.

On returning to the sugar manufactory of Quebrada, we passed through what is called the Pueblo Viejo. It is said to have been the site of the ancient Huarco, where Pizarro and Almagro met in one of their conferences. We also skirt the hacienda of Montulvan, formerly belonging to the celebrated O'Higgins, one of the heroes of Independence. This estate was presented to the valiant old man by the Peruvian Government; but it is now in the hands of an Italian company, having its head-quarters at Lima. Another tunnel is reported to be on the estate of La Imperial, and accredited to have been made by the Conde de la Vega, when viceroy at Lima. But I did not care to see it, as I have no faith in such work having been done at any time by Spanish priests, or viceroys.

Mr. Swayne has got four estates here, namely, Quebrada, Casa Blanca, Huaca, and Carillos, all of which are communicable one with another by tramways. The ploughing on these is done by steam ploughs. Besides, he has a farm near Cerro Azul, another close to Chilial, and a hacienda at Ungara on the southern side of the second range of hills, that run transversely through the valley, and south of the Cañete river. His property in this valley includes an extent of more than ten thousand acres, and has an annual produce of more than two millions of dollars' worth in rum and sugar.

At the Quebrada I first saw Chinese labourers on the coast of Peru. Their treatment is exceptionally good, and on Mr. Swayne's different properties they number beyond fifteen hundred. They have their joss-houses, and their opium-smoking saloons, without both of which it would be as difficult to make them work as the proverbial impossibilities "to wash the blackamoor white, or make the leopard change his spots." There is a hospital for them, which is daily attended by the Doctor from Cañete town, and they seem to be as happy as the day is long.

Owing to the state of ill-health in which I was when down at Cañete, I regretted very much not being able to explore any more of it. But I brought away with me some specimens of skulls from the Cerro del Oro, procured through the kind assistance furnished by Mr. William Renwick. These form part of the instalment which I sent to the Anthropological Institute of London, that were exhibited on the 1st of April in this year, and about which a paper was read by Professor Busk, F.R.S., President of the Society. In the illustration of these the celebrated craniologist, Dr. J. Barnard Davis, of Henley, took part, and I believe they created considerable interest at the meeting.[1]

Besides these relics of humanity I obtained some slings that were found in the graves, with a few specimens of little wooden idols, one of which is very curious, as representing the large lobes of the ears of a warrior with a cocked hat, and holding what appears to be a shield in his hand. He is not armed, and may therefore be supposed to be doing only the "head-work." In this we have such a case of enlarged ear-lobe as is spoken of by Mr. Harrison,[2] although in the case before us certainly not traceable to the Incas.

I did not leave Cañete at all satisfied with the

[1] *Vide* Appendix A.
[2] "Journal of the Anthropological Institute of Great Britain

account of the conquest of these Chincha valleys given by Garcilasso de la Vega, whose book I studied during my stay of a week at Mr. Swayne's

WOODEN IDOLS FROM HUACA.

sugar estate of La Quebrada. The more I read of this work, the more it appears to me as made to order,—to glorify the Incas, and by consequence to re-glorify the Spaniards who conquered them.[1]

After the nineteenth chapter, in which it is

and Ireland," July and October, 1872, p. 190. On the Artificial Enlargement of the Ear-Lobe. By J. Park Harrison, M.A.

[1] Prescott says, "His commentaries are open to a grave

denied that, according to some false rumours, the war lasted here for several years instead of months, we are brought back to Cuzco to witness the principal festival of the Sun, and the preparations made for it. But this chapter terminates with an account of how Capac Yupunqui, the general, and brother of Pachacutec, sent once more for another army, that he wanted to punish some of these Yuncas, who were not only disobedient, but actually rebelled against the new laws, and customs introduced by the Incas. Thence it was supposed that their dereliction of common sense must have arisen from these people being accustomed to commit unnatural crimes, such as caused the destruction of Sodom and Gomorrah in the days of old. For this there was only one cure, namely, that "el suave govierno de los Incas"

objection, and one naturally suggested by his position. Addressing himself to the cultivated European, he was most desirous to display the ancient glories of his people, and still more of the Inca race, in their most imposing form. This, doubtless, was the great spur to his literary labours, for which previous education—however good for the evil time on which he was cast—had far from qualified him. *Garcilasso, therefore, wrote to effect a particular object.* He stood forth as counsel for his unfortunate countrymen, pleading the cause of that degraded race before the tribunal of posterity." ("History of the Conquest of Peru," p. 129.) Although there are few writers for whom I have a deeper respect than for the illustrious historian of Mexico and Peru, I believe him to be too lenient in his judgment here. Garcilasso might have affected the glorification of his own race without trying so earnestly to disparage, as he does, everything done by their predecessors on the coast.

(the mild government of the Incas), as Garcilasso styles it, "should make prisoners of all those who were known to have rebelled,' and in one day burn them alive,—have their houses knocked down,— their crops scattered about,—their trees torn up by the roots,—so that no memory should remain of anything they had planted with their hands. The women and children were burnt for the sins of their fathers, without anything of humanity being considered as involved in it, because they had been guilty of a vice which the Incas detested with the most fervent earnestness."

Then we have eight chapters devoted to an account of the religious ceremonies to the Sun at the capital, as well as of military and civil discipline. These devotions to the Sun included the sacrifice of goats, sheep, and cows,—because they were his property. The details are too minute to transcribe. So after all this worship the General Capac Yupanqui went back again to carry his invasion farther north. In his previous visit he had only destroyed the Chinchas of the Cañete valley, whereas he comes now with ministers, arms of war and ammunition (it is a pity we are not told of what kind they were), commissary stores, and everything necessary to invade the beautiful valley of Runahuanac, governed over, as already mentioned, by Chuqui-Mancu, the lord of four valleys. The disputed philology of the word

' Op. cit. chap. xix. p. 195.

Runahuanac occupies more space than I care
to devote to it. It appears, however, to be
not only the name of the valley, but of a
river, in crossing which many of the invaders were
drowned. In these times the valley was densely
populated, as may be seen by any one who wanders
through it in the present day. On the first
attempt at crossing of the river, the King Chuqui-
Mancu came to meet the invadors, and several
bloody battles took place. The Yunca king, not
being up to the strategy of war, made battle
in the valley of Huarcu (now Cañete) instead
of Runahuanac, and was therefore defeated. It
took only one month to do this, according to Garcilasso de la Vega, but Señor Larraburo y Unanue
says it cost the Inca eight months' fighting, with
an army, as I have before stated, four times
renewed, and requiring one hundred and fifty
thousand men. Others say the war lasted four
years—a period, probably, much more likely than
either of the previous.

But hunger soon made the people importune
Chuqui-Mancu to give up; for, although it is not
stated so, we may suppose it natural that the Incas
chief did here as he did elsewhere, namely, tear up
the crops, and destroy the watercourses. The Incas
people had begun to threaten the Yuncas that they
would soon hand them over to their old enemies,
the neighbouring Chinchas, or, we may suppose, as
many of them as were left after the general burning
mentioned in the previous page. But the subjects

of Chuqui-Mancu, having their patience worn out by the length of the siege, with its accompaniments of thirst and hunger, came out in a multitude to the Inca, and, "going down on their knees, asked mercy and pardon for their faults, adding that they rejoiced to become vassals of the Inca, since the Sun his father, sent him to conquer the whole world."

The Inca's uncle and nephew received them with much meekness, made them presents of clothes and other things, sending them all back contented to their homes. To this succeeded the surrender of the other three provinces; and then, all the people, not conscious of the good that was brought to them by the children of the Sun, boasted that the Incas took four years to subdue them—that they conquered them by hunger and not with iron. Moreover, they said a great many things about their own deeds and their bravery, "besides several other items of talk which we don't care to mention," says Garcilasso, "because it does not affect history." Very true and trite indeed.

As a trophy of this victory, he continues, the Incas built, in the valley of Huarcu, a fortress, small in compass, but grand in proportions, and of wonderful workmanship. The sea beat on it, and injured it; and "it was left for many centuries (muchos siglos) without repair," which was the cause of its being so destroyed when I passed there in 1560."

[1] Op. cit. p. 209.

Garcilasso seems to forget it was less than two centuries previous to the coming of the Spaniards that these valleys were conquered by the Incas; and that, therefore, if the fortress in question had evidence of "some centuries" of decay, it was out of the question that it could ever have been built by the Incas. Yet this I believe to be the one of which Mr. Markham

PERUVIAN PREHISTORIC POTTERY-WARE.

writes, "The best preserved Inca edifice of which I took measurements is at Hervay."[1]

Previous to my departure from Lima, I got from Mr. Richardson a copy of some prehistoric crockery-ware, which, on showing to an archæological friend of mine there, were said by him as

[1] "Journal of the Royal Geographical Society," vol. xli. p. 323. London, 1871.

known to have been taken out of burying-grounds in some part of the Chincha valley. If such be the case, and that the Yuncas in this part, or their predecessors, were the artificers of these beautiful things, they can hardly be considered as the savages, which many parts of Garcilasso's book would lead us to believe.

In several portions of the Cañete valley we see groves of olives, which were brought out some years ago, by Senor Don Francisco Carabantes, from Seville. In the valley are also vines, the original of which were introduced from the Canary Islands, by Don Antonio Rivera. There is a copper-mine in this province, in the district of Coayllo, but it has been abandoned.

All through Cañete are about twelve to fifteen sugar-cane establishments for the manufacture of sugar and rum. Of these Senor Laraburro y Unanue writes:[1]—

"In all these plantations there are some differences which are worthy of being noted. That of Unanue attracts attention by its splendid Gothic palace, without a rival in South America (if we are to believe some travellers), and by its railroad, that places in communication the most remote parts of the farm, as well as facilitates the transport of the sugar-canes. The manufactory of Montalban (O'Higgins) is famous for its sugar-refining, according to the best systems practised

[1] "Correo del Peru," vol. i. No. x. p. 77.

in Europe. That of Aroma (Don Pedro Paz Soldan's) for the beauty and picturesqueness of its hillocks. Whilst Hualcara (Ramos's) is well known for the excellence of all its products. The same can be said of Santa Barbara (formerly belonging to Mr. Carillos, and now owned by Mr. Swayne). But those of the Huaca, Casa Blanca, (White House) and La Quebrada, (the ravine) of Mr. Swayne, surpass all the rest, not only by their discipline, but by their steam-engine works, that are the most perfect in the valley. They likewise realize the largest amount of products."

To meet the trade daily increasing in Peru, vessels of the Pacific Steam Navigation Company—one of the best managed, and therefore one of the most successful, companies in the world—ply twice a week from Callao to Cerro Azul, the port of Cañete, and *vice versâ*. In case of a considerable shipment required, the large steamers of the Straits line will touch here.

From Cerro Azul to Callao is a distance of less than eighty miles by sea; and Cerro Azul is the southern boundary of the Callao jurisdiction. I prefer, however, asking my readers to accompany me on a visit to Pacha-Cámac, which may be seen, by the map, to lie between this and Lima. For we can go the voyage at any time by sea.

CHAPTER IX.

Inca progress to Pacha-Cámac and Rimac.—Account of it by Garcilasso de la Vega.—Cuys Mancu, or Hatun Apu, Lord of Pacha-Cámac and valleys adjacent.—Temples of Pacha-Cama, and Dolphic Oracle of the Rimac.—Message sent to Cuys Mancu.—Machiavellianism of the Incas.—Craft of Capa Yupanqui.—Treaty of the Incas with the Yunca Chiefs.—Conditions of same.—Unconditional surrender of Cuys Mancu.—The Devil coming to have a finger in the pie.—Author's visit to Pacha-Cámac.—Cyclopean work.—Mr. Steer's tracking.—Evidence of niches for idols as of sacrificial fires in supposed Temple of the Sun.—Skulls with sutures in the frontal bones.—General conglomeration of ruins.—Unsatisfactory results.—What Stevenson says of Pacha-Cámac. —Wonderful messengers.—Dr. A. Smith's opinion.

THE King, Chuqui Mancu, having been subdued, according to Garcilasso, as well as orders given to him that the government, laws, and customs of the Incas should be introduced to his people, the conquerors passed on from Huarcu (or Cañete) to annex the valleys of Pacha-Cámac, Rimac, Chancay, and Huaman. This last-named place may be observed on the map as Huaura, near to Supe—a little farther northward. The Spaniards afterwards gave to it the title of Barrancas, or the banks. All these were governed over by a powerful chief, named Cuys Mancu, who did not presume to call himself king, for there was no such word amongst the Indians, but whose official rank was expressed by the title of Hatun Apu—that is, Great Lord. A glance at the map will show my readers what an extensive territory these valleys included. The names mentioned cannot give half an idea of its greatness. For in it are included the valley of Lurin, near to Pacha-Cámac—the large and formerly densely-populated valley of Huatica in the triangle, formed by Chorillos, Lima, and Callao, and bounded on the west by the Pacific Ocean,—the valleys of Ancon and of Pasamayo, which have burying-grounds in them with thousands and thousands of bodies,—the valleys of Chancay and Huacho, with all the signs of an enormous population intervening.

Before getting to Pacha-Cámac, Garcilasso tells us that the Incas, with the natural brightness which God gave them, had first started the idea of Pacha-Cámac, which signified a great being— the maker and sustainer of the universe. This faith was spread throughout all territories both before and after their conquests. It was because this spirit was invisible that they made neither temples nor sacrifices to him as they did to the Sun; but they adored him interiorly in their hearts, with great expressions of demonstrative devotion of head, eyes, arms, and body, when the name was pronounced. This doctrine having been spread about with the fame of the Incas, it had been adopted by the predecessors of Cuys Mancu, who built a temple at Pacha-Cámac, and gave the same name to the valley in which they founded it—which in these times was one of the most famous on the coast. In the temple the Yuncas had their idols,—figures of fishes, as well as of the female fox.[1]

The temple of Pacha-Cámac was one of the most solemn edifices of the kind in Peru. Here the Yuncas made sacrifices, not only of animals, but of men, women, and children.

In such things I may interpose they did no more than their conquerors. For Polo de Ondegardo, the first writer who mentions the Incas, speaking of their sacrificial doings at Cuzco, says, "On these occasions they killed the girls, and it was necessary they should be virgins, besides offering them up at special seasons, such as for the health of the Inca—for his success in war—for a total eclipse of the sun—on earthquakes, and on many other occasions suggested by the devil."[2]

Besides the temple of Pacha-Cámac there was another in the valley of Rimac, four leagues farther north than the former.[3] The term Rimac signifies

---

[1] Op. cit. c. xxx. p. 208.

[2] *Vide* Mr. Markham's translations of "Rites and Laws of the Incas." Op. cit. p. 161.

[3] In "Peruvian Antiquities," by Mariano Eduardo Rivero, p. 168, I find the following note :—"Tradition relates that the celebrated temple of the idol Rimac, in the valley of Huatica, was continuous to Limatambo ; and that the destroyed town has

one that speaks. The Deity, therefore, was the Delphic oracle of this part of Peru. Some of the Spanish historians confounded the temple of Rimac with that of Pacha-Cámac; but, it appears, they were entirely different.

A similar message to that formerly sent to the Chinchas was now forwarded to Cuys Mancu—namely, that Pachacutec had come to show him and his people the true religion of the Sun—that they should give up their idols and conform to the Inca's government, laws, and manners—and that he proposed in the first place a peaceable surrender, as he purposed to enforce his religion whether they liked or not. To which the great Cuys Mancu, having called all his nobles, ministers, and soldiers about him, sent a reply—that his vassals had no need of another master—that they had no want of other laws than their own—and that they did not require knowledge of any gods than those they had—that they adored their Pacha-Cámac, the creator of the universe,—that they likewise worshipped Rimac, who spoke to them, and gave them answers when they consulted him. They also venerated the she-fox for its caution and astuteness, and the sea, because it gave them so much fish. But the Sun they did not care for, as their ground was hot and dry enough; so they begged the Inca

passed into that of Magdalena." That this is a mere conjecture, without any foundation as regards the site, may be seen hereafter.

not to molest them, as they did not need his
Empire.

Then the Incas came out with their Machiavellianism—although I believe the author of that system was not born in these days. They rejoiced that the Yuncas had such veneration for Pacha-Cámac, whom they themselves adored interiorly as the highest god. So they proposed not to make war, but to have a general palaver, and invited Cuys Mancu to the conference. This latter had already set out with an army of men to defend his territory, but the General Cupac Yupanqui sent to him a request not to fight till they talked more over their gods, as he wished to tell him that the Incas, besides adoring the Sun, also worshipped Pacha-Cámac. Although they did not build temples to him, nor offer sacrifices, because they had not seen him, and did not know what sort of a being he was, interiorly in their hearts they worshipped him, and therefore there was every reason why the Incas and the Yuncas should be brothers, and friends, instead of fighting. Moreover, Pachacuteo would guarantee that, for the future, the Inca kings, besides adoring Pacha-Cámac, and holding him for creator and supporter of the universe, should worship and adore the oracle, Rimac, on condition that the Yuncas would come over amongst the children of the Sun—a god better deserving of adoration than either the earth or the sea, the she-fox or any animal. He suggested, likewise, that they should obey the Inca, his brother, who was a son of the Sun, and the pattern of everything clement, pious, just, and merciful—that they would do well to consider these things over dispassionately, and come to the peaceful arrangement proposed, instead of offering to resist the power of the Incas, that no force of arms was able to subdue.

So, after a short truce, peace was concluded on the following conditions:—"That the Yuncas should adore the Sun as the Incas do; that they should build for this worship a temple apart (*templo aparte*), like that of Pacha-Cámac, but no more human blood should be shed, as it was against the law of Nature to kill a man that he should be offered up in sacrifice.¹ That they must remove their idols from the temple of Pacha-Cámac, because he, being the creator and lord of the universe, was only to be adored in their hearts, and not with idols—that for the better ornament and grandeur of the valley of Pacha-Cámac, they should found a house of selected virgins,² in combination with the Temple of the Sun, in the style which they had it in Cuzco—that the King Cuys Mancu should hold his rights, as well as the other Curacas or chiefs,—obeying the Inca as supreme lord, to follow the laws, customs, and

¹ See extract from Polo de Ondegardo, at page 149 of this chapter.
² Which they never did, or of which, at all events, no vestige remains at the present day.

manners of the latter—that the Incas should maintain much esteem and veneration for the oracle Rimac, and send orders to all his kingdoms to observe the same."

After the conclusion of this treaty, and everything was arranged for the Inca executive in the valleys of Pacha-Cámac and Rimac, the next step was for the General Copac Yupanqui and his nephew to return to Cuzco, with an account of their mission to the Inca. In this journey they were accompanied by Cuys Mancu, in order that the Inca king should know him, and give him thanks with his own hand. Nothing is said of Chuqui Mancu, who was not so easily brought to terms as the other. But Cuys Mancu went; the great Inca came out from Cuzco to receive him, and he was overpowered with feastings and with presents—all the Incas of the royal blood being bidden to the feasts to do him welcome. These things passed, Cuys Mancu was sent back rejoicing, and "perfectly convinced that the Inca was a true son of the Sun, worthy to be adored and served by the whole world."*

I must confess that it shakes my faith in Garcilasso's narrative when I find him continuing—as I am now about to quote—in the same strain of seriousness with which the previous account was written, and in the very sentence succeeding the last:—"It must be known that as soon as the Devil (*El Demonio*) saw that the

* Op. cit. c. xxxi. p. 211.

Incas were about to lord it over the valley of Pacha-Cámac, and that his temple stood emptied of the many idols it contained, he put himself up for the particular lord whom the Indians adored," and more bosh to the same effect. In part of Prescott's work on the "History of the Conquest of Peru," we find the Devil spoken of in the same serious manner.[1] The dreadful battle of Puna was caused by Pizarro "having abandoned his wretched prisoners, ten or twelve in number, to the tender mercies of their rivals of Tumbez, who instantly massacred them before his eyes." Then the people of Puna sprang to arms, and with fearful yells and menaces went in to battle. But Hernando Pizarro conquered them, having put them into a state of panic-strike by his terrible array of steel-clad horsemen, with the stunning reports and flash of fire-arms. "Yet the victory was owing, in some degree, at least if we may credit the conquerors, to the interposition of Heaven; for St. Michael and his legions were seen high in the air above the combatants, contending with the arch-enemy of man, and cheering on the Christians by their example." This story is told with such seriousness, as being translated from Montesinos, I am almost afraid to desecrate its gravity by suggesting that, according to what I have been taught on the subject, the arch-enemy of man, being up in the air, must have been out of his

[1] "History of the Conquest," chap. i. p. 144.

element, or like a fish out of water; so that we need scarcely wonder at his being conquered. At all events, it is quite clear that the Devil in old times has had his fingers in many pies amongst the Peruvians.*

It was not until a few weeks previous to my departure from Callao that I was able to visit the ruins of Pacha-Cámac. As we are here on the spot with the Incas and Yuncas of old, I deem this an appropriate place for giving my account of it. Premising that I am indebted to Mr. William Sterling, managing director of the Lima and Callao Railway, for having kindly supplied me with horses for my party and self. These consisted of Lord Cochrane; Mr. J. B. Steer, a celebrated North American explorer, from the University of Michigan; Mr. John Schumaker, of Valparaiso; Mr. Woodsend, of the London Bank of Mexico and South America, at Lima; and Mr. George Wilson, the son of our Vice-Consul at Callao. We started from Lima for Chorillos by the first train, at 8 a.m., taking with us some commis-

* Cieza de Leon devotes considerable space to the pranks of the Devil in Peru. In chap. xlix. and after, much is left out by Mr. Markham as "unfit for translation"—I should suppose from its indecency. He says (page 182), "In all parts where the holy Evangel is preached, a cross is placed, at which the Devil is terrified, and flies away." Chapter cxviii. is devoted to accounts of a Chief, who, when he wished to be converted, "saw the Devils visibly." As he sometimes "saw them when he was sitting with a glass of liquor before him" (p. 416), perhaps their colour was blue.

sariat necessaries, and a few large sacks to bring anything back, that might be worth appropriating.

At Chorillos we met the horses sent down for us by Mr. Sterling—three mules with provender and sacks having gone ahead on the previous day. Here, too, we were received by Senor Don Vicente Silva, Colonel and Commissary of the National Guard, and Prefect of Lurin, to whose hacienda at San Pedro, two miles from Pacha-Cámac, we were invited on the day before, and from whom we received the most courteous attention during our night's stoppage at his house.

The road going eastward from Chorillos passes, at the distance of a few hundred yards outside of the town, one of those grand old forts, with high walls, bastions, embrasures, and a wonderful work of architecture, that are so plentiful over Peru. I expressed to Mr. Schumaker my desire to have a sketch of it, but unfortunately time did not permit him to do more than the five excellent drawings of what we saw at Pacha-Cámac, and which accompany this chapter.

Our ride, after passing by the hacienda of Villa,[*] only half a league distant from Chorillos, was along the sea-shore. This style of journey occupied more than half the way. We started from

---

[*] The old fortress and the hacienda in this place are the property of one of the Goyanaches—family of the late Archbishop of Lima, who is said to have died worth twenty-five millions of dollars.

GENERAL VIEW OF PAGSA-CAUAO INCLUDING ANCIENT CITY, AND RUINS OF BURIAL HOUSES.

Chorillos (after breakfasting at the Hotel San Pedro) at ten o'clock, and reached the ruins of Pacha-Cámac at about two p.m.

Whilst Senor Don Vicente Silva proceeded to his house to make preparations for our breakfast, we commenced our explorations. The immense size of the débris,—of huacas, temples, city, and burying-grounds, at once convinced me that nothing more than a cursory inspection could be taken. A Cycoplean mass of earthwork is before us as we enter on the sacred place of these ruins. This is more than two to three hundred feet high, and forms a semi-lunar shape, that is beyond half a mile in extent, stretching with its concave side to the south. We mounted to the top by a roundabout passage on horseback; but here the place was such a confused mass of wreck, that a measurement was impossible unless we could stop a week at it. The first glance showed what Dr. Archibald Smith, writing of it, describes [1] "like the temple of Cholula on the plains of Mexico;—a sort of made mountain or vast terraced pyramid of earth."

Mr. Steer commenced by tracking the topmost terrace. One ledge he found 248 paces, or yards, in length, whilst some of the lower ones were only 150. The height between four of these terraces is from six to eight feet each; but there was so much

[1] "Peru as it is." By Archibald Smith, M.D. London, Richard Bentley, 1839. Two volumes. Vol. ii. p. 306.

disintegration of stone walls about, and such a quantity of earth mixed up with them, that the measurements were very difficult to be defined. I did not ask him to attempt any further, when he told me, after half an hour's pacing and calculation, that the top measured ten acres square, and this at a height of nearly 300 feet from the base.

On the western side, and about twelve feet beneath the highest part, is a row of arched recesses, or alcoves, high enough to admit a man of ordinary stature to stand upright in any of them. From each end of these, but on the terrace above, are the remains of a large wall, about three feet thick, and stretching backwards to the east. The wall facing north is built of stones outside and of adobe, or sun-dried brick inside, whilst that fronting the south has adobes in its fore-part, and stones within. One can scarcely imagine these recesses could have been used in worship of the Sun, from the simple reason of their facing towards the setting of that luminary instead of its rising. Unless, indeed, we were to allow the faculty mentioned by the poet Moore of—

"The sunflower turns to its God when he sets,
The same look that it turn'd when he rose."

Much of these walls are washed over with a red paint, and in three or four places are square niches, apparently of the same shape and size as we see in the ruins of Pagan

CHAP. IX.] GRECIAN SCROLLS AT PACHA-CÁMAC. 159

temples on the lowlands. Of this colouring—
done probably with ochre—Dr. Smith likewise
remarks, that, although executed many centuries
ago, it is as inviolate and fresh on the mud
plaster, as if it were the work of yesterday.
He further adds, "By-the-bye, it may not be
impertinent to mention, that, among these paintings, we find what is called the Grecian scroll,
which, if I am not mistaken, the Grecians bor-
rowed from the Egyptians. This may serve to
throw some light upon the origin of Pacha-Cúmac.
Like that of Mexico,—nay, with still more
emphatic gesture,—the gigantic architecture of
Peru points to the Cyclopean family, the founders
of the temple of Babel, and of the Egyptian
pyramids. I believe that the temple of Pacha-

RUINS OF REPUTED TEMPLE OF THE SUN AT PACHA-CÁMAC.

Cámac was standing when that part of the coast was conquered by the Incas, so that there is no knowing its age." [*]

From one side, going towards the north, is the relic of a wall, which is covered with soot—possibly the remnant of fires to make sacrifices—and nothing can better illustrate the conservative tendency of the Peruvian climate than the fresh appearance of this soot. Two questions at once suggest themselves whilst I am resting here: If this were a Temple of the Sun, built as it is on the top of a large huaca or burial-ground—for

ARTICLES TAKEN FROM GRAVES IN THE BURYING-GROUND AT PACHA-CÁMAC.[1]

right under where I am seated—though a few hundred feet below—Mr. Steer and Mr. George

[*] Op. cit. p. 306.
[1] 1, Copper chisel; 2, flute of sheep shank; 3, smoking pipe of deer's horn; 4, copper implement; 5, terra-cotta figure; 6, wooden bowl; 7 and 8, grinding-stones with grinders.

CHAP. IX.]   DISINTERRING BODIES.   161

Wilson, accompanied by four Chinamen, are, with pick-axe and spade, disinterring bodies—why should we find niches for heathen deities and evidences of sacrificial fires? Or whose hands carried up the enormous quantities of earth, that fill every space, and allow no definition of rooms, halls, or indeed of anything but the clay itself, and the walls cropping up from amongst them?

On the uppermost terrace I saw two sticks stretching sideways out of the clay, and, having the place opened, found three bodies inside, with the same style of swathing as those taken down lower—the only difference being that the grave was lined with stone. Some of the old Yunca people I should suppose buried here in the Temple of the Sun by the Incas—if I am to believe

VIEW (FACING EAST) OF RUINS AT PACHA-CAMAC.

that the Temple of the Sun was built on the top of a Yunca huaca, and afterwards filled with clay. On the centre plateau, descending about seventy feet, I observed some graves opened, which were lined with sun-dried adobes; but in the lower ground, where Mr. Steer and Mr. George Wilson have dug, and are still taking out relics, they are buried very thickly together, and simply in the clay. It was from these that we got several bodies, so very old that, on opening the wrappings in which they were enveloped, they all fell to pieces. I managed, however, to get together a few score of skulls for the Anthropological Museum. We likewise obtained no inconsiderable number of curiosities. Amongst them were the matters designed on the accompanying engraving, together with a lot of rude figures of wooden faces. Some of these were stuck in the cloth encircling the head, and not a few of the heads had bags of coca-leaves fastened on the top. Several of the female bodies had with them the toilette of "a lady of the period," consisting of a very small apron of about ten inches in width, and four inches deep, with strings attached for fastening them round the loins.[*] All of these human remains were rolled round with cloth, and encircled with rope in the same style as those we got at Chosica—hereafter described. The eye-sockets of

[*] Garcilasso de la Vega speaks of these as the dress of married ladies. Mr. Markham's translation, vol. i. chap. xiii. p. 57.

many were stuffed with masses of cotton flock, and some of the men had slings enclosed in their wrappings. In the skulls I brought with me were two with holes, evidently caused by the stroke of stones flung from slings, and two others having frontal fissures like those I had previously obtained at the burial-place of Pasamayo, about ten miles north of Ancon, on the Lima and Huacho railway.

Accompanied by Mr. Schumaker, I rode over to a distance of about a quarter of a mile, northward from the great mound, to where was a very interesting ruin of a square building. It might have been a place for worship of some kind, for although the edifice was only about twenty yards each side, the inner rooms were full of square niches.

VIEW (FACING WEST) OF PREVIOUSLY-MENTIONED ACCREDITED TEMPLE AT PACHA-CÁMAC.

The walls of this were about two yards in thickness, made of *Adobones*, although on a stone foundation. Several of these niches had bevelled cornices of perpendicular direction, and one or two of them were rounded at top. On the opposite side of this was an arched vault, which in the original state, and judging from the level of the circumjacent ground, was from eight to ten feet in height. Even still it is beyond five feet, reaching up to my chin as I stand before it. In three of the niches alongside of this are horizontal indentations of about six to eight inches wider than the niches themselves; and these have on them marks of cord pressure into the adobe when fresh,—suggesting that from them hung down pieces of cloth, fastened in by wood, to hide the faces of their deities from the vulgar gaze. From this, towards the west, ran out two strong abobe walls, each two and a half yards in thickness, which apparently constituted part of the enclosure of the temple in the days of its integrity. The basement of these walls is built with large masses of stone, fitted into one another with perfect art, without any mortar or cement.

Besides the similarity of the frontal suture to some of those skulls I had dug up at Pasamayo, as already mentioned, many obtained here had bits of copper in the mouth, like several of those last named. All through the ruins of the town, inside the walls of what once seemed houses, as well in large squares, skulls were everywhere lying about, together with the different bones that belonged to them. Thus extensive excavations had been made here by the treasure-hunters. Many small bits of crockery-ware were scattered amongst the ruins, and I saw two very large vases, each capable of holding from twenty to thirty gallons. But their enormous size prevented my bringing off either of them. They were from four to five feet in height, and of proportionate rotundity. Neither of them, however, were perfect, as each had been broken, to a certain extent, from the manner in which they had been tossed about as useless, by men who came here only to seek silver and gold.

Whilst I was with Mr. Schumaker during his sketching of the last small temple, Lord Cochrane rode over to the ruins of some old walls, which stood about three quarters of a mile distant in the direction of Lima. On his return, he told me they stretched away from east to west, or from the sea inland to a length that he could not attempt to calculate. I therefore concluded that these were some of the boundary walls of the old city.

From the topmost part of the mound, and looking seaward, we can observe the Pacha-Cámac group of islets, ten in number, that seem like so many volcanic boulders, either dropped into the sea, or pushed up out of it. The largest and most northern has the shape of a sugar-loaf, and is remarkable by being covered with a whitish something that may be guano of bird or seal, or might be a soda efflorescence.

In his notice of Pacha-Cámac, Stevenson[*] likewise goes in the Garcilasso de la Vega track. "In September, 1533," he says, "Don Francisco Pizarro arrived at Pacha-Cámac, a large town belonging to the Indians, where a magnificent temple had been built by Pachacutec, the tenth Inca of Peru, for the worship of Pacha-Cámac, the creator and preserver of the world. This rich place of worship was plundered by Pizarro, and the virgins destined to the service of the Deity, though in every respect as sacred as the nuns of Pizarro's religion, were violated by his soldiers. The altars were pillaged and destroyed, and the building was demolished. However, when I visited it in 1817, some of the walls still remained, as if to reproach the descendants of an inhuman monster with his wonted barbarity." Then wandering amongst the remains of this temple, Stevenson enters into a strain of moralizing about the impiety of Pizarro's work in destroying "an edifice destined by its founder to be a monument of national glory, or even personal honour;" and more of the same kind, of what is scarcely removed from rant. He goes on about "the remains of a building once sacred to a large portion of our fellow-creatures, and raised by them in honour to

[*] Op. cit. vol. i. p. 144.

the Great Father of the universe, wantonly destroyed by a being, in whose hands chance had placed more power than his vitiated mind knew how to apply to virtuous purposes,"—concluding with the climax of—" we cannot avoid cursing him in the bitterness of our anguish."

I can scarcely consider the term "rant" as too severe applied to such sentiments. Because, even independent of the uselessness of cursing Pizarro, it might be a matter of justice to inquire whether he is the party who ought to receive the malediction. For Mr. Stevenson seems to me rather rapidly coming to a conclusion, that the founder of this edifice was Pachacutec, instead of inquiring into the possibilities of its having been made a ruin of by that Inca's brother and son, who were the invading parties here, or perhaps by the original founders of it—possibly the Yuncas—to prevent its being turned to use by invaders. All the revelations of ancient historians about this place incline me to the belief that Pizarro found it in 1533 as it was in 1817 when Stevenson visited it, and as it stood in the month of April last, 1873, when Lord Cochrane, myself, and our party were on the top of it. If it were not so, how account for its being now filled up with clay? We have no relation of any fighting, as a feature of the "conquest," having been at Pacha-Cámac, or in the neighbourhood. We find no record of by whom, or wherefrom, were brought the hundreds of thousands of tons of clay that fill up those rooms, or altar-places. In fact, we see but one large building on the top of this immense mound or huaca, and there exists no indication as to where the house of the nuns stood. Was it inside the walls of the temple, or in the town? Until these points be settled, I cannot help looking on the whole of the story of the plunder of this place by Pizarro, and the violation of the nuns by his soldiers, as a piece of braggadocio, founded on imposture. The ancient Peruvians, whose history was wiped out by the Incas, were, most probably the builders of Pacha-Cámac. And if such a thing be proved, as probably it may be, by further investigations amongst the mounds, it will reveal another illustration of how the mighty spirit of truth seems advancing, before all things, to be the great triumph of the nineteenth century—the triumph of our humanity, and our civilization.

On our way to Don Vicento Silva's house we crossed a pretty suspension bridge over the river Lurin, and along a road, as wide as any highway in England, perfectly level, and shaded on each side with trees. The village of Lurin has nothing remarkable except that its houses, in anticipation, no doubt, of earthquake contingencies, are built of reed and mud—called *Kinshin*.*

---

* This resembles what in West Africa is styled the "wattle and dab"—a framework of bamboo stems over which clay mortar is slapped on.

It has a most melancholy-looking little plaza or square, over which towers a spacious chapel, with a huge dome—a house of worship apparently large enough to hold the populations of two or three towns of the same size. In the valley of Lurin, or as it was formerly styled Pacha-Cámac, there are seven sugar-cane plantations, besides that of Senor Silva; and wherever we go John Chinaman is prevailing. Here, as in many other places in Peru, there is a legend that at a place called Chimeroo, not more than ten leagues distant, the gold is concealed, which was being sent from Cuzco to Cajamarca for the release of Atahualpa, and that the Indians, who were the bearers thereof, either scattered about, or hid, it as soon as they heard of their monarch being murdered. It was a pretty tidy sum—eleven thousand llamas, each carrying a hundred pounds in weight of gold,—or eleven hundred thousand pounds of the precious metal, as we are told by Rivero, Tschudi, Prescott, and many others.'

I rode back to Lima in company with Lord Cochrane and Mr. George Wilson, together with our *arriéro*; the last-named having charge of two mules, that carried more than fifty skulls, with other items of our excavations, on their backs.

' No less than half a dozen different places in Peru are accredited with the storage of this strayed money—Caxma and Yupanqui amongst them.

It is impossible to conceive anything more dreary and desolate than this road—through soft sand half-way up to the horses' knees, and with a line of rocky hills three to four hundred feet high on either side of us. Not a drop of water to be seen anywhere—no well, rivulet, or azequia, till we came within six or eight miles of Lima, where we passed over one of the streams from the Rimac river, that debouches above Lima to water the valley of Huatica. The distance from Lima to Pacha-Cámac is calculated to be only eight leagues, and from Chorillos five. But I think a couple of leagues might be tacked on to the first named, without much fear of exaggeration.

Writing of the Chasquis, or messengers of Peru in the time of the Incas, we are told by Stevenson[1] that the Incas had relays of messengers on all the principal roads, who relieved one another in carrying messages from the coast to Cuzco, or *vice versâ*. The distance from Cuzco to Lima Stevenson makes out only a hundred leagues, or three hundred miles; but I believe it is nearer double that amount. By means of Chasquis, we are asked to believe, " the court of the Incas was supplied with fresh fish from the sea near Pacha-Cámac, —probably from the Bay of Chilca,—where a village of Indians is still employed in fishing. It is the place to which Pizarro was directed

---

[1] Op. cit. vol. ii. p. 65.

by the Indians, when in search of a good harbour before that of Callao was discovered. The distance from this part of the coast to Cuzco is more than a hundred leagues, yet, so vigilant and active were the Indians, Garcilasso affirms "*that the fish often arrived at Cuzco alive.*"

After this, surely no statement of Garcilasso can be doubted; unless, perhaps, by some one who might be credulous on the point of the fish not being acclimatized to the rarefied atmosphere on the Andes' summit of 14,000 to 15,000 feet, over which they had to cross in their journey of beyond one hundred leagues. If the *modus operandi* of this transport were known, I feel confident it would be highly appreciated by Mr. Frank Buckland.

On the morning after my return from Pacha-Cámac, I consulted other works that were in my possession, which had been written by actual visitors to this historic place, for the purpose of seeing how far I could have depended upon them. Opening Rivero's book,' I found as follows, under what the author styles the particulars of the history of Pacha-Cámac:—"On the conical elevation, near the bank of the sea, 458

---

* "Peruvian Antiquities." By Mariano Edward Rivero, Director of the National Museum, Lima, &c. Translated by T. L. Hawks, D.D., LL.D. New York: Putnam and Co., 1853. Page 288.

feet above its level, are found the ruins of the ancient temple of Pacha-Cámac. At the foot of this hill are seen at the present day the decayed walls of the edifices, which were intended to receive the strangers who came on pilgrimages from the most distant provinces of the empire to present their offerings to the deity."

Commenting on Senor Rivero's account, as I proceed, I have here to observe, that at the foot of the hill in question there are no decayed walls of edifices. Moreover the term "hill" is scarcely applicable to what Dr. Smith styles a "made mountain," and such as I believe it to be.[1] At a distance of about 200 yards from its base we find ruined walls, supposed to be ruins of the town of Pacha-Cámac. But that they were intended to receive strangers, who came from a distance for the pilgrimage, seems to me an assumption, for which I cannot recognize any proof. In the next paragraph Senor Rivero says, "The whole was surrounded by a wall of adobes, nine feet in width, and probably of considerable height, for some parts of it are twelve feet in height, although in its average extent it is not more than four or five." Such a wall as is here described only exists at the northern side of the town—running from the sea inland, and separates all the ruins from the desert track to Lima. He

---

[1] *Vide* page 157.

continues, "The material throughout the whole fabric is not hewn stone, as in the edifices of Cuzco, but adobes, easily crumbled." What fabric may be meant here? The "ancient temple of Pacha-Cámac? decayed walls of edifices? or the wall surrounding the whole?"—because, although no hewn stones are in either of the two last, the chief component of the structure on top of the hill is from hewn stone; and the quarry whence they may have been taken, as of a like geological formation, is only about half a mile distant, before crossing the iron bridge over the river Lurin.

Then "the upper part of the highland, or ridge, which is about 100 feet high, is artificially formed by walls—each one thirty-two feet in height, and from seven to eight feet wide. In the most elevated part is seen the temple, with the sanctuary of the deity towards the sea. Its door was of gold, richly inlaid with precious stones and coral; but the interior was obscure and dirty—this being the spot chosen by the priests for their bloody sacrifices before the idol of wood, placed at the bottom of the enclosure, the worship of which succeeded the pure and abstract worship of the invisible Pacha-Cámac. At present there remain of this temple some niches only, which, according to the testimony of Cieza de Leon, contained representations of several wild beasts; and we have detached fragments of paintings of animals made on the wall upon the whitewashed clay. We can, however, still distinguish the place of the sanctuary, according to the description of the early chroniclers."

The only thing on the high building at the period of my visit which could be taken for a sanctuary of the deity are the niches, of which Mr. Schumaker has taken a sketch. The whole of this mound appears to me artificial. But I could not discover where had been any place for door of precious stones, coral, and gold; because the building, whatever it was in old times, has lost all shape or form, leading to being recognized, by being filled up with earth. There is no whitewashed clay, unless that can be called so (Hibernically) which is of a red colour. I saw no traces that could be indicated as paintings of animals.

"The opinion is erroneous," he goes on to say, "which deems these ruins to be the Temple of the Sun. It is one, however, which has been adopted by almost all modern authors, although diametrically opposed to that of the historians contemporaneous with the conquest, as well as to the account given by Hernando Pizarro, brother of Francisco, and destroyer of the temple."

My readers will see by this, we are informed that the ancient temple of Pacha-Cámac was, according to Rivero, not the Temple of the Sun. Yet consulting a work of his fellow-traveller,

Dr. Tschudi,[1] we are told, "Pacha-Cámac was the greatest deity of the Yuncas, who did not worship the Sun till after their subjugation by the Incas. The temple of Pacha-Cámac was then dedicated to the sun by the Incas, who destroyed the idols which the Yuncas had worshipped, and appointed in the service of the temple a certain number of virgins of royal descent. In the year 1534 Pizarro invaded the village of Lurin (two miles away from Pacha-Cámac); his troops destroyed the temple, and the Virgins of the Sun were dishonoured and murdered."

But instead of the old temple of Pacha-Cámac being converted into a Temple of the Sun, as Tschudi says, I find again, on returning to Rivero,[2] "Outside of this edifice (that was the old Pagan temple, with its doors of gold and coral and precious stones) there were in Pacha-Cámac a Temple of the Sun, a royal palace, and a house of virgins— monuments erected by the Incas, Pachacutec, and Yupanqui. According to our investigations, the Temple of the Sun extended from the foot of the mountain,[3] on which was situated the temple of Pacha-Cámac, towards the north-east, and on the

---

[1] "Travels in Peru during the years 1838 and 1842." By Dr. J. J. Von Tschudi. London: D. Bogue, Fleet Street, 1847. Page 205.

[2] Op. cit. p. 290.

[3] The "made mountain," he might have said, as I believe it to be the work of human hands.

side towards the north-west, as far as the Lake of Sweet Water, and at the foot of the mountain from the south-east of the temple of Pacha-Cámac to the house of the chosen virgins."

Not a vestige of any ruins, save of old walls, of the same character as the rest, existed in the direction indicated when I was there last April. From the chief mound on top of which the ruins of the old building described by me are found, both in a north-east and north-west direction, extend smaller mounds to the distance of half a mile, where they are bounded by the river Lurin. But I must ask a few questions. If the Incas had a Temple of the Sun here when Pizarro came, and that it was a different building from that on the high mound, how does it happen that it has disappeared, whilst the relics of the old Pagan temple remain? If the latter, according to Tschudi, had been converted into a Temple of the Sun, who filled it up with clay, so as that we can now walk on its very summit, with all the walls underneath our feet as we look down? Not being able to find or invent a reply, I lay aside the works of Senor Don Mariano Edward Rivero and Dr. Tschudi, to ruminate on the old fairy story of "Jack and the Beanstalk," as well as on what Stevenson tells us of some people's belief that Don Quixote was buried at Trujillo.

CHAPTER X.

Calláo Bay.—Earl Dundonald and the island of San Lorenzo.—Cutting out of the "Esmeralda."—The concrete works of Mr. Hodges.—Pacific Steam Navigation Company.—First appearance of steamboat on the Pacific.—Earliest report of Pacific Steam Navigation Company in 1843.—Hardihood of directors.—Present status of the Company.—Organization in Calláo.—Programme of sailings.—Large trade created by it.—Additional steam lines.—Floating-dock of Calláo.—Original establishment.—Utility to Pacific shipping.—Muelle y Darsena (mole and dock); great work of Brassey and Co.—Calláo trade for 1872.—Imports and exports.—Guano existing in deposits.—Amount of supply for future.—No fear of Government securities.—New discoveries of nitrates and of silver-mines.—Immense increase of Custom-house receipts.—Port dues.

From Cerro Azul we have a little over seventy miles of sea voyage, in which, after passing by Pacha-Cámac and Chorillos, we enter one of the finest bays in the world at Calláo.

This harbour is situated in lat. 12′ 6″ S. and long. 79° 45′ W. The port can be entered (if coming as we are from the south) through the Boqueron channel, which separates the island of San Lorenzo from La Punta (the Point)—a low peninsula composed of the *débris* of marine shells, and rubble of ordinary paving-stone size,

the latter of which is being constantly added to
by the surging in of the ocean. Another entrance
is by going round San Lorenzo to its northern
extremity, whereon a lighthouse stands, and straight
into the anchorage. San Lorenzo is about four
miles in length, and a mile in width. It is a barren
mass of brownish grey colour, without the semblance of vegetation, except, as I am told, some
wild potatoes that grow on the top, which is about
eleven hundred feet high.

On entering the Boqueron channel, and looking
up the side of the island, one can recognize the
figure of a cross, made with what appear large
clumps of basalt, or some volcanic-looking boulders—no doubt the work of the early Spanish
padres. The island is considered as about six
miles distant from Calláo, and it has its old historic memories. The brave Earl Dundonald,
very early in his operations on this coast, was able
to liberate from this island thirty-seven Chilian
soldiers, who were imprisoned by the Spaniards
for seven years.[1] They had been forced to work
in manacles, and at night were chained by the
legs to iron bars in a filthy shed. "Cochrane
established a laboratory in San Lorenzo, and while
rockets and fire-ships were being prepared there,
he sailed hither and thither, capturing treasure-
ships belonging to the Spaniards, and intercepting

---

[1] *Vide* "Chambers' Miscellany," part iii. p. 27.

treasure-trains inland." In September, 1819, he came from Valparaiso to attack Callao; his indomitable spirit determined to give no peace to the Spaniards till they were rooted out of the Pacific shores. He was accompanied by a squadron of seven vessels, with two fire-ships, and four hundred soldiers to act as marines. He sent a flag of truce, challenging the Viceroy of Peru to fight him ship for ship, which was, of course, prudently declined.

But his greatest feat in Callao bay, subsequent to the storming of Valdivia already recorded, was the cutting out of the Spanish war-frigate "Esmeralda." This is so graphically described by Stevenson[*] that I am tempted to give it in his words—more especially as he at the time was secretary to Lord Cochrane, who was Vice-Admiral of Chili; and Stevenson was a sharer in the attack :—

On the 3rd of November, 1820, his lordship astonished the inhabitants of Callao by sailing through the narrow passage that lies between the island of San Lorenzo and the mainland, called the Boqueron. Never had the Spaniards known a vessel of more than fifty tons attempt what they now saw done with a fifty-gun frigate. Expecting every moment to see us founder, the enemy had manned their gunboats, and formed themselves in a line, ready to attack the instant

[*] Op. cit. vol. iii. p. 269.

they should observe us strike. To witness which the batteries were crowned with spectators—but, to their utter astonishment, we passed the strait, leaving them to ruminate on the nautical tactics of the admiral of the Chilean squadron.

Having passed the Boqueron, a ship and a schooner hove in sight. The ship proved to be English, the schooner to be the "Alcance" from Guayaquil, bringing news of the revolution and declaration of independence, and having on board the ex-governor, with other Spanish authorities. Guayaquil had followed the example of the other South American cities in the manner in which she threw off the colonial yoke. The Spanish mandatorios were deposed, and a new Government established on the 9th of October, without any bloodshed, or even insults offered to the authorities set aside.

The adventurous spirit of Lord Cochrane immediately formed the project of performing the most gallant achievement, that has honoured the exertions of the patriot arms in the new world. The two Spanish frigates, "Prueba" (Proof) and "Venganza" (Vengeance), had left the coast of Peru, and the only vessel of respectable force at Callao was the frigate "Esmeralda." She was at anchor in this port, guarded by fifteen gunboats, two schooners, two brigs of war, and three large armed merchantmen, besides the protection of the forts and batteries on shore, and a floating boom surrounding all the vessels, open only on the north side, lying close to the shore of Boca Negra. His lordship determined on cutting out the frigate, the brigs, and schooners, with as many of the boats and merchantmen as might be possible. This daring enterprise was to be executed by volunteers alone. But when the act was proposed, on the 3rd of November, to the crews of the different vessels, the whole of them wished to share in the glory of the undertaking. On this account it became necessary to issue the following proclamation, which was received with the enthusiasm, that the voice of a hero causes when he speaks to those who know his character:—

"Soldiers and Sailors,—To-night we will give a mortal blow to the enemy; to-morrow you will present yourselves before Calláo, and all your companions will look on you with envy. One hour of courage and resolution is all that is necessary to triumph. Remember that you are the victors of Valdivia, and fear not those who have always fled before you.

"The value of all the vessels taken out of Calláo shall be yours; and, moreover, the same sum of money offered by the Government of Lima to the captors of any vessel of the Chilean squadron shall be distributed amongst you. The moment of glory is at hand. I hope, Chileans, you will behave as you have hitherto done, and that the

Englishmen will act as they are accustomed to do, both at home and abroad.

"Nov. 4th, 1820. COCHRANE."

On this day, the 4th of November, fourteen boats belonging to the Chilean vessels of war were manned, and left the ships, filled with volunteers, at half-past ten at night. But this was only intended by his lordship to exercise the men. On the 5th, being the day determined on by the admiral for the gallant enterprise, the signalman of the flag-ship was sent to the signal-staff erected on the island of San Lorenzo, where he hoisted two or three flags, and was answered by the "O'Higgins." The "Lantaro," "Independencia," and "Araucano," immediately weighed anchor and stood out of the bay, leaving on board the "O'Higgins" (the admiral's ship) the boats and volunteers. This *ruse de guerre* completely succeeded, and the Spaniards were persuaded that they had nothing to fear that night, for they supposed that some strange sail had appeared in the offing, and that our vessels had gone out in pursuit of it. All being thus ready, at ten o'clock at night we again embarked in the boats, and proceeded towards the inner anchorage. The boats, containing two hundred and forty volunteers, proceeded in two divisions—the first under command of Captain Crosbie of the flag-ship —the second, of Captain Guise, of the "Lantaro," both under the immediate direction of his lordship. At midnight we passed the boom. Lord Cochrane, being in the first boat, was hailed from a gunboat, but, without answering, he rowed alongside her, and, standing up, said to the officer, "Silence or death! Another word, and I'll put you every one to the sword!" Without waiting a reply, a few strokes of the oars brought the boats alongside the "Esmeralda," when his lordship sprang up the gangway and shot the sentry; the one at the opposite gangway levelled his musket and fired. His lordship returned the fire and killed him, when, turning round to the boats, he exclaimed, "Up, my lads; she's ours!"

The soldiers and sailors now boarded her in every direction, and possession of the quarter-deck was immediately taken. The Spaniards flew to the forecastle, where they defended themselves, and kept up a continued fire of musketry for seventeen minutes, when they were driven below and obliged to surrender. We had scarcely obtained possession of the quarter-deck when a gunboat, close astern of the frigate, fired a shot into her. The shot tore up the deck under the feet of Captain Coig, commander of the "Esmeralda," and wounded him severely. It also killed two English sailors and one native. But the officer and crew of the boat immediately abandoned her.

The frigate was in an excellent state of defence, and her crew under good discipline. The men were all sleeping at their guns, and the guard of marines on the quarter-deck. So prompt were the latter, when his lordship jumped up the gangway, that they appeared as if they had been ordered out to receive him. Indeed, had not the men in the boats, under the command of Captain Guise, boarded almost at the same moment behind the marines, the admiral and many others who accompanied him on the starboard side must have fallen by their fire. His lordship at this time received a shot through the thigh, but until the ship was ours he paid no attention to the wound except binding a handkerchief round it. After which he stood on one of the guns of the quarter-deck and laid his leg on the hammock netting, where he remained till three o'clock in the morning, and then went on board the "O'Higgins" to have it dressed by the surgeon.

Well might Captain Downes, of the United States war-ship "Macedonia,"[3] have said in a despatch to General San Martin, "I do most sincerely congratulate Lord Cochrane upon the capture of the 'Esmeralda.' The exploit was executed in a gallant style never surpassed." Well, too, did Sir James Mackintosh say in the House of Commons:[4] "Lord Cochrane is such a miracle of nautical skill and courage; his cause of banishment from his country is so lamentable; his adventures have been so romantic, and his achievements so splendid, that no Englishman can read

[3] Op. cit. vol. iii. p. 299.   [4] Idem, vol. iii. p. 279.

them without pride that such things have been done by his countryman, and without solemn concern that such talents and genius should be lost to the land that gave him birth."

But not less remarkable than the courage shown in capturing the "Esmeralda" was the ability with which she was taken out of her barricaded position. "It was the intention of Lord Cochrane," continues Stevenson,* "to clear the bay according to the instructions given; but being wounded, and the resistance made by the Spaniards on board proving much greater than was expected, Captain Guise ordered the cables to be cut, which being done, the frigate began to drift from her anchorage. The batteries were pretty active during the engagement, and when the 'Hyperion' (English frigate at anchor in the port) and 'Macedonia' (United States frigate in same position) sheeted home their topsails, and began to move out of the way of the shot, the firing increased. These ships showed two lights—one at the mizen peak, the other at the jibboom—as distinguishing signals, which, being observed by Lord Cochrane, he immediately ordered the same to be shown on board the 'Esmeralda.' Thus she was brought out of the anchorage with less damage than either of the other two sustained. Indeed, excepting the shot from the gunboat, the 'Esmeralda' sustained none whatever."

* Op. cit. vol. iii. p. 297.

With this we find the "Esmeralda" had, from the lists that turned up, three hundred and twenty persons on board, besides some visitors—the latter, no doubt, from what had taken place the previous day, not suspecting any danger.

On the following day, when the prisoners were mustered, their number amounted to only a hundred and seventy-three; thus their loss was inferred to be a hundred and fifty-seven, besides several wounded, who were sent on shore with a flag of truce. The loss of the attacking party under Lord Cochrane amounted to eleven killed and twenty-eight wounded."

Although the capture of the "Esmeralda" must have proved not only a death-blow to the Spanish naval forces in the Pacific, but have given additional strength to the cause of Independence and South American emancipation, this great victory was not appreciated by General San Martin, whose petty jealousy, exhibited in his treatment of Lord Cochrane, is one of the greatest blots on the memory of the self-elected Dictator of Peru. From this time for two years afterwards, the paltry vanity of San Martin, added to his lack of honesty in breaches of promise, of justice, and humanity, made his name odious to every lover of the principles of truth and right. But at the end of 1822, and whilst residing on his estate at Quintero, Lord Cochrane received the following communication from Peru—a document that reflects much credit on the Congress of that Republic:—

"The sovereign constituent Congress of Peru, contemplating how much the liberty of Peru owes to the Right Honourable Lord Cochrane, by whose talents, valour, and constancy, the Pacific has been freed from our most inveterate enemies, and the standard of liberty has been displayed on the coast of Peru, resolves, that the junta of Government, in the name of the Peruvian nation, do present to Lord Cochrane, Admiral of the squadron of Chile, expressions of our most sincere gratitude for his achievements in favour of this country, once tyrannized over by powerful enemies —now the arbiter of its own fate.

"The junta of Government, obeying this, will command its fulfilment, and order it to be printed, published, and circulated.—Given in the Hall of Congress, Lima, the 27th of September, 1822. (Signed) Xavier de Luna Pizarro, President; Jose Sanchez Carrion, Deputy Secretary; Francisco Xavier Marreategui, Deputy Secretary.

"In obedience we order the execution of the foregoing decree. (Signed) José de la Mar, Felipe Antonio Alvarado, El Condé de Vista Florida. By order of his Excellency Francisco Valdivieso."

---

* Stevenson, Op. cit. vol. iii. p. 463.

† Creditable though this document be, the general public will regret to know, it was the only recompense given to the man

The island of San Lorenzo, likewise, deserves notice now-a-days as we pass it by. During the last year, a governor has been named to it by President Pardo. There are nearly three hundred workmen living thereon, part of whom are employed in the quarrying for Mr. Hodges, C.E., in reference to his great work of the Muelle y Darsena (the mole and dock); and the remainder are employed in Messrs. Harris and Co.'s smelting furnaces.

The first thing to attract attention in the harbour of Callao, as we round the Punta, is the extensive machinery for making concrete which has been put up here by Mr. Hodges; and the next is the great extent of yards, engine-shops, and manager's residence of the Pacific Steam Navigation Company. When the eye ranges over these, and takes in the stores, as

who, before all others, was the main instrument in achieving Peruvian independence; whilst General San Martin, who made himself Dictator chiefly by the help of Earl Dundonald's labours, was rewarded with a pension for life of 20,000 dollars per year, and a present of a large sum of money. Better late than never. It may be hoped that the existing Peruvian Government will follow the example recently set by one of the most eminent of Brazilian statesmen, who moved in the Parliament at Rio de Janeiro, that Earl Dundonald's family should receive a further reward due to them for their father's service, in achieving the freedom of Brazil. The motion was received with enthusiastic applause, and without a dissenting voice, and was soon followed by an award of 40,000*l.* Those who appreciate the sense of justice due to such services, will join me in saying,—" May it be no less in Peru!"

well as the large number of steamers in the bay, we can at once comprehend how the Pacific Steam Navigation Company has come to be the greatest British power on the West Coast of South America.

It may not be *mal-à-propos* here to relate an incident connected with the commencement of steam navigation on the waters of the Pacific.[*] The first steamer that arrived on the coast of Peru was one called the "Telica," its captain and owner, Senor Metrovitch, having made the voyage with it, under sail, from Europe round by the Straits of Magellan to Guayaquil, where he took on board the machinery, together with the Colombian flag, and several passengers. After a trial trip in the river of Guayaquil on the Sunday before departure, he set out seaward in the direction of Callao. But, delayed in his voyage on account of the fogs along the coast, the supply of fuel got short, and the captain became exasperated by the complaints of his passengers, which were heaped upon him to increased aggravation one day, whilst they were breakfasting in the port of Guarmey. Whereupon Metrovitch discharged a pistol into a barrel of powder, causing the steamer to fly up into the air (*hizo volar el vapor*). All of the passengers and crew perished, with the exception of a few that were on shore, and a man named Tom

[*] From a volume published in Spanish at Lima in 1871, about the Railway of Arequipa.

Jump, who, standing at the ship's bow at the moment of the explosion, leaped into the water, and swam to land. The hull of the steamer may still be seen at Guarmey.

"The most curious part of the notice," says the writer, "and for which I am indebted to the amiability of Señores—Captain in the navy Don Aurelio Garcia y Garcia, Don Frederick C. Fremdt, and Colonel Don Manuel Odriozola—the most curious, I repeat, is that this affair happened forty years before steam navigation was established between Europe and America. One of my informants, M. Fremdt, had been a passenger on board the 'Telica.'"

In the first report of the directors of the Pacific Steam Navigation Company, of a meeting held at the offices, in Austin Friars, London, on Friday, the 18th of August, 1843, it appears there was some little stumbling-block at the threshold of its operations, by an accident to the Chile steamer, as well as by the books on the Pacific stations being allowed to fall into arrear, and no accounts therefore forwarded to England. At this time the steamers of the company were limited to two, the "Peru" and the "Chile." They had likewise purchased a schooner for the purpose of keeping up communication between Calláo and Panama; but, owing to calms and currents, this vessel was sailed at a loss. The "Peru" and "Chile" had, at the first, been limited to the navigation of the coast between Calláo and Talcahuano in Chile,—the latter near the Arauco bay, and whence coal was obtained. The services of the steamers were then prolonged northward to Guayaquil,—a short time previous to the sale of the schooner. At the period of which I am writing, the paid-up capital of the company was only 91,630*l*., added to which the loan of 20,000*l*. made up a sum of 111,630*l*. In the account presenting such statement there was shown a loss of 13,695*l*. 8*s*. 10*d*. Yet that this did not frighten the directors may be assumed from the following resolution which they adopted:—"The directors deem it their duty, however, before closing this report, to call the attention of the proprietors to the necessity of *sending a third steamer to the Pacific*, to provide against casualties, or any interruption to the traffic in which the two are now engaged, in the event of either being laid up for temporary repairs."

Looking at the large fleet of steamers in the bay whilst I am penning this, one may nevertheless admire those bold buccaneers of Austin Friars, having the hardihood to propose a third boat for the Pacific in the face of such a loss. Because at the period the company was but an experiment, which possibly never would have weathered the storm of such a "heavy blow and sad discouragement" to its financial operations, if it had not for its promoters and managers such men as Mr. William Wheelwright,* the founder and originator of the company, Mr. George Petrie, who is still manager at Callao, and Mr. Richard Just, in the same position at Liverpool. Let us see how it has progressed from its three steamers thirty years ago.

The company was organized in 1839, and in February, 1840, was obtained the charter of incorporation. Its head-quarters in South America are at Callao. The brain and heart of the company's works are in a comparatively small office in the Callo del Muelle (the Street of the Mole); but those works cover an area of over 60,000 square yards, at a portion of the old Callao town, called Chucuito. They comprise stores convenient to the Custom-house, and from which a mole, with locomotive and steam-cranes, assist in loading and discharging. A little farther on is the house of the manager, with extensive stores underneath, as well as another mole with steam-crane. Spacious iron and brass foundries; carpenters' and blacksmiths' shops, in which is a quantity of steam-power; a steam washing-house for the linen of the steamers worked by Chinese, and capable of turning out 1000 pieces of linen per day; a steam-bakery, with one of Perkins' ovens large enough to hold 124 four lb. loaves at a

---

* This indefatigable friend of South America—and most amiable of men—died at his residence, Gloucester Lodge, in the Regent's Park, London, on the 26th of September this year, and whilst the proofs of this work were going through my hands.

baking; brass casting apparatus; a residence for the workmen in an enclosed block of buildings called "Glasgow Terrace," wherein there is likewise a well-fitted theatre; a butchery, with enclosure of stalls for cows and sheep, needed in the provisioning of steamers. There is also an hospital, which was opened in 1865, but had to be closed in 1869, when the Peruvian Government enacted the hospital tax law referred to elsewhere.

In the year 1870 the steamers of this company brought to England about 106,000 bales of cotton, amounting to nearly 9,500 tons.

The line of this company's steamers in connexion with South America, from Liverpool, has hitherto been bi-monthly in their voyages, carrying cargo, passengers, and her Majesty's mails. Although that just referred to has been running for little more than three years, yet it appears that the "company contemplate, early next year, having a supernumerary fleet of some twenty steamers, of between 3,000 and 4,000 tons each, in order to maintain weekly communication to and from Liverpool."

Of the new arrangement the following itinerary is proposed:—

From Liverpool every Saturday; from Bordeaux every Tuesday; from Lisbon every Friday; touching at Rio de Janeiro every Saturday; calling at Monte Video every Thursday; arriving at

Valparaiso every Wednesday. From Valparaiso every Thursday, calling at Monte Video every Monday; at Rio de Janeiro every Saturday; arriving at Liverpool every Thursday. Each alternate steamer is to proceed as far north as Calláo, stopping at Arica, and Islay,—going and returning.

Besides these the company has steamers running four times a month between Calláo and Panama. Those of the 14th and 28th of each month bring mails and passengers from Calláo, destined for England, the Continent, United States and elsewhere, by the royal mail steamers from Colon, on the opposite side of the Isthmus of Panama. The first-mentioned steamers return to Calláo (whence, it may be needless to state, there is almost daily means of passage along the coast), leaving Panama on the 10th and 26th of each month, thus effecting the communication, within a month, between Calláo and England or the Continent. The third steamer on this line is that which leaves Calláo on the 22nd of each month to correspond with the New York steamers, as well as the Mexican and Californian lines from Panama; and the fourth leaves Calláo on the 6th of each month for the French Compagnie Transatlantique, to and from Colon.

I have elsewhere shown the amount of hospital tax paid by the Company's steamers. In Calláo, at the offices and works, they have about 480 hands employed, independent of the commanders, officers, and crews of more than twenty steamers that are daily arriving and departing for different parts of the coast.

Last year the company had forty-four steamers comprising their fleet; whereas now they have fifty-four, with an aggregate of 106,980 registered tons, and a combined force of 19,680 horse power. Sixteen of its vessels were laid to sail from Liverpool out hither, and through the Straits of Magellan, in the five months from the end of July, 1872, to the end of December in the same year.

Between Calláo and Valparaiso there is a bi-weekly steam communication to Valparaiso besides the line of Magellan Straits steamers. There are generally from ten to twelve of the company's steamers in the Bay of Calláo, arrivals and departures being of daily occurrence. Since the first of this year the Pacific Company has had an opposition in a line of French steamers of the "Compagnie Générale Transatlantique" between Valparaiso and Panama, touching at Calláo. Messrs. Ismay, Imrie, and Co., of Liverpool, have commenced, on the 5th of October 1872, a second series of steamers for the West Coast of South America—"The White Star Line"—to come through the Straits of Magellan to Calláo. With these, German steamers have begun to voyage through the Straits from Hamburg to Calláo, the first of

which, the "Karnak," together with the first of
the White Star Line, the "Republic," arrived
at, and left Calláo in the month of December
last year.

As proofs of the large trade created by the
Pacific Steam Navigation Company, I may add a
few facts. During the single month of May in the
year 1872 its steamers conveyed from Calláo, either
via Panama transit, or through the Straits of
Magellan, more than 5,000 bales of cotton. From
Saturday evening, the 7th of December, to Monday
morning, the 9th of the same, or in the space of
thirty-six hours, there arrived in the Bay of
Calláo the following steamers of this company
with the corresponding cargo:—

The "Quito," from San Jose and intermediate ports, with 1,769 packages and 506 in transit.
The "Trujillo," from Panama, Guayaquil, and Payta, with 3,081 and 1,124 in transit.
The "Pacific," from Valparaiso and intermediate ports, with 757 and 74 in transit.
The "San Carlos," from Pisco and intermediate ports, with 256 and 77 in transit.

Total for Calláo . . .	5,863
In transit . . .	1,871
Grand Total . .	7,734

Before going ashore, we must have a look round
and see what other matters are to be noticed in
the Bay of Calláo. Besides the immense forest of
masts, we cannot help observing the floating dock
and the new Muelle y Darsena (mole and dock),

being constructed by Mr. Hodges, C.E., for Messrs. Thomas Brassey and Co., of London.

The floating dock is one of the most important institutions on the Pacific coast of South America.

The privilege for this dock was granted by the Peruvian Government on the 14th of April, 1863, to Mr. George Petrie, manager of the Pacific Steam Navigation Company, with the obligation to form a separate company to carry out its objects.

The Dock trust was to have the exclusive privilege for twenty years for the establishment of docking accommodation in the Bay of Callao. On the 16th April, in the same year, Mr. Petrie announced in Callao " The Callao Dock Company," capital 500,000 dollars (75,000*l.*), in 500 shares of 1,000 dollars each, of which half the number should be offered to the public of Peru. 404 shares were at once taken there, and 250 shares in England as soon as Mr. Petrie could proceed to place them. The dock was made at Glasgow by the eminent firm of Randolf, Elder, and Co., for a sum of 42,000*l.*; the whole expense of freight, insurance, &c., from Glasgow being at the cost of the Dock Company.

The material, consisting of plates, rivets, angle-irons, pipes, machinery, &c., was sent out by sailing vessels, and amounted to nearly 2,900 tons in weight. The launch-ways were constructed

by Mr. James Anderson, who is still the dock
master. The structure is called the St. George's.

It draws only four feet of water. The measurement in length is 300 feet, and in breadth
100 feet outside, inside 76 feet. It can be put
down sufficiently to take in a vessel of twenty-one
feet draught, and can lift about 5,000 tons of dead
weight. It is sunk by opening the valves and letting water in, and pumped out by a pair of steam
pumps of twenty-five horse-power each. As it has
been from the beginning, so it is still, i.e. the following tariff of charges for the use of the dock is
to be calculated by measurement, viz.—

For Steamers and Ships of War:

    1 sole (3s. 9d.) per ton for first day.
    75 cents of a sole ,, four following days.
    50 ,, ,, subsequent days.

For Sailing Vessels:

    50 cents of a sole per ton for first day.
    25 ,, ,, following days.

From these rates 33 per cent. has to be allowed
to the Peruvian Government, and a reduction of
25 per cent. is made to the Pacific Steam Navigation Company; use of dock hawsers, stages, blocks,
shores, &c., 50 soles (10l.) for vessels under 500
tons, and 100 soles for those over 500 tons.

The following are facts with reference to this
dock that may be depended on:—

    1. That it is perfectly rigid and firm as it was

when first launched six years ago, in spite of all the weight that has been put on it.

2. That a vessel of any tonnage can be lifted in from an hour and a half to two hours, according to its weight.

The foregoing details have been given to me by Mr. Noel West, who is the very efficient manager of the dock in Callão. Last year the company paid 12 per cent. to the shareholders, whilst reserving 5 per cent. for a depreciation fund.

When I was leaving Callão in May of this present year, I was informed by Mr. James Hodges,[1] C.E., the principal of the great work of the Muelle y Darsena, that he had then seven hundred men employed on it, together with three locomotives, fifteen steam engines, and a steam dredger, two tugs, and thirty barges. These combined powers manage to put *in situ* from 2,000 to 2,500 tons of material per day. Of this, from 40 to 60 blocks of concrete form no unimportant portion,—each block weighing ten tons. At an angle from the turn of the inner bay, going up to the old mole, and crossing down a length of 1,200 feet, opposite the parish chapel, they are filling up what is to be a

---

[1] As a guarantee of the solidity and perfect nature of the work, I may add that this is the gentleman, who built the Victoria Bridge over the St. Lawrence near Montreal, in 1853 to 1859. In the last-named year it was opened by the Prince of Wales on behalf of her Majesty.

large embankment of reclaimed ground, necessitating nearly 500,000 tons of earth. In the works of the Punta they turn out from 536 to 560 blocks of concrete (ten tons each) within the fortnight.

The proceedings at this mole had been carried on in a slow manner, till the original concessionists, Messrs. Templeman and Borgmann, of Lima, handed it over to Messrs. Thomas Brassey and Co., of London, on the 13th of July, 1870. These world-renowned contractors sent out Mr. Hodges to do the work.

It may be understood by a few figures what is the extent of this undertaking.

The dimensions of the blocks of concrete are 8ft. 2 in. by 4 ft. by 3 ft. 3¼ in., and the average weight of each 8 tons. The depth of water here may be guessed from the fact of seven layers of blocks being required to come up to low-water mark.

The area of the mole and dock over all is to be 984 feet by 820 feet—806,880 superficial feet. Besides this, there is a large space of water and old pier place to be reclaimed, approximately, 490,000 superficial feet. The whole is to be completed in June, 1874.

It appears that the primary concession, granted by the National Government to Messrs. Templeman and Borgmann for this work implies the following privileges:—They are to hold it for sixty years, for the first ten of which it is to be an exclusive privilege. At the end of ten years the Government may claim the right to purchase it, and when sixty years shall have terminated, it will belong to the nation.

All vessels above 10 tons entering the Bay of Callao must pay 10 cents. of a solo per ton register, for which they can make use of the dock, by means of their boats, in shipping provisions and so forth. Ships of war of any nation are not to be charged.

Vessels entering the dock of above 10 tons are to be charged 75 cents. of a solo per ton for all goods landed or shipped.

Owners of goods will have to pay the actual present cost of landing and shipping, with a reduction of 5 per cent. on same.

In no case can the charge exceed 2 soles 50 centanos per ton measurement, and 1 solo 50 centanos per ton weight: that is, in fact, from 9s. to 10s. in the first case (measurement), and from 5s. to 6s. in the second (weight).

I have not been able to ascertain what are the terms or conditions of purchase in case the Government should be disposed to effect this at the end of ten years.

Messrs. Brassey and Co. have likewise, together with the concrete manufactory, a forge and saw-mill worked by steam, close to the new molo.

From statistics supplied to me by Senor Don

Manuel Palacios (late Captain of the Port in this city), I find the following number and tonnage of vessels entered and cleared during the first six months of the present year, 1872 :—

SHIPS ENTERED.

Nationality.	Number of Ships.	Registered Tonnage.	Average Tonnage of Cargoes.
Peruvian	103	31,932	42,470
British	103	88,472	117,668
North American	46	48,582	64,014
French	43	22,093	29,384
Italian	21	12,067	16,049
German	12	9,259	12,315
Central American	35	11,806	15,705
Swedish	19	10,938	14,647
Others	10	5,166	6,870
Total	482	240,317	319,622

CARGOES ENTERED.

Species of Cargo.	Number of Ships.	Registered Tonnage.
General Cargo	84	50,678
Lumber, chiefly from United States	49	25,846
Coal	33	38,039
Railway Plant	1	1,047
Wheat and Flour	33	8,710
Chinese Immigrants	15	11,544
Cattle	1	150
Guano from Guanape	15	14,000
,, Macabi	24	18,047
Fruits	156	16,073
Ballast, coastwise	34	23,506
,, foreign	37	32,110
Total	482	240,317

Class of Ships.	Number of Ships.	Respective Tonnages.	Number of Passengers.
Sailing Ships	482	240,317	42
Steamers	236	180,176	22,554
Coasters	319	3,072	84
Total	1,037	423,565	22,680

Whilst I cannot account for the omission, in the previous summary, of 6,535 Chinese amongst the passengers entered (which thus makes a total immigration to the country of 29,215, instead of 22,680), I may point to the fact, that the cargoes cleared include no Chinese, although their engagement is supposed to be only for a term of eight years.

SHIPS CLEARED.

Nationality.	Number of Ships.	Registered Tonnage.	Average Tonnage of Cargoes.
Peruvian	188	29,012	38,586
British	96	83,236	110,704
North American	49	54,265	72,172
French	39	19,266	25,624
Italian	15	9,290	12,356
German	15	10,643	14,155
Central American	38	13,089	17,408
Norwegian	3	1,410	1,875
Swedish	17	0,674	12,857
Others	10	6,023	8,011
Total	470	235,908	313,758

Cargoes Cleared.

Specimens of Cargo.	Number of Ships.	Registered Tonnage.
Guano for England	4	5,239
,, France	11	4,614
,, Belgium	17	16,778
,, Havana	4	1,313
Assorted Cargoes	168	25,140
,, ,, and Fruits	12	4,255
In Ballast for Ballestas Islands	1	159
,, Guanape ,,	74	73,982
,, Macabi ,,	38	34,512
,, Coastwise	47	20,009
,, Foreign Ports	94	49,901
Total	470	235,908

Class of Ships.	Number of Ships.	Tonnage.	Passengers.
Sailing Vessels	470	235,908	657
Steamers	239	159,288	22,243
Coasters	298	2,933	323
Total	1,007	398,129	23,223

Balances of Previous Tables.

	Tonnage.		Numbers.
Imports	240,317	Passengers came in	22,680
Exports	235,908	,, went out	23,223
Surplus of Imports	4,409	Surplus left the country	543

Of the vessels entered and departed the highest amount of tonnage was English, then in succession, North American, Peruvian, French, and Italian.

Vessels with guano are less in number than in the last six months of 1871. This may be partly accounted for by the fact that many ships left the guano islands of Macabi and Guanape for their destinations without calling at Callao. During the present year, however, an edict has been passed, rendering it obligatory on all vessels laden with guano to touch at Callao before they start for abroad.

Amongst the fifteen vessels that brought Chinese, ten were Peruvians, two French, two Portuguese, and one Dutch. They embarked from Macao 7,206 Chinese, of which number 6,535 arrived in Callao—showing a loss of 671 in transit—that is, an average of ·093, or nearly ten per cent.

At the time of the foregoing table being compiled by the Captain of the Port, there were eighty foreign vessels in the Bay of Callao.

That the greatest number of craft trading to Callao are British will appear at once from an extract of the commercial circular, published by Messrs. Bryce, Grace, and Co., of this city, on the 28th of May last. This gave the names of 133 vessels cleared, sailed, and loading at different foreign ports—for Peru—the larger number being for Callao. They are classified as follows:—

Nationality.	Tonnage.
British	55,813
North American	42,619
French	6,404
Norwegian	1,349
North German	2,936
Salvadorian	1,651
Others	1,879
Total	112,656

It appears to me more than probable that no small amount of this shipping may be credited to the exaggerated reports that have been circulated in England, the States, and on the Continent, about enormous supplies of recently-discovered guano deposits. The *Field*, in its issue of the first week of June, 1872, prints the following statement:—

"PERUVIAN GUANO.—The supply of Peruvian guano receives an immense accession from an unlooked-for quarter. We learn from private sources that a vast deposit of guano has been revealed some distance to the south of Lima, and several miles inland. The guano lies under successive beds of black salt (?), nitrate of soda, and borax. The deposit consists of many millions of tons."

This no doubt refers to the neighbourhood of Pisco, nearly opposite the Chincha Islands, about which some absurd rumours were got up in Lima, but that I ascertained, on inquiry, were perfectly foundationless. The statement[1] that the Peruvian Government has still available 300,000,000*l.* sterling of guano, is so enormously misleading, and so entirely without proof, that I consider it my duty to say it has no foundation.

Another report was published at Callao in the month of May last, with reference to an extensive deposit of guano having been found recently on the mainland near to Supé, which is only ninety-

[1] Made by Mr. Consul Vines of Islay, and published in Consular Reports for 1872.

one miles north of Callão, and is the northern boundary of the Callão Consular Jurisdiction. This guano was said to extend to Gramaudel, Colorado Grande, Punta de Santander, Casma, Caleta de Mongon, and the vicinity. It was accredited to be calculated at about 1,000,000 tons, and to be equal, if not superior in purity, to the guano of the Chincha Islands.

Guano being, since its discovery in 1836, one of the principal sources of Peruvian wealth, I have done all in my power, since my arrival in Callão, to ascertain its probable actuality as regards future supplies. I have been informed, after very cautious inquiries at the Guanape and Macabee Islands, that the former are calculated to possess still about 500,000 tons, and the latter to have approximately 750,000 tons. This report comes to me only a month ago,* when at Guanape there were forty-seven vessels loading at the rate of 600 tons per day; and fifteen ships at Macabee, loading at the rate of over 300 tons per day.

Added to the quantity just mentioned at the Guanape and Macabee Islands, I am assured, on the best authority, that the guano on the Lobos Islands, which are situated farther north, does not exceed 750,000 tons. So that the whole exportable guano which Peru possesses to-day may be safely estimated as under 3,000,000 tons.

* In the month of November, 1872.

The large number of seals and sea-lions, which frequent the localities where guano is found, makes it extremely probable that some of this deposit is left by these animals, as well as by birds. Corroborating impressions of such conviction have been conveyed to me by Mr. Steer, from the University of Michigan, in the United States, who has collected, bottled up, and analyzed specimens which he knows to have been deposited by seals, and which is perfectly analogous to the guano of commerce.

Statement showing the nett product of Guano sold in 1871 in the consignments to Europe and to Messrs. Dreyfus Brothers and Co.

Consignments.	Tons sold.	Nett Product.		Sterling.		
		Soles	c.	£	s.	d.
Great Britain	111,456	4,066,210	73	767,083	8	3
France and Mauritius	106,736	3,990,267	16	738,866	1	10
Belgium	77,825	3,093,391	60	580,010	18	6
Germany	24,615	888,109	20	160,520	0	0
Italy	5,571	217,027	80	40,602	11	3
Holland	6,886	318,170	02	59,658	0	1
Spain	30,511	1,187,183	48	222,596	18	0
	363,200	13,740,065	99	2,576,262	7	5
Dreyfus Bros. and Co.	30,526	1,116,690	92	209,379	11	0
	393,726	14,856,756	91	2,785,641	18	5

Guano existing in the deposits of the consignments on June 30th, 1872:—

	Tons.
Great Britain	187,757
France and Mauritius	68,416
Belgium	6,174
Italy	9,330
Spain	10,628
United States	99,521
Actual Tons	381,826

On the voyage, to August 31st, 1872:—

	Tons.
Great Britain	24,892
France and Mauritius	7,931
Belgium	25,509
Spain	937
Italy	580
Holland	3,625
United States	2,187
Tons (register)	65,661

Loading on August 31st, 1872:—

Great Britain	8,137	
France and Mauritius	7,104	
Belgium	7,459	
United States	1,550	
		24,250
Tons (register)		89,911
Add 33 per cent. (approximate) for actual tons		29,670
Actual Tons		119,581

Relating to the future supply of guano I have to add, that during arrangement of materials of this work, the following appeared in one of the London papers (July 15th). I put it here for the object of adding my testimony to the statements of his Excellency, Senor Don Pedro Galvez, the Peruvian Minister Plenipotentiary, although I have had no communication with that gentleman on the subject:

"PERUVIAN BONDS AND GUANO DEPOSITS.—Noticing the calculations, founded on a report of the British Consul at Callao, as to the supposed insufficiency of the guano deposits in Peru as a

guarantee for the external debt of that nation, the
Peruvian Minister in London writes :—The quantity of guano in the deposits of Peru cannot be
calculated with any certainty, neither can an
approximate measurement be obtained. At present
the Government is quite satisfied as to the quantity remaining, and there is not the least ground
to fear that the guano will be finished within the
next ten years, calculating the demand to be,
more or less, about 500,000 tons per annum.
Assuming that Mr. Hutchinson's calculation is
correct,[1] there is still no cause for alarm. Supposing the stock of exportable guano on the
island to be 3,000,000 tons, and the quantity in
stock or on the way to be 500,000 tons, which is
putting it at a very low figure, we have a total
of 3,500,000 tons. This, at the net price of
8l. 10s. per ton, gives us the sum of 29,750,000l.,
which we can calculate upon as disposable for
the payment of the Peruvian Loan of 1872,
36,800,000l. But of the amount of this loan
15,000,000l. are by the terms of the contract to
be exclusively applied by degrees, during a period
of several years, to various public works in contemplation, which when completed are to form
one of the guarantees offered to the bondholders.
In the same loan is also included the sum of
15,000,000l. of the loan of 1870; this has been

[1] As it appeared amongst Consular Reports, published by the
Foreign Office in May, 1873.

employed in the construction of railways, some of which are completed and others very far advanced, and these works, like those in contemplation, are an additional guarantee to the bondholders. Another security for the bondholders is the nitrate of soda, the demand for which increases every year. In 1871 the exportation of this article was 200,000 tons; this, at 16*l.* per ton, gives a sum of 3,200,000*l.*, on which the Government could levy a tax of 10 per cent., and this would give us 320,000*l.*, or nearly enough for the service of the loan, even supposing the demand did not increase. The development of the country is such that during the year 1871 the Customs produced 1,200,000*l.*, and this source of income is increasing immensely every year. If we add to this the fact that already upwards of 1,000,000*l.* of the loan of 1872 had been paid off, I think that even taking, as I have, Mr. Hutchinson's statement as a basis on which to form a calculation, I have at least shown that there is no cause for the alarm of the bondholders."

In this I firmly believe, from my two years' experience of Peru. I therefore have no hesitation to endorse the conclusion, that "there is no cause of alarm to the bondholders:" whilst I cannot consider it other than highly improper to allow such an unwarrantable assertion, as that of three hundred millions of pounds sterling* of guano still

* *Vide* p. 206.

existing, to go before the public without being contradicted. There seems to me not the slightest danger in Peru for guarantee of its external debt. The progressing prosperity of the Republic may receive a cogent illustration by the following figures:—

Returns for Customs of Callao during Eleven Months of 1872.

1872.	Currency.		Sterling.		
	Soles.	c.	£	s.	d.
January	303,185	87	56,847	7	0
February	303,514	52	56,908	19	5
March	305,148	39	57,215	6	6
April	316,294	05	59,305	2	8
May	371,830	00	69,718	2	6
June	403,027	63	75,567	13	7
July	402,468	46	75,462	16	9
August	414,956	67	77,804	7	6
September	408,380	21	76,571	5	9
October	472,388	49	88,572	16	10
November	537,196	66	100,724	7	6

Another item of evidence of the increasing trade at Callao may be educed from the fact that Senor Morales rented the mole-tax from 1st October, 1870, to 30th of September, 1872, for the sum of 85,000 soles, or 15,937*l*. 10*s*., whilst the same concern, put up to auction, was rented by the same gentleman from 1st October, 1872, to hold on till 30th September, 1874, for the sum of 169,200 soles, or 31,725*l*., nearly double the first amount, at the nominal exchange of 45*d*. per sole.

No better proof of the monthly increasing trade

of Callao need be adduced than what is proved by this last table. From which it may be observed, that in the month just passed (November, 1872), the Custom-house receipts amounted to 537,196 soles, or 100,724*l*. 7*s*. 6*d*., being an excess over the preceding month of October in the same year of 64,808 soles 17 c., or 12,151*l*. 10*s*. 8*d*. A glance at the table will likewise show that each successive month had a progressive increase over its predecessor, till the Revolution in July put a temporary check to it.

The Government has published that the receipts of the several Custom-houses in the Republic for the ten months of the present year, ending 31st October, show a total of 5,740,656 soles 87 c., or 1,076,373*l*. 3*s*. 3*d*.

Not only, in the words of the Minister, does the demand for nitrate of soda increase every year, but, what is better, the supply is found to exceed the demand. And no doubt that further explorations through the province of Tarapaca, where Iquique and Pisagua are situated, will show, as is being done daily, new sources of this wealth. Moreover, the railroads of Mr. Meiggs are already leading to discoveries of silver—a great excitement being recently created in the neighbourhood of Chilete, on the Pacasmayo railroad, by the extraordinary argent riches of that district.

I have received from Major Williamson, United States' Consul, a longthened table of statistics of the particulars of North American commerce with this port of Peru for the year beginning 1st October, 1871, and ending the 1st October, 1872. I must, however, make a synopsis of it, as the whole would occupy too much space. By this table I learn that in the quarter from 1st December, 1871, to 31st December same year, twenty-six merchant vessels bearing the United States flag came into this port of the aggregate of 24,297 tons. The cargo of these consisted of lumber, 5,469,000 feet; wheat, 41,750 bushels; coals, 3,706 tons; sperm oil, 3,937 gallons—said cargoes being valued at 758,945 soles, or 146,468*l.* 17*s.* 1*d.* Of those ships, twenty-five left, one being sold, and fourteen of them sailed with guano—the united cargoes of their 23,750 tons being estimated at 948,750 soles, or 177,890*l.* 12*s.* 6*d.* In the quarter from 1st of January to 31st of March, 1872, there came in twenty-eight United States vessels with an aggregate of 29,588 tons, consisting of coals, 10,234 tons; lumber, 1,814,000 feet; wheat, 34,000 bushels, 30,900 railway ties, valued at 1,084,110 soles, or 203,270*l.* 12*s.* 6*d.* These ships all sailed, fourteen of the lot being with guano cargoes; and the value of total cargoes being 985,172 soles 87 c., or 184,719*l.* 18*s.* 3*d.*

The quarter from 1st April to 30th June shows twenty-seven North American vessels of the aggregate of 29,934 tons, and cargoes valued at 433,935 soles, or 81,362*l.* 16*s.* 3*d.* Of these vessels thirteen

CHAP. X.] PROGRESS IN TRADE AT CALLAO. 215

left with guano, two were sold, two remained in port at the end of the quarter; and the total cargo brought away by those that sailed valued at 696,980 soles, or 130,683*l*. 15*s*.

In the last quarter, from 1st July to 30th September, the number of United States vessels entering was thirty-seven of 40,266 tons, and cargo valued at 1,364,705 soles, or 255,882*l*. 3*s*. 9*d*. All of these sailed together, with some that had remained from the previous quarter, comprising an aggregate of 46,615 tons, and a value of cargoes of 1,408,450 soles, or 264,084*l*. 7*s*. 6*d*. Of these twenty-seven left with guano.

Of French and Italian shipping at Calláo I find the following during the respective years :—

FRENCH.

Years.	Arrivals.			Departures.		
	No. of Ships.	Tonnage.	Crews.	No. of Ships.	Tonnage.	Crews.
1864	147	75,842	2,504	141	72,965	2,423
1868	144	78,193	2,595	141	76,870	2,460
1870	151	79,268	2,635	139	76,903	2,421

ITALIAN.

Years.	Arrivals.			Departures.		
	No. of Ships.	Tonnage.	Crews.	No. of Ships.	Tonnage.	Crews.
1860	183	87,332	2,568	190	90,640	2,570
1870	141	73,422	1,987	135	70,037	1,891

MOVEMENTS OF MERCHANT SHIPPING IN CONNEXION WITH THE
PORT OF CALLAO DURING THE YEAR 1869.

Flags.	Entered.			Cleared.			Total.		
	Ships	Tonnage	Crews	Ships	Tonnage	Crews	Ships	Tonnage	Crews
Peruvian	301	26,412	1,524	335	32,804	1,730	636	59,246	3,254
North American	254	266,097	4,594	267	266,639	4,601	521	525,636	9,199
English	734	639,540	20,064	749	649,022	21,255	1,483	1,278,712	41,246
French	130	76,768	2,424	141	76,878	2,469	280	152,646	4,886
Italian	183	87,222	2,669	190	90,298	2,570	373	177,932	5,134
German	36	24,056	637	39	26,088	653	77	50,144	1,287
Swedish	39	23,113	579	44	23,498	636	83	46,611	1,204
Norwegian	65	35,790	867	62	34,446	748	127	64,236	1,712
Portuguese	6	1,027	97	8	1,635	89	16	3,049	175
Belgian	6	7,313	143	7	6,332	121	13	13,635	274
Danish	1	472	18	...	...	...	1	472	18
Russian	1	671	16	2	1,305	28	3	1,876	44
Greek	1	326	7	1	326	15	2	654	22
Central American	10	9,062	194	37	13,875	660	47	17,937	854
Guatemala	6	1,760	77	3	740	27	11	2,400	104
San Salvador	29	18,948	634	37	11,762	358	66	30,641	992
Chilian	2	102	10	...	...	...	2	102	12
Argentine	...	766	16	1	417	14	3	1,105	31
Sandwich Islands	1	464	11	2	596	16	3	1,060	20
English Steamers	236	166,160	8,178	235	166,769	8,073	474	333,619	16,148
	2,072	1,340,002	44,639	2,140	1,349,695	44,729	4,212	2,740,648	89,367

The amount of coal imported in British vessels in 1869 exceeded 30,000 tons. But in 1870 it amounted to over 36,000.

The value of cargoes by American ships (United States) imported to Calláo in 1869, consisting principally of lumber, railway material, wheat, ice, cattle, and coal, is estimated at about 2,063,000 dollars (386,812*l*.). The weight of coals by American ships having been 17,560 tons.

Dues on shipping coming to Calláo or other ports of Peru are paid for six months. Peruvian ships in the coasting trade, and under 200 tons burden, pay only every twelve months. The following are the principal dues:—

1. Light dues . . . . . ¼ real per ton.
2. Tonnage dues . . . . . 2 reals „
3. Port dues—1st ports . . . 8 dol. per ship.
   „   2nd „ . . . 5 „ „
4. Water dues, per ton of water . . 4 reals per ton.
5. Ballast dues—Ballast . . . 1 dol. „

The water thus costs 1¼ dollar per ton at ships' tackles. The ballast 2 Bolivian dollars per ton on board.

Consignee of ship is paid . . . 150 dol. = 22*l*. 10*s*.
Commission on freight . . . . 5 per cent.
Recovery of freight . . . . 2½ „
Purchase of return produce . . . 2½ „
Payment of duties and disbursements . 1 „

Goods may be bonded for five years on condition of paying only storage.

The ratio of increase in the Calláo trade may be estimated by the fact, that the revenue of the Custom-house at the port for the single month of May of the year (1871) was 325,089 soles 22 centavos—60,954*l*. 3*s*. 9*d*.; whereas in May, 1861, it was 166,027 soles 24 centavos—31,130*l*. 1*s*. 3*d*.,—thus doubling in ten years.

We likewise find the preponderance of British trade may be assumed by another fact, that there arrived in Calláo on one day, the 24th of September in this year, 1871, no less than twelve vessels from foreign ports, representing the aggregate of 8,842 tons, classified as follow :—

	Vessels.	Tons.
British	8	6,969
Swedish	2	1,904
French	1	442
American	1	327
		9,842

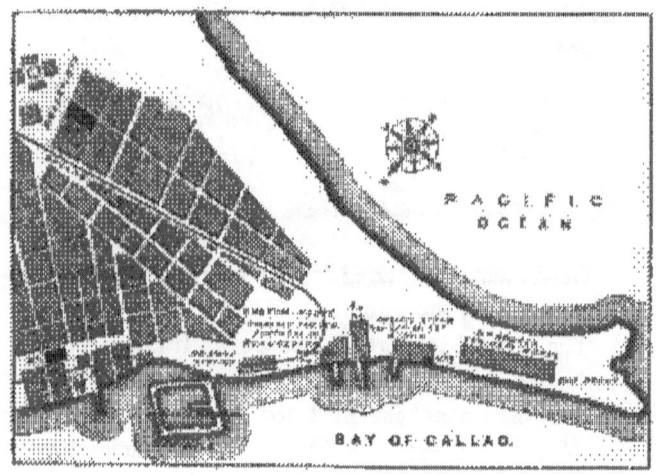

CALLAO.

CHAPTER XI.

The "Painter" at Calláo.—Its different appearances.—Analysis of water during its existence.—Extent of "Painter" on the whole coast of Peru.—Author's observations of appearances of water.—Frezier's writings about Calláo.—Earthquake of 1746.—Number of convents and of chapels.—Dreadful effects of earthquake.—On shore at Calláo.—Lima and Calláo Railroad.—Club.—The royal fort.—Its great size and extent.—Fight for independence.—Bombardment of Calláo by Spanish fleet in 1866.—The native hospital in Calláo.—Revenue of Beniticencia Society.—Hospital tax on shipping.—Silver in Peru.—Misfortunes of 1868.—Parish of Santa Rosa.—La Punta.

STILL in the bay of Callao, and previous to our going ashore, there is an interesting peculiarity here, worthy to be noticed—more particularly as I am not aware of its having been discussed by any previous writer on Peru.

This is called "the Painter"—the palpable evidences of which consist in a changed colour of the sea water (most generally to a muddy white),—an odour most fœtid, nauseous, and depressing,—with the accompaniment of the white paint on ships and boats, inside as well as outside, becoming totally discoloured, and often partially black. Some persons attribute this to conveyance of miasmatous matter from the Andes, by means of the river Rimac, into the sea. Others say it proceeds from the decomposition generated in the bay by the excreta of Callao washed into it. In neither of these, exclusively, have I faith. Because, knowing that the whole coast of Peru is super-volcanic, as well as believing that Callao bay has been the crater of an extinct volcano, I am induced to attribute this emanation chiefly to submarine volcanic action, generating sulphuretted hydrogen gas. The vicinity of Callao, too, is generally of that boulder or rubble formation in its upper geological stratum, through which such gas could be eliminated without any difficulty. Although met with at Callao in its most aggravated form, the "Painter" is likewise found along the coast as far as San José de Lambayeque, nearly five hundred miles north. From the end of December until April, is the time when this phenomenon mostly exists.

I have before me an analysis of the sea water of Callao, bottled up during the existence of "the Painter," and having some mud from the bottom of the bay contained therein. This was sent by Mr. Hodges to London, and was there analyzed by Mr. T. Keates, F.C.S., Consulting Chemist to the Metropolitan Board of Works, &c. Mr. Keates reports that, after being allowed to rest, the water poured off proved to be sea water, and that the black mud left, after the water had been decanted, was in a state of active decomposition—large

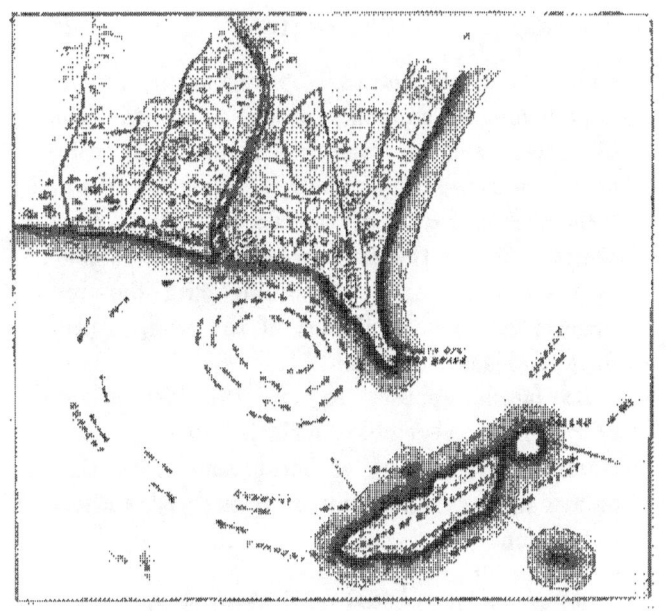

PLAN OF CURRENTS RUNNING INTO CALLÃO BAY.

quantities of sulphuretted hydrogen gas, as well as sulphate of ammonia, being given off. The black colour of the mud was found to be owing to the presence of sulphate of iron, which was formed as a result of the decomposition mentioned. Whilst this latter was due to the sulphur of the organic matter combining with the iron present in the mineral part of the mud, to produce the black sulphide.

So far it appears to me, the idea of an origin from vegetable malaria coming down from the Andes, or of local causes, be they animal or vegetable, may be considered without foundation.

1000 parts of the mud dried at 230° Fahr. yielded,—

Water	769·6
Dry mud	230·4
	1000·0

100 parts of the dried mud yielded by analysis,—

Organic matter	10·50
Chloride of sodium, alkaline sulphates, &c.	6·43
Salts of lime	3·75
Alumina of oxide of iron	16·00
Silicious matter	63·25
Loss	·07
	100·00

Mr. Keates further tells us, "This mud appears to be ordinary river mud, or silt deposited at the mouth of a river, and lying in sea water.

It contains a considerable quantity of vegetable and some animal matter, and under the microscope shows abundance of diatomaceous remains."

As perhaps a few of my readers may not understand the penultimate word of this last extract, I shall explain it, according to Sir Charles Lyell's definition:—"There is a variety of dry deposits in the earth's crust, now proved to have been derived from plants and animals, of which the organic origin was not suspected until of late years, even by naturalists. Great surprise was therefore created by the recent discovery of Professor Ehrenburg, of Berlin, that a certain kind of silicious stone, called tripoli, was entirely composed of millions of the remains of organic beings, which the Prussian naturalists refer to microscopic infusoria, but which most others now believe to be plants. They abound in fresh-water lakes and ponds in England, and are termed Diatomacea by those naturalists who believe in their vegetable origin. The substance alluded to has long been well known in the arts—being used in the form of powder for polishing stones and metals. When examined with a powerful microscope, it is found to consist of silicious plates or pustules, of the above-mentioned Diotamaceæ, united together without any visible cement. It is difficult to convey an idea of their minuteness, but it is estimated there are 41,000 (forty-one thousand) millions in every cubic inch.

The remains of these Diatomaceæ are pure silex."

Mr. Keates further adds, that when the mud was sent to him, the organic matter which it contained was rapidly decomposing. "It was in a very fœtid state, and was giving off a large quantity of the gas called sulphuretted hydrogen."

No doubt it was. And equally probable that if this mud were examined, at the place from which it was taken, it might have given different results. For it is more than probable that the change of temperature between Callao and London, as well as transition from the natural condition to that of being bottled up, must have caused no trifling chemical reaction in the elements of which it was composed.

The supposition of its deadly influence from being on the banks of the river, and therefore intermittingly exposed to the influence of a tropical sun on the ebb of tide, leads to erroneous inferences on the part of the analyst. Because the Painter locale is not near the river, and the chief part of the bay of Callao, which is affected by the rise and fall of tide, is covered with rubble, devoid of any mud.

That the current, sweeping as it does round the bay, and past the mouth of the Rimac, brings from that river a considerable quantity of drift, there can be no doubt. But if these were the causes of "the Painter," why should we have it only at intermittent periods—in fact, only for a few months of the year—and then always previous to the heavy rains, which may be supposed to bring down, on the floods, a greater quantity of silt than when the river is very low?

During one of several periods that I was enjoying the hospitality of Mr. Hodges, and when "the Painter" was in full blow (in the month of January last), I took notes of its appearance. Mr. Hodges' residence is on the edge of the bay, in what was formerly the "ice-house," when this part of Peru was supplied with that article from Wenham Lake, and before the monopoly for its artificial manufacture was given to a company in Lima. This house is built of wood, and is situated on the very shore of Calláo bay, between the stores of the Pacific Steam Navigation Company and the railway station to Lima. In the course of a few days I observed the water of the bay under four different aspects.

1st. Ochre-brown, with somewhat of a reddish tinge, and opaque. This, when examined under the microscope, showed animalculæ of a spheroid or circular form, and of like colour to the water. In twelve hours after it was—

2nd. Of a dark green, and still thick, aspect, in which by the microscope was visible another class of animalculæ of an hour-glass form, round and broad at each end, but contracted in the centre. Although there was but one drop of water under the glass, a large number of these jumped about.

3rd. The next morning, or in fourteen to sixteen hours afterwards, the water was a muddyish white. This time the smell in the harbour was most pungently nauseating. It is considered the "true Painter" period when white paint becomes black, and headaches are general with everybody under its influence. No animalculæ were visible through the microscope in this state of affairs. From the second to the third condition, I may add that in the intervening period we had a shock of earthquake at about five o'clock in the morning, and during the occurrence of which, it may be conjectured, submarine volcanic action destroyed all the animal life of these insects seen the two days previously.

4th. This is the ordinary water of Callao bay, different in its colour in proportion as it is near to the drainage outlets of the town, or to the neighbourhood of the current, which flows through the Boqueron Channel. This latter meets the larger sea-stream coming from the south round the north end of San Lorenzo Island, and which makes a back-water detour of the bay, as shown by the sketch in previous chapter.

The present site of Callao, it may scarcely be necessary to add, is some distance to the north of the city which was destroyed by the terrible earthquake of 1746. That occurred thirty-three years after the visit of M. Frezier, Ordinary Engineer to the King of France. Frezier's description of the coasts of what he styles "Chily and Perou" was published in Paris in 1716—157 years ago—and gives a very lucid account of every place at which he touched.

Senor Paz Soldan[1] tells us, that at half-past ten o'clock on the night of the 28th October in the fore-mentioned year, the earthquake came on : "It could not be well described or conceived as a simple shaking of the earth, but as a convulsive throe, by which the heaving up of the sea-bottom in one place, and its depression in another, caused an enormous wave to sweep over the town, and at one gulp to destroy 5,000 inhabitants."

Frezier, thirty-three years previous, set down the number of inhabitants at 400 families, although they themselves claimed 600.

The old city of Callao was of triangular form, and was surrounded by walls, with bastions and buttresses, built up when the Marquis of Mansern was Viceroy. These fortifications cost 369,000 dollars. In 1671 the Viceroy, Count of Leinus, declared it a city, and in 1694 it had an excellent mole, constructed of stone from the island of San Lorenzo.

[1] "La Geografía del Peru," p. 655.

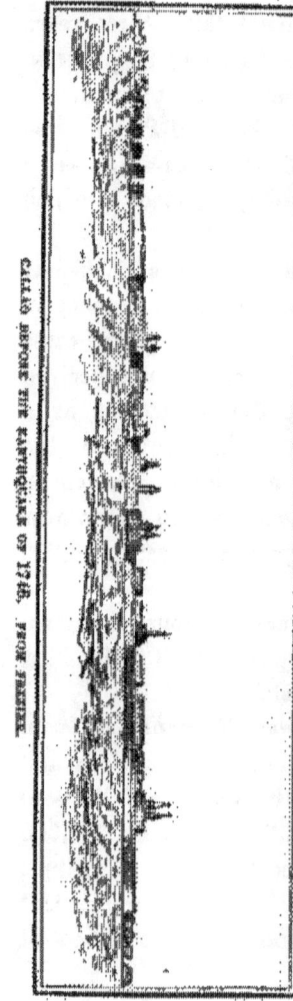

CALLAO BEFORE THE EARTHQUAKE OF 1746. FROM FREZIER.

But the earthquake did not spare these more than any of the religious buildings. At the time of its occurrence, together with the Viceroy's palace and the Governor's house, both near the sea, were the six chapels of La Matriz (the parish chapel), San Augustin, the Jesuits', Santo Domingo, San Francisco, San Juan de Dios, and La Merced. There were also five convents of religious orders — the Dominicans, the Augustins, the Cordeleros, the Fathers of Mercy, the Jesuits, and the Brothers of the Hospital of San Juan de Dios (Saint John of God). Besides these, each of the thirteen bastions of the walls was named after a saint, as—1, Saint Michael; 2, Saint Ignacio;

3, Holy Cross; 4, Saint Catherine; 5, Saint James; 6, Saint John the Baptist; 7, Saint Dominick; 8, Saint Philip; 9, Saint Louis; 10, Saint Lawrence; 11, Saint Francis; 12, Saint Peter; 13, Saint Anthony—all being, of course, in the Spanish tongue, from which I have translated them.

In less than three minutes the whole town of Callao was either swallowed up, swept away, or demolished into ruins. Only a few hundreds of the total population are said to have escaped—some of these reported as washed over to the island of San Lorenzo—an incident in which I have no faith. The Jesuit priest, Father Lozano, wrote an account of it to the Reverend Bruno Morales, of the same company, residing in Madrid, giving a description of the dreadful catastrophe. From this, as well as the relation given by Senor Paz Soldan, it would appear to have been precisely the same kind of thing, which took place in 1868, as already described, at Arica. For there was a like sweeping in, and sweeping out, of a Cordillera of volcanic wave. Out of all the monks in the six convents, there was only one saved—the Padre Arispe, of San Augustin. How he managed to get off we are not told. The Viceroy at the time was the Conde de Superunda, and his heroic exertions to assuage the miseries of the dreadful calamity deserve immortal record.

Going ashore at Callao, we find ourselves in the middle of one of the most bustling of places at the molo. The odor of this at once strikes us as nothing of an improvement on "the Painter" which we have left in the bay. The examination of our luggage at the "Resguardo" is conducted with great courtesy. We land, not at the old molo, but at the new stairs of Mr. Hodges' great work; and the first large building which attracts the attention of strangers is the spacious edifice of the railway station. Besides the offices for tickets and stores for luggage and cargo, it has an up-stairs series of apartments, in the most extensive of which we find the club of Calláo. This was organized in 1867, and is the club of the English-speaking community here. It has a spacious verandah, overlooking the sea, excellent and well-supplied reading-room, with two billiard tables.

The first sod of this railway was turned on the 30th of June, 1850, by Senor Don Ramon Castilla, at the period President of the Republic; and it was opened for traffic on the 5th of April, 1851, although not completely finished till 1852. The distance hence to Lima is only seven miles. The Callao station is 12 feet, the Bella Vista station 48 feet, and the Lima station 465 feet above the level of the sea. The original contractor was a native Peruvian, Senor

Don Pedro Candamo, from whose hands it passed into those of an English company.

The Lima and Chorillos Railway was laid down by the same company, and was opened for traffic in November, 1858. This is nine miles long from Lima to Chorillos, which latter may be said to be the Brighton of the Peruvian capital. Some few years ago, Chorillos was a very small fishing village, but now it is a most fashionable bathing-place, and owes its first rise to General Castilla, who was the owner of much property there. The Chorillos station is 137 feet above the level of the sea.

The affairs of this company, of which the head-quarters exist in London, are excellently conducted by a local manager, and two consulting directors here. The manager, Mr. William Stirling, to whom I am indebted for these details, has likewise furnished me with the following statistics of the railway operations :—

INCREASE OF RAILWAY TRAFFIC.

"The Annual Traffic Receipts of the Railways during the ownership of the present Company have been as follows:—

	1867.		1868.		1869.		1870.	
	£ s. d.	Soles c.	£ s. d.	Soles c.	£ s. d.	Soles c.	£ s. d.	Soles c.
Passenger and luggage traffic	79,863 8 9	391,413 0	72,388 18 9	144,354 0	63,847 11 0	64,257 0	61,794 8 9	241,827 0
Goods traffic	25,123 0 1	3134,277 0	16,146 12 6	185,449 0	51,023 3 9	258,510 0	64,110 11 6	312,721 6
Total traffic receipts	104,716 8 9	6,526,615 0	89,549 11 3	2,627,733 0	112,761 16 3	212,847 0	125,935 1 9	391,245 0
Annual increase	...		...		10½ per cent.		14·3-10 per cent.	
Proportion of working expenses to revenue	50 per cent.		54 per cent.		62½ per cent.		47 per cent.	
Number of passengers carried	1,340,677		1,230,030		1,267,811		1,353,628	
Net tons of goods carried	...		...		60,714		81,015	
Number of train miles run	...		...		104,540		123,570	

"For the eight months of the present year ending with October, 1871, there is an increase in the passenger traffic of 79,000 soles, equal, to 13,687*l*. 10*s*., over the same months of last year, while the goods traffic is almost exactly what it was in 1870."

Of its traffic in 1872 Mr. Stirling has supplied me with the annexed:—

NOTE OF TRAFFIC FOR THE NINE MONTHS ENDING
SEPTEMBER 30, 1872.

Number of passengers carried on the Calláo line	1,004,961
" " " Chorillos line	461,310
Total	1,466,271

	£	s.	d.
Receipts from passengers and luggage	100,936	14	0
Number of tons of goods carried, 99,989.			
Receipts from goods traffic	58,369	19	0
" other sources	3,569	9	0
Total receipts	£162,876	2	0

There are two barracks in Calláo, and one at Bella Vista, which latter is about a mile outside of town, on the line of railway to Lima. Adjoining the Custom-house is the military and naval Intendencia. Together with the three Catholic chapels of the town, there is likewise a Protestant church (having a school attached), of which the manager of the Pacific Company for the time being, the British Consul for the time being in Calláo, and the United States' Consul for the time being in the same place, are trustees. It was originally built, and the ground on which the building was raised, bought by funds raised through Mr. Petrie, and friends, in 1864. Part of material for building was likewise given for it by Mr. Wheelwright.

The church is vested in the foregoing trustees

for the use of the English-speaking Protestant community in Calláo. These trustees were appointed in 1869, when the title-deeds were made out in their names.

At Bella Vista is a foreigners' burial-ground, originally enclosed by the British Government in 1830, but now under management of a committee.

There is not much that may be deemed worthy of remark in the architecture of Calláo—its chief public building being the old fortress, Real Felipe, erected some time between 1770 and 1775, nearly thirty years after the great earthquake. It is said to have cost the Spanish Government thirty millions of dollars—a sum considered so large that the king of the period, Philip III. of Spain, ironically ordered a telescope to be carried to the top of his palace in Madrid, that he might have a look at the fortifications. Covering nearly twenty acres of ground, it has very thick walls, and parapets about twenty feet high on the sea side. It contains two round towers—the Torreon de la Patria, and the Torreon de San Fernando. Between it and the sea is the smaller tower of Santa Rosa, and these are accredited, at the time of Earl Dundonald's exploit in the capture of the "Esmeralda," to have mounted a total of 300 guns. In the great fight for Independence, the fortress stood out for eighteen months when besieged by Bolivar and the patriots of the time,—only surrendering from sheer starvation on the 22nd of January, 1826.

The last famous battle in which it was engaged was the celebrated bombardment of Calláo by a Spanish fleet, under General Castro Mendez Nunez, on the 2nd of May, 1866. That squadron came up here fresh from its unopposed battering at Valparaiso; and after allowing six days for neutral vessels to leave, opened its fire on the town. From a description of the event by Mr. William De Courcey, of Calláo, who was an eye-witness (published in the *South Pacific Times*),[1] we are told that the Spanish commander-in-chief addressed a circular to the Diplomatic Corps in Lima, "allowing four days for the foreign inhabitants to move themselves and effects, as he would positively raze the port and city of Calláo." Whilst such was his assurance, that he publicly declared, and it was as positively asserted, that he invited the captain of a French man-of-war, then in the harbour, to take a glass of wine at the Governor's house before he would burn it down. Although the Spanish fleet did not fire the first shot until thirteen minutes after twelve o'clock, at two minutes past five in the evening, they had all got such a peppering, as obliged them to beat a retreat. The squadron consisted of thirteen

---

[1] The English newspaper of Calláo, and one of the best conducted journals in South America. Edited and owned by Mr Isaac Lawton, from Jamaica.

HOSPITALS IN CALLÁO.

sail, six of them being first-class frigates, with an aggregate compliment of 275 guns, and 500 supernumeraries brought out by three transports. The 2nd of May is, therefore, the great holiday for Calláo and Lima.

In Calláo we have also the Prefect's house, a theatre, and the hospital of Guadaloupe, down near the Oroya railway station. The market-place is nearly half a mile outside the centre of the town, and on the inside of it (for the railway runs by the opposite) is erected a cross to celebrate where one of the ships in the great earthquake of 1746 was driven up. Near to the sea, at the northern end, we find a sugar manufactory belonging to Mr. Ramos, of Lima. This is quite close to the Oroya railway station, at the other side of which is the Guadaloupe Hospital.

This institution is under the management of the Beneficencia Society of Calláo; but its chief revenue is derived from a tax levied on all shipping that comes into the port, under a decree of the National Government, dated 27th October, 1868.

In a sanitary point of view, the hospital could not be in a worse position. It is admirably managed by the good sisters of charity under the Beneficencia Society. It has a ward, called the St. George's ward, devoted to sick sailors speaking English; and the Board of Trade has appointed Dr. T. A. Roe, formerly of the Royal Navy, as medical inspector, to watch the condition of our sick seamen. Joined to his assiduity and attention, Doctor Roe has effected several useful reforms in the establishment.

The decree already mentioned provides:—

"Art. 3. An established hospital revenue will be formed in favour of this charitable society (the Beneficencia), obliging all foreign and national sailing-vessels and steamers to pay the sum of four cents. of a sole every six months, for each and every ton register, and that the said society will be obliged to assist and receive all seamen from all foreign and national sailing-vessels and steamers free of all charges whatsoever."

I have ascertained by inquiries that English and North American trading ships, with the Pacific Company's steamers, have paid since the date of passing that Act as follow:—

BRITISH SHIPS.

	Soles.	c.	£	s.	d.
From January to December, 1869	8,174	6 =	1,541	5	4
„ January to December, 1870	9,240	16	1,742	3	0
„ January to September, 1871	4,401	20	829	16	2
	21,816	12	£4,113	4	6

PACIFIC STEAM NAVIGATION COMPANY'S STEAMERS.

	Soles.	c.	£	s.	d.
From January to December, 1869	800	0 =	150	16	8
„ January to December, 1870	1,200	0	226	5	0
„ January to September, 1871	1,400	0	263	19	2
	3,400	0	£641	0	10

NORTH AMERICAN VESSELS.

	Soles. c.	£ s. d.
From January to December, 1869	5,077 68 =	957 6 11
„ January to December, 1870	5,658 20	1,066 16 1
„ January to September, 1871	3,140 56	592 2 5
	13,876 44	£2,616 5 5

These calculations into currency, made at the average rate of exchange for the three years, of 45¼d. per sole, constitute a sum total of 7,370l. 10s. 9d.

This does not, however, include payments of hospital tax by German, French, Italian, Spanish, Chilian, Peruvian, or ships of any other nation. And these by the lowest estimate of a rough guess at their numerical proportion, may be calculated at 3,000l. during the time indicated; in fact, showing a contribution of about 3,000l. per annum from all the shipping to the hospital. By their own account the Beneficencia Society has a rent of 77,279 soles—(at 45d. per sole, 14,489l. 16s. 3d.)—of which they consider the ships pay 16,800 soles (3,150l.), the rest being derived from land and household property.

The Beneficencia expended the last year, 1870, 67,871 soles (12,725l. 16s. 3d.), leaving a surplus of 9,408 soles (1,764l.).

Throughout all its history, the name of Peru has been associated with unbounded mineral wealth; and the tales that are told of the immense hoardings up of silver and gold turned out, since the conquest of the Incas by Pizarro in the

sixteenth century, seem almost fabulous. Mines
have been, and still are, worked with varying
success. But I have no doubt that an enormous
impetus will be given to this class of enterprise,
more particularly in the copper and silver mines,
as soon as the railways of Mr. Meiggs shall be
completed. These metals are found at many
places between the coast lines and the centre
range of Cordilleras;—notably so of silver at
Cerro del Pasco on the Oroya line,—at Salto and
Gualquayoque behind Trujillo,—and at Chiliété,
interior to Pacasmayo.

On the island of San Lorenzo, at the south
and west of Calláo Bay, there has been lately
erected an establishment for smelting ores. This
is managed by Colonel Harris, who represents
the only English mining company now working
in Peru. Amongst the projects submitted to
President Pardo, that were brought before the
extraordinary session of Congress, called together
on the 9th of November, 1872—the anniversary
of the battle of Ayacucho—was one for the establishment of a school of mines.

Going southward from the railway station
along a plank road, we see evidences of what
is being done by the foreign element in Peru.
To the right, this planking leads down to
Chucuito, and half-way to the Puntá.* These

---

* The Punta is now becoming the fashionable bathing-place
for the Chalacos (as the Calláo residenters are styled).

are in the parish of Santa Rosa, which is extra-parochial to that of Calláo. We pass for the first few hundred yards between the rails and the old fortress; then skirt the house where Mr. Hodges dwells. Next to that we come to the stores of the Pacific Steam Navigation Company; and if we turn downwards, skirt the fortress of Santa Rosa, to the comfortable dwelling of Mr. Petrie, attached to the company's works. Following towards the point, we arrive at the new stores, erected by Messrs. Dockendorff and Co., and near the extremity to the extensive concrete works of Mr. Hodges. At the Punta we find four hotels—the Grand Hotel of Senor Rivero being the largest. From this returning to the back of Santa Rosa chapel on the Lima and Callao railroad, there is now a locomotive engine with carriages running, so as to correspond with the trains from Lima. If we take this train either up or down, we can have a view of the extensive foundries of Messrs. De Courcey, and Clarke; of the spacious iron yards of Messrs. Deansiro and Dartnell; of the steam flour-mill at Chucuito; of the railway works; of the gas establishment; and of a new line of store-houses being built on the embankment behind the old fortress,—in front of the Pacific Ocean.

During the year 1868, Callao was visited with a triad of misfortunes. On the same evening that the great volcanic wave swept over Arica, came a similar one, though less in volume, to menace Callao. Accompanied as it was by terrific earth-shakings, many of the inhabitants fled to Lima and Bella Vista. Nearly at the same period, a large portion of Constitution Street, close to La Matriz, or the parish church, was consumed by fire; and, to crown all, appeared the yellow fever, which swept away in a short time nearly two thousand of the inhabitants.

CHAPTER XII.

Hygiene of Callao.—Senor Paz Soldan's calculations of increase of population.—Mortality at the native hospital.—Excess of deaths over births in the town.—Census of population.—Chinese immigration.—Mortality of Chinese immigrants in the middle passage during the last decade.—Mortality of same in 1871 and 1872.—Law of Congress prohibiting Chinese immigration in 1856.—Its reauthorization by Congress in 1861.—Particulars of contracts.—Mission of Peruvian embassy to China.—Existing convention between Peru and Portugal touching emigration from Macao.—Coolie immigration to the West Indies.—Sir G. Young's paper on the subject.—Difference of mortality in Guiana and Callao.—Speculators in the Chinese immigration.—National Company of Navigation.—Its intended extensive monopoly.—Decree revoking the concession.—New bill for import duties.—Monopoly of nitrate of soda.—Guano from Mejillones.—General *resumé* of railroads in Peru.—Drainage of Callao by Mr. Clarke.

I REGRET that my two years' experience of Callao do not give me the same favourable results of its comparative mortality as I find recorded by Senor Paz Soldan.[1] In 1860, he tells us, there were 729 births, and 365 deaths all through the year. During my time I took careful note of the statistics, furnished by the Beneficencia, or Benevolent Society's Registrar, and therefore on data

[1] "Geografia del Peru," p. 361.

that cannot be disputed. This latter gentleman published in *El Porvenir*, the local newspaper, a table of the deaths in connexion with the native cemetery of Callāo, from its inauguration on the 1st of January, 1862, to the 31st of December, 1871. From it I learn that in these ten years there has been a total of 11,561 interments, amongst which are recorded 3,980 cases of fever. Of these last-named, the yellow fever year of 1868 shows 1,454, whilst during the very last year of all (1871), which was considered a normal year, and whilst I have been commenting on these things in the Callāo press, we have had 629 cases of fever amongst the mortality. Contrary to what happened in the year 1860, noticed by Senor Soldan, from the tables published by the Registrar before mentioned, I find we have had in 1871:—

Births at Callāo during the year			.	1,251
Deaths	„	„	„	. 1,570
Thus showing an excess of	.	.	.	. 319 deaths

over the births. The supposition, therefore, that Callāo has from 22 to 25,000 inhabitants, appears to me only a wild guess. I take from *El Commercio*, Lima paper, of 5th of August, 1871, the following statement with reference to the population of this city:—

"The Census of 1859 gave to Callāo 18,792 inhabitants; that of 1862, 17,539; and that of 1866, the last taken, 14,801."

Therefore, instead of increasing, it would appear

to be diminishing in population. Moreover, as the yellow fever committed great havoc in 1868, and no census has been attempted since 1866, I am inclined to think that from 15,000 to 18,000 is a very approximate calculation of the present inhabitants of Calláo.

From the "Estadistica del Callao," published by the "Sociedad de Beneficencia," I learn that there were buried in the native cemetery from 1st January to 30th June, 1872, the number of 911, and in that of Bella Vista, 91. Out of this total 278 were cases of fever. That fever is endemic to the town, and proceeds, in the opinion of every one, from the absence of all attempts at hygiene.

During the six months indicated, the number of births recorded amounts only to 614, whilst the number of deaths reached 1,002—thus leaving a surplus of 318 deaths over the births in the space of six months.

Another fact evidencing the decrease of population in Calláo is seen from what I am told in a statistical table, published by the former Captain of the Port, Don Manuel Palacios, in his report to the Minister of War and Marine, to the following effect:—

"In the same six months just referred to, I there find of the passenger traffic to and from Calláo—arrivals, 22,680; departures, 23,233, showing a surplus of 549 who have left the country."

Some of the mortality tables of the Guadaloupe Hospital, given to me by the Mother Superioress, Madame Stephanie, are before me, and I translate them:—

In September, 1871, there were 483 patients in the hospital, of whom 53 died in the month, or at the rate of nearly 11 per cent. per month. Of these there were 117 Chilians, who had been working on the Oroya railroad, and of whom 17 died.

In October, 1871, there were 471 patients in the hospital, of whom 42 died—a mortality of 9 per cent.

In November of the same year there were 445 sick in the hospital, of whom 46 died, or 10·33 per cent. during the month.

The month of December, 1871, shows a total mortality of 39 out of 691 patients, or 5·66 per cent. during the month.

In January of this year there were 699 patients, with a total mortality of 57, or 8 per cent.; and in February there were 755 in the hospital, with a mortality of 48, or 6·33 per cent. in the month.[1]

Connected with the mortality of this hospital, the most important feature is that of the Chinese.

I have heard from the Mother Superioress of the Sisters of the Native Hospital in Cállao, that since the 1st of January to the end of October,

---

[1] The foregoing gives an average of 8 per cent., which is exactly what we find recorded of the great plague of London in A.D. 1663.

CHAP. XII.]   MORTALITY OF CHINESE.   245

1871, their books show of statistics in reference to the Chinese:—

    Entered the hospital 733
    Came out convalescent . . . 519
    Died 214

Thus constituting a death-rate of nearly 30 per cent. in ten months.

This fatality amongst the Chinese in the hospital is well worthy the attention of all humanitarians. In the middle passage from Macao it is not so bad, although even there it has reached in some cases to 31 and 26 per cent. during the voyage of a hundred days.

It occasionally happens that Chinese mutiny on the passage, although this is said to be a voluntary emigration. And whilst their engagements are accredited to be from five to eight years, I cannot ascertain that a shipment of any back to their own country has ever been made.

The following is worthy of attention, particularly as it is, like all my statistics, derived from official sources : —

During the year 1870 a few dreadful cases occurred of the burning of ships containing Chinese bound to this port. In normal voyages it may be seen by the ensuing tables that 7 per cent. die on the middle passage, whilst 30 per cent. have departed this year in the native hospital at Callao.

IMMIGRATION OF CHINESE TO CALLAO.

Year.	Arrived.	Sailed from Macao.	Deaths on Passage.
1860	1,413	2,007	594
1861	1,440	1,860	420
1862	1,003	1,716	713
1863	1,628	2,301	673
1864	6,410	7,010	600
1865	4,540	4,794	254
1866	5,929	6,543	614
1867	2,184	2,400	216
1868	4,266	4,387	121
1869	2,291	2,366	75
1870	7,544	7,917	373
Totals	38,648	43,301	4,653

Deaths were 7 per cent. on the voyage from Macao to Callao.

The Captain of the Port in 1871, Senor Palacios, has furnished me with the following :—

SUMMARY OF CHINESE IMMIGRATION FROM JANUARY 1 TO SEPTEMBER 30, 1871.

Month.	Sailed from Macao.	Arrived.	Died on Passage.
January	1,810	1,693	117
February	.	.	.
March	1,650	1,579	71
April	2,244	2,128	116
May	1,119	1,064	55
June	1,777	1,648	129
July	721	543	178
August	372	366	6
September	.	.	.
Totals	9,693	9,021	672

Showing an average mortality during the voyage of 7 per cent.

From our present Captain of the Port, Senor Don Juan A. Moore, I have obtained the following statistics, showing the immigration of Chinese up to the end of September quarter, 1872, with the mortality on the voyage :—

IMMIGRATION OF CHINESE INTO CALLAO, FROM JANUARY 1 TO OCTOBER 3, 1872.

Date of Arrival.		Nationality of Ship.	Name of Ship.	Tons.	Embarked in China.	Died on the Voyage.	Arrived at Callao.	Mortality per cent.	Consignees.
1872.									
January	20	French	Mille Jonnes	785	432	39	393	9	Canovaro.
,,	21	Peruvian	Hong Kong	488	314	8	306	2½	,,
,,	24	,,	Providencia	574	416	5	411	1¼	Figari.
February	12	,,	Peru	570	400	10	390	2½	,,
,,	12	,,	Callao	1,049	629	19	610	3	Compania Maritima.
March	24	,,	Lola	690	598	4	588	¾	Ugarte.
April	12	,,	Fray Bentos	410	375	6	369	1½	Figari.
,,	24	Portuguese	Cecilia	533	380	8	372	2	Compania Maritima.
,,	25	Peruvian	Clotilde	1,314	760	9	751	1¼	Candamo.
May	16	Dutch	Johann den Villen	494	260	13	247	5	Canevaro.
,,	17	Peruvian	Lama Canevaro	1,043	739	192	547	26	,,
June	11	Portuguese	Emigrante	965	499	107	392	21½	,,
,,	12	Peruvian	Rosalia	816	457	64	393	14	Dinaly Filgueira.
,,	13	,,	America	1,662	690	105	585	15	Compania Maritima.
,,	30	French	Antares	401	263	82	181	31	Canevaro and Co.
August	31	Peruvian	Camilo Cavour	854	650	57	593	8½	,,
September	10	,,	Sara	638	346	23	323	6¾	Ugarte.
,,	12	,,	Hong Kong	458	314	37	277	11¾	Canevaro.
,,	16	French	Canadienne	853	507	19	488	3¾	Compania Maritima.
,,	19	Peruvian	J. Bigam	387	193	7	186	3½	Ugarte.
,,	23	,,	Callao	1,049	695	10	685	1½	Compania Maritima.
,,	22	,,	Providencia	574	422	10	412	2½	Figari.
,,	27	,,	Peru	570	406	34	372	8½	,,
,,	28	Dutch	Inrust	636	453	45	408	10	Canevaro.
,,	29	French	Radama	487	305	4	301	1¼	,,
October	3	Peruvian	Macao	603	436	39	397	9	Compania Maritima.
			Total	—	11,933	956	10,977	—	

Average Mortality about 8 per cent.

Few subjects connected with trade in Peru deserve so much attention from the world of humanity as that relating to the Chinese labourers brought hither. On the 6th of March, 1856, the immigration of Chinese was prohibited by law of Congress, but another law of the succeeding Congress again authorized it in 1861. To prove any of the horrors of this traffic may be unnecessary, when we find in the table just quoted that in this year, 1872, the French barque "Antares," Captain Natle, arrived in Calláo at the end of June last with a cargo of Chinese from Macao. Out of 263 put on board at the port of embarkation, only 181 reached Calláo —having had the appalling mortality of 31 per cent. on the voyage. Eighty-two had died.

The run from Macao to Calláo averages from 100 to 120 days.

The mortality in the previous table, therefore, of 82 out of 263, or 31 per cent. in the "Antares," of 105 out of 690, or 15 per cent., in the "America," and of 64 out of 457, or 14 per cent., from the "Rosalin," proves that there is a serious cause for inquiry into this matter.

The Chinese are contracted for during a service of eight years at the rate of 450 dol., or about 75*l*. per man. During their period of service they receive generally 4 soft dol., i. e. 13*s*. per month for their food supplies, besides getting a pound and a half per day of sweet potatoes, rice, yuca (a kind of arrowroot), and Indian corn—that is to say, a pound and a half of vegetable material. They are not, however, so well fed as this on all the haciendas.

Since the elevation of Senor Don Manuel Pardo to the Presidency, on the 2nd of August last, his Excellency has made public his intention to send a Plenipotentiary to China, chiefly with the object of establishing the Chinese immigration on a better footing. For several months that mission was arranged to go in the Peruvian war-frigate "Independencia." But the latter plan was set aside, and it was despatched per mail steamer *via* San Francisco. Senor Don Manuel A. Garcia y Garcia is the Minister Plenipotentiary appointed, and Senor Don Frederico Elmore, first Secretary of Legation, together with a staff of officials. The mission set out from Calláo per mail steamer on the 22nd of December last.

The existing convention under which Chinese are brought into Peru is one celebrated between the respective High Contracting Parties at Lisbon on the 24th of February, 1872. And that is founded on a previous Treaty, concluded between Peru and Portugal on the 26th of March, 1853, called a "Consular Convention." The text is based on the fact, that the peninsula of Macao, in China, being owned by Portugal, the contingencies of exportation should be carried out in a legal manner, according to the provisions of Portuguese law. Such a rule is still observed, although it appears that the Chinese Government has recently forbidden emigration to Peru.

Every Chinaman coming to Peru is furnished with a copy of contract, printed in Spanish and Chinese, by which he is bound for a period of eight years. Four hundred and fifty dollars are paid by the owner of farm, or employer in other labour, to the contractor, for this service. One item of the terms of agreement provides that "the period of service of eight years being concluded, the Chinaman is free to dispose of his labour—no debt of any kind being sufficient to impede his liberation, as any such debt must be recovered by the laws of the country." But there being no security given for his return at the end of service, this liberation rarely proves more than a delusion.

It may not be out of place to contrast the present condition of Chinese who come to Peru, in the relations already stated, with what we learn from Sir G. Young's paper, read at the last meeting of the British Association at Brighton, under the title of "Is the Asiatic emigration to the West Indies likely to be a permanent fact in modern geography?"

Of the mortality in this latter immigration Sir George says:—

"It would be asked if it were possible that the results of the introduction of Africans during the time of the slave-trade could be matched by the immigration of Asiatic volunteers, brought from a greater distance by Government ships, under a system liable to be stopped at the first outcry of philanthropists, and so closely guarded that, as we learn from the last report of the Emigration Commissioners, the mortality during the middle passage had been reduced to below 20 in the 1,000,—a better rate than obtained in many parts of England."

The mortality of 2 per cent. in the passage contrasts vividly with that I am obliged to record of Chinese immigration to Peru.

Again, Sir George speaks of mortality in Guiana:—

"The mortality for the first ten years was frightful; the Commissioners lately in Guiana estimated that it reached 10 per cent. per annum."

As antithesis to this, I must point out that in my last year's report on the trade of Callão,[1] I had to show a mortality to the enormous rate of 30 per cent. in the ten months to end of October, amongst the Chinese at the hospital of Guadaloupe in this city.

Sir George continues:—

"In 1851, one-third of the whole number introduced within six years was already dead. The improved regulations of this passage, however, and the very great efforts of the planters and Colonial

[1] Published by the Foreign Office, amongst Commercial Reports from her Majesty's Consuls. Presented by order of her Majesty to both houses of Parliament.

Governments had brought down the mortality to a mere fraction of the former death-rate. In Guiana and Trinidad it fluctuated between 3 and 4 per cent.

"An important Government department was charged with the supervision of all matters, in which the interests of the coolies were affected. A special labour law, on which great pains had been spent, was administered by stipendiary magistrates, in order to secure them work at fair wages. Medical aid was provided gratuitously, and no estate was without its hospital. After 20 years of this improved, and still improving, system, we found in Guiana that, of a population of 200,000, one-fourth, or 49,000, were immigrants from Asia, while 6,000 more were children of those immigrants, called creole coolies in the colony. In Trinidad, with a population of 100,000, there were 24,500 immigrants, and 5,500 creole coolies,— making 130,000 in all. The female sex was as yet sadly deficient in numbers. The Colonial Office insisted on a minimum of 40 to every 100 males who were recruited, and would increase the proportion but for the extreme difficulty of making up the quota, without resorting to women of a character likely to neutralize all the benefits intended by their introduction. At the present time there were in Guiana women in the proportion of 42·21 to every hundred males, showing that the equalizing influence of the rising generation was beginning to tell."

After instituting an interesting comparison of the relative working qualities of the coolies and negroes, Sir George concluded by saying, that he was inclined, though not without hesitation, to stake his credit, as an observer, upon the permanent establishment there of the negro, with a reservation, however, in favour of the Chinaman, if the Chinese immigration were resumed.

To the statement already mentioned as given to me by the Superioress of the Gundaloupe Hospital in Callao, referring to the mortality of Chinese in the last year, I regret having no more favourable one for the present. These two items of 7 to 8 per cent. mortality on the voyage, with 30 per cent. in the hospital during 10 months, are matters pre-eminently calling for investigation.

In the Lima newspaper, *El Pueblo*, of the 20th December, I find the following:—

"From 20th January of present year up to date, 32 ships, solely engaged in the Chinese traffic, have arrived at Calláo. They brought a sum total of 13,380 Chinese coolies. Having taken on board 14,494 at Macao, there died on the voyage 1,114, or 7 and $\frac{7}{8}$ per cent. In the year 1871, the Chinese immigration had amounted in its totality to 11,812 individuals—this year being an excess on the previous one of 1,478."

By a reference to my Trade Report of last year, it will be seen that 7 per cent. was the mortality on the middle passage.

"Thus," continues *El Pueblo*, "we have had in the past and present year brought to Peru 25,192 colonists, representing for the speculators in human flesh a capital of 11,714,280 dols., equal to 1,757,142*l*., if we calculate the worth of each colonist at the sum of 465 dols., or 69*l*. 15*s*., which is the minimum value."

The term "colonist," in this case, appears to jingle with the expression of "speculators in human flesh,"—more especially as there is no provision in the Peruvian system of immigration for the female element.

In the month of March last (1872) a Decree was attempted to be passed,—was approved of by the late President Balta, and sanctioned by the Finance Minister of the time, Senor Don Felipe Masias. Although the document bears date the 9th of March, it only appeared in a Lima paper, *La Patria*, on the 1st of June, when the originator of the scheme, Don Rufino Pompeyo Echenique, was on his way to England, *viâ* United States, by the steamer that started two days before publication, to procure the necessary capital for the work.

The absurdity of trying to crush all existing maritime interests, by such an extensive monopoly, caused universal indignation, and it was rescinded by the same minister, Don Felipe Masias, a few days after its publication. The following is the official announcement of the affair, under the title of "National Company of Navigation:"—

Lima, March 9, 1872.

In consequence of the present proposal of Don Rufino Pompeyo Echenique, and having to view the following considerations, viz.:—

That guano, saltpetre, and other products of raw material exported to foreign ports necessitate the employment of a considerable amount of shipping; that the investment of capital in a company, for the purpose of shipping, to the extent of 100,000 tons, would be advantageous and in every way profitably secure; that besides those advantages, assured to the country by the investment of so much capital, its industry would be protected or favoured by guaranteed cheap freights; that these provisions, which the company and the country would derive from the existence of a mercantile marine of the extent indicated, will be better understood, as the transports would offer, at reasonable prices, to carry all articles necessary to extend the national products; that by means of vessels, constructed with specific conditions, to provide convenient or cheap passages, a considerable immigration would be facilitated, at low rates, to families abroad; that the plant, indispensable for the railways in construction, and for the works of irrigation that have to be undertaken, the possession of a mercantile marine would provide the cheap transport of the productions of the country and of the workmen needed to cultivate the ground to be irrigated; that in view of these great results, it is indispensable to procure the services of such shipping, it cannot possibly be denied that the concession solicited is a means of protection; that the grant of those means will invite no prejudice of any kind in the State, but, on the contrary, adjust effective economy, and, what is indispensable, fix certain conditions which will insure the standing of the projected company:

It is accorded to Don Rufino Pompeyo Echenique, as a means of protection for the immediate establishment of the company proposed with the following title, "Compañia Nacional de Navogacion" (National Navigation Company), the concessions following:—

1st. The Government guarantees to the company, for a term not exceeding nine years, that it will be solely in the ships of the company, to the extent of its power to comply, that the Government will transport all articles of whatever class, for account of the Government, that have to be brought from foreign parts, and from points that are under the sphere of action of the company.

2nd. Equal guarantee is conceded, and for the same time, for as much as it is possible for the company to transport, of all products, articles, and objects of national dominion, or property of whatever kind or nature they may be.

3rd. Whether or not the actual contracts for providing coal have terminated, the company will furnish coal, for the said term of nine years, all that the Government requires, at the strictly cost price, embarked in Europe, charging the corresponding freight, insurance, commission, and the usual charges customary, in a commercial point of view; the Government making the respective payments on receipt of the articles.

4th. The Government will impose the conditions on these parties in charge of the construction of railways and public works, on account of the State, and on those who may rent or hire such railways or properties from the State, that they use only the shipping of the company, under pain of indemnification to the same, in transporting every kind of material required, and to buy or purchase from the company, on the terms stipulated in the above clauses, all the coal necessary for the use of those railways or properties which the company are able to furnish.

5th. The nine years which are referred to in the first and second clauses will commence to go into operation from the moment one or other of the ships of the company receives the first cargo, and commence to comply with the stipulations, as regards the Government, and the contractors of the State from the time when the company have one or other of their sailing-vessels in seagoing condition.

6th. The ships of the company will be, at all times, free of every inconvenience of a fiscal character in all the ports and creeks of Peru.

7th. The company undertakes not to charge, under any motive or any pretext whatever (in cases where it refers to the clauses 1, 2, 3, and 4), more freight or commissions than those current in the place or places where, and at the time when, they receive the cargo.

8th. The company are obliged to provide accommodation, if needed, in every one of their ships for fifty emigrants, allowing the Government to proportion the charge for the passage, and healthy and abundant food, of each emigrant 2s. daily for adults, and for boys from two to thirteen years of age 1s. The days will be calculated from that on which the ship sails from the port of departure till the day when she arrives at the port of destination. If, for whatever motive, the voyage is delayed, they will not recover, on any pretext whatever, more than 12l. sterling for an adult and 6l. for each boy.

9th. The company obliges itself to place its management in such a manner that each ship will, at least, make three round voyages every two years. If six months pass, counting from the date of the document of this concession, it will be considered made without effect.

Passed to the Direction of Administration, in order that they may extend the corresponding document.

[Rubric of his Excellency the President]
(Signed)   FEIJPE MASIAS.

This was abolished by the following documents,

which came to light a few days after the first was published:—

By Supreme Decree of the 9th of March last, issued by the Minister of Finance, a privilege for nine years has been granted to Don Rufino Echenique to establish a navigation company, with the exclusive right to transport all produce, objects, and articles, of every description, being national property, as well as those belonging to railroad companies and public works, which in future may be established, and to sell to the Government, and to the companies referred to the coal they may require.

Such a concession is an infraction of the constitution, because it restrains the liberty of industry. It is equally contrary to the law of privileges, as it does not refer to an invention, nor the introduction of a new industry; it also violates the laws in force as to contracts with the State; and, finally, it involves an usurpation of faculties of Congress, as far as it exonerates the company referred to from the payment of all fiscal dues.

In consequence, the undersigned deputy proposes:—

That the first representation be made to the Government to derogate the Supreme Decree of 9th March, as it is an infraction of the constitution and the laws.

(Signed)   RICARDO W. ESPINOSA.
Lima, June 3, 1872.

DECREE revoking the Concessions granted to Don Rufino P. Echenique :—

Lima, June 4, 1872.

On reconsideration of the petition of Don Rufino Pompeyo Echenique, in which he asks the concession of certain privileges for the establishment of a National Navigation Company, the Decree of 9th March granting them is hereby revoked, and consequently the corresponding document extended by the Notary Public is to be cancelled.

Signed by the President and the Minister of Finance.

So that the very persons who sanctioned the affair (the late President and Minister), were the same who squashed it in three days after its publication.¹

The following is substance of a bill on imports which has been introduced by the Minister of the Interior, in pursuance of the recommendation of President Pardo, at the opening of Congress, on the 2nd of August last, and which came into law on the 1st of April, 1872.

Article 1.—Ten per cent. duty to be charged on

---

¹ Since my return to England I have seen account of a demand made by Senor Echenique for what he calls "compensation" regarding his losses in this speculation. The Government of President Pardo, however, at once crushed his claims, by denying the possibility of such a monopoly to be sanctioned by the State.

merchandise, now duty free. The following articles only are free from all duties:—Anchors and kedges of iron, tar, quicksilver, live or stuffed animals, iron buoys, pitch, fire-engines with utensils, banknotes, iron-chains, iron anchor stocks, ships, extincteurs, dried fruits (except cocoas), waste, felt for ships, shackles for anchors, instruments and tools when introduced by mechanics, but according to the law; printing-presses and utensils, scientific instruments when introduced by professors; machinery of all kinds (except sowing machines), money, gold in powder or paste, presses and articles for printing on stone, plants or herbs, silver in paste or manufactured, newspapers, produce of fish caught by national ships, ships' masts, seeds, printers' inks, vegetables, ornaments, such as vases or other articles of good taste (but subject to the law); articles for use in national hospitals (subject to law); articles for public companies, subject to agreement made between the contractor and the Government; personal effects (according to law); national produce which may return to the country, having been proved to be such; articles belonging to the steward's department of ships, and for consumption on board, excepting such as may be re-shipped or transhipped with this object; provision and merchandise imported by whaling vessels to the value of 400 soles, as per tariff; straw (toquilla and macora) and coal.

Article 2.—Five per cent. more will be charged

on the value of goods in all the Custom-houses in the Republic.

Article 3.—Special duties are charged on the following:—

		Currency.		Sterling.		
		Soles.	c.	£	s.	d.
Aguardiente of all kinds	Per dozen	4	20	0	15	9
„ in jars or barrels to 30 degrees	Per gallon	1	20	0	4	6
Beer and Cider	Per dozen	1	75	0	6	0½
„ „ in barrels	Per gallon	2	10	0	7	10½
Aguardiente, in jars or barrels, over 30 degs.	„	2	10	0	7	10½
Liquors or sweet wines	Per dozen	3	50	0	13	1½
Champagne and wines of that class (excepting Asti)	„	5	60	1	1	0
Wines of Borgoña, Brussels, Chopric, Sherry, Madeira, Port, and Vermuth	„	3	50	0	13	1½
The above in barrels	Per gallon	1	00	0	3	9
Wines of other kinds	Per dozen	2	00	0	7	6
	Per gallon	0	50	0	1	10½
Cigars of all kinds	Per lb.	0	88	0	3	3½
Tobacco of all kinds	Per 100 lbs.	28	00	5	5	0
Cards (playing)	Per gross	4	20	0	15	9
Coffee	Per 100 lbs.	7	00	1	6	3
Cocoa	„	4	00	0	15	0
Cheese	„	4	00	0	15	0
Tallow	„	3	00	0	11	3
Common Soap	„	5	00	0	18	9
Candles of all kinds	Per lb.	0	12	0	0	5½
Biscuits	Per 100 lbs.	2	00	0	7	6
Butter	„	12	50	2	6	10½
Tea	Per lb.	0	25	0	0	11½
Sugar of all kinds	Per 100 lbs.	4	80	0	18	0
Flour	„	1	80	0	6	9
Wheat	Per 135 lbs.	1	80	0	6	9

Article 4.—The Government to give to the

Chamber immediately a report in detail of the results produced by the changes now made in duties to be charged by the Custom-house, so that Congress may consider what alteration may be necessary.

For the two months after this law came into operation, I find, by *South Pacific Times* of June 28th, the following proof, in spite of this enactment, of the steady progress of trade in Callao :—

The receipts of the Callao Custom-house for the last two months have been—

In April	.	S. 366,138 91
In May	.	403,086 66
	Total	S. 769,224 57

The revenue from this source, during the same months last year, was—

In April	.	S. 316,294 05
In May	.	371,330 46
	Total	S. 687,624 51

It will thus be seen that, notwithstanding the activity in March, to avoid the payment of the augmentation of 25 per cent. in the import dues, this has been sufficient to produce an increase of S. 81,600 06 as compared with the two months' same of the preceding year. Another law relating to the taxing of exports is also under the consideration of the Government. It provides—

Article 1.—In the exportation of saltpetre, will be charged 50 per cent. on the difference between the cost price and the market value, which is to be decided by a commission to be appointed.

Article 2.—In the exportation of the raw material (caliché), a duty of twenty-five cents, will be recovered on every 100 pounds.

Article 3.—The Government to adopt any means that may suit to collect this duty.

Article 4.—This law to commence and take effect six months after its publication.

The latter law, however, in respect to Article 1 of 50 per cent. on the profits, has been altered by establishing the production of the nitrate of soda, to a Government monopoly—the State paying two soles and 40 c. (or about twelve shillings) per quintal (100 lbs.) to the producers, and reserving to itself the privilege of fixing a market price to purchasers of the article. For the Peruvian Government knows, now that the whole realizable amount of guano cannot be calculated at over 3,000,000 of tons, the nitrate of soda to make artificial manures must become more valuable in the European markets.

An addition to this has been made in proposing to have the nitrate sold at the markets of Iquique and Lima.'

' My readers may, however, see by referring back to my

From the port of Mejillones, which is between Chilo and Peru, the Pacific Company's steamer "Penguin" took a load of guano to England in the month of November.

As nothing can be more intimately connected with the progress of Peru than its railways, I append herewith translation of part of a paper read last year by Mr. Hohagan, C.E., before the Royal Geographical Society of Berlin. These have appeared in the memoirs of the Society, but some errors, typographical and general, have been corrected for me by Mr. John Meiggs, brother of the great contractor:—

The following Government railroads are now in course of construction, or have been completed by Mr. Henry Meiggs:—

Names of Railroads.	Length in English Miles.	Cost in Peruvian Soles.	Equivalent in Pounds Sterling.	Will be finished in the Year
		Soles.	£	
Callao and Oroya, now about half finished	130	27,600,000	5,175,000	1874
Mollendo and Arequipa—working—gives Government 3 per cent. until 1872, after that date 4 per cent.	107	12,000,000	2,250,000	1870
Arequipa to Puno, in construction, about half finished	222	32,000,000	6,000,000	1873
Puno to Cuzco, just begun	230	25,000,000	4,687,500	1874
Chimbote to Huaras, just begun	172	24,000,000	4,500,000	1876
Ilo to Moquegua, will be finished this year	63	6,700,000	1,256,250	1872
Pacasmayo, Guadalupe, and Magdalena	83	27,100,000	1,331,250	1878
Total	1,007	131,400,000	25,200,000	

Chapter on Saltpetre at Iquique, that this monopoly is being done away with.

According to this, the kilometer costs Government 108,536 soles 80 c., or 20,350*l*. 10*s*.; and it is certain that Mr. Meiggs is the contractor of highest rank known.

Besides these, the following State railroads are to be constructed by private individuals:—

Names of Railroads.	Length in English Miles.	Cost in Peruvian Soles.	Equivalent in Pounds Sterling.		Will be finished in the Year
		Soles.	£	*s.*	
Tacna to Bolivia—part Government has in it, 80,000 soles at 15,000*l*.	108	6,000,000	1,125,000	0	1876
Lima to Huacho, finished up to Chancay	80½	4,000,000	750,000	0	—
Pisco to Ica, finished	48	1,455,000	272,812	10	—
Paita to Puira, in construction	68	1,800,000	337,500	0	—
Lima to Pisco, not yet begun	144	10,000,000	1,875,000	0	—
Huacho to Sayan, in construction	36	2,400,000	450,000	0	—
Total	484½	25,655,000	4,810,312	10	

Projected Railways to be Commenced soon.

Names of Railroads.	Length in English Miles.	Cost in Peruvian Soles.	Equivalent in Pounds Sterling.
		Soles.	£
Chancay to Cerro de Pasco—private	120	Not known to outsiders.	—
Oroya to Chanchamayo—State	80	,,	—
Tacna to Puno—State	301	,,	—
Salaverry to Ascope—State	40	,,	—
Oroya, Jauja, and Ayacucho—State	240	,,	—
Oroya and Cerro de Pasco—State	40	,,	—
Trujillo to Eten—private	148	,,	—
Huacho to Lambayeque—private	560	,,	—
Total	1,529	210,000,000	39,375,000

PRIVATE UNDERTAKINGS—RAILWAYS ABOUT HALF FINISHED.

Names of Railroads.	Length in English Miles.	Cost in Peruvian Soles.	Equivalent in Pounds Sterling.
		Soles.	£
Cerro de Pasco to Pasco (silver mines)	15	Not known.	—
Iquique to the Noria (saltpetre district)	37	,,	—
Pisagua to Sal de Obispo	35	,,	—
Eten to Ferrenafé	28	,,	—
Total	115	,,	—

RAILWAYS ALREADY WORKING.—ENGLISH COMPANIES.

Names of Railroads.	Length in English Miles.	Cost in Peruvian Soles.	Equivalent in Pounds Sterling.
Arica to Tacna, with 6 per cent. security	39½	Soles. 6,000,000	£ 1,125,000
Callao to Lima and Lima to Chorrillos	15½		
Total	55	6,000,000	1,125,000

With these data to calculate upon, we arrive at the result that there are now in Peru, lines traced with an aggregate length of 2,979 English miles, and a total value of 382,250,000 soles, or 71,671,875*l*., so that to every ten square miles, and for each thousand inhabitants, there is one English mile of line.

To the amount above stated ought to be added the sum of 65,800,000 soles, or 10,087,500*l*. spent chiefly upon water-works, besides the immense sums required for the ramifications of some railways, for which Mr. Meiggs has also contracted, and which cannot be quoted at less than 125,000,000 soles, or 23,437,500*l*.

The details of mortality in Calláo already submitted by me having demonstrated a sad state of hygiene, I am happy in being able to add that, to afford some remedy for this state of things, there has been drawn up, in the month of September of this year, by Mr. Thomas Charles Clarke, C.E., a scheme for the sewerage of Calláo. The temperature of Calláo being rarely below 65 degrees Fahrenheit, or above 77, it ought to be one of the healthiest towns in the world—more particularly as it has almost always the pure wind blowing into it from the South Pacific.

The details I have already submitted will show how such a scheme is needed. Mr. Clarke's plan is to consist of—1st, a main outlet for sewerage; 2nd, pumping station for lifting the sewage; 3rd, line of main sewage; 4th, branch sewage; 5th, flushing and ventilation of sewers. To this succeeds the estimated cost of eighteen miles of sewers with junctions, forty inspection and ventilation shafts, twenty-five flushing chambers, and forty gullies with gratings—the whole amounting, in Mr. Clarke's estimate, to 494,958 soles, or 92,748*l*. 7*s*. 6*d*.

The station for pumping (to be worked by a windmill, with an auxiliary steam-engine) is fixed at the Calláo side of river Rimac. By these

CHAP. XII.]   PLAN OF SEWERS.   269

machines, calculating a provision for 30,000 inhabitants (which I believe to be an over-estimate), and allowing 25 gallons per day for each person, or a total of 750,000 gallons of water daily, no doubt that a new era of health would dawn in Callao. Mr. Clarke has been the supplier of a similar system to this, and with perfect success, to the cities of Oxford and Portsmouth in England. The plan has been received favourably by the municipality of Callao at its meetings. But the only action taken in the matter up to the time of my departure from Callao was an advertisement from the municipality for plans for the construction of sewers through the town, as well as for a general slaughter-house These were to be received at the municipality up to the 31st of January, 1873, and a premium of 2,000 soles (or about 400*l.*) to be given for the design of sewers, and 200 soles (or 40*l.*) for that of a slaughter-house—both plans to become property of the municipality.

CHAPTER XIII.

From Callao through the Huatica valley.—Bella Vista.—
Viceroy's palace.—Custom-house stores.—Spasmodic efforts to
make suburban residences.—Ruins of old city of Huatica.—
Ruins of castles, temples, and fortresses.—Senor Cerdan's
pamphlet about water-supply.—Tracking the Pando burial-
mound (huaca) by Mr. Steer.—Measurements converging to
multiples of 12.—Extraordinary dimensions.—Made up of
small sun-dried bricks.—Masses dislodged by earthquake.—No
notice of these things by Rivero.—Huaca de la Campana
(Marongo, or Arambolu).—Legend about this mound.—Characteristic features of architecture.—Filled up with earth.—
Fortress entitled San Miguel (Huatillos).—Adjacent temple.—
Wedge-shaped walls.—Fortresses to protect old city and
burial-ground.—Ancient temple of Delphic Oracle Rimac.

There are few portions of Peru which I have
visited, that seem to me more worthy of a searching exploration than the valley of Huatica, whereto
I am about to introduce my readers. What I
mean by exploration is such a one as that recently
conducted by Mr. Smith for the *Daily Telegraph*,
in Assyria, amongst the ruins of Babylonia and
Mosul, as well as what has been done by Dr.
Henry Schliemann in Priam's Troy. In one of
the letters of Mr. Smith,[1] describing his visit to
Babylon, he says, "The first mounds I exa-

[1] Vide *Daily Telegraph*, June 25th, 1873.

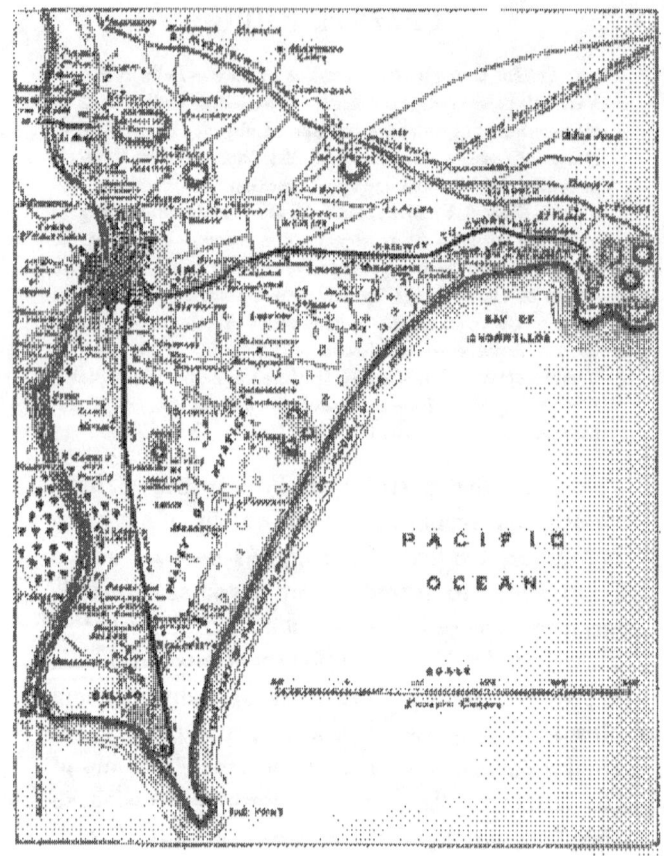

PLAN OF HUATICA VALLEY.

mined were those of the ruins called now Babil, but sometimes Miyolliba; it is the most northern set of mounds. These ruins consist of one vast oblong mound, surrounded by some smaller mounds, and the ruins of a wall which had once enclosed its structure." Quite similar to what we find in the Huatica valley, as will appear by the accompanying illustrations.

From Callão our way lies through Bella Vista, situated about a mile to the east, and on the road to Lima. It is the only stopping-station of the train between these two cities on the upward journey; but, on the downward, all the trains halt at the back of Santa Rosa church, whereby easier communication can be had with many parts of Callão, and from where the train starts for "the Point" (La Punta).

Bella Vista was founded in 1747—the year after the great earthquake—by the then Viceroy, Conde de Superunda. It certainly deserves the name, on account of the pretty view that can be had from the top of what was the Viceroy's palace in times gone by. This is now the property of a Lima gentleman, Don Pedro Bezanillo. It is situated in front of a very handsome and capacious plaza, or square, having a circular flower parterre, surrounded with iron railings, and ornamented with a fountain. Behind Don Pedro's house in the parallel square is what formerly was the chief barracks in the epoch of the Spaniards; but, shortly before my leaving the country, it was converted into a lying-in hospital. Besides the passenger line of rails to Bella Vista, there is a track for train communication between the Custom-house and its corn stores, which form a considerable building here. In the same square as the old barracks we find a Government iron foundry, in which are done all the iron works necessary for keeping the Peruvian navy in order. A considerable portion of property in this town belongs to Senor Don Gregorio Real, who was Alcalde (or mayor) of the Municipality during the first year of my residence here; and more of it is the property of Senor Gregorio Garcia, who was President of the Beneficencia Society when I left Callao. Both of these gentlemen deserve credit for trying to make Bella Vista a suburban residence. But although it ought to be healthy from its position at a height of forty-eight feet above Callao, and exposed to the fullest of the pure breezes from the South Pacific, all the spasmodic attempts to make it appreciated have failed, and its average mortality shows the same rate as Callao.

Between Callao and Bella Vista, on the side next the sea, is the site of the former race-course with its grand stand, beneath which is a liquor-shop, under the style of the "Derby Arms." Still nearer to the sea than this runs a line of rails by which Mr. Hodges procures, from a farm called Chacra Alta, material of earth as filling stuff for the piece of ground that is being reclaimed near the old mole of Callao. It is a pleasant feature of daily life amongst the native indolence with which one is encompassed in Peru, to see a train of twenty trucks, making a journey out here of two miles, and doing it ten times in the day, bringing in a daily contribution of about 800 tons of material.

RUINED WALLS OF OLD CITY OF HUATICA.

Near Bella Vista we see also partial tracks of a line of rail that was formerly planned to Magdalena, but had to be given up on account of some landed proprietor refusing a concession.

Our road, now on horseback (in company with my friend Senor Don G. Salcedo y Ruiz, from Talambo), is to have a look at the old ruins in the valley of Huatica. So, skirting a very long wall, with loop-holes for muskets, that stretches to

a mile in length behind the old barracks of the
Viceroy, we find ourselves, after half an hour's
ride, in the midst of what I believe to be the ruins
of the old city of Huatica. I may add that, in the
country all around, extending from the railroad to
the sea, and as far as this, not more than four

VIEW FROM WEST SIDE OF HUACA OF PANDO.

miles from Calláo, I counted seventeen different
huacas (as they are entitled here), but some of
which have no appearance of being burial-grounds.
I therefore set them down as residences, castles,
or fortresses. The burial-mounds of various sizes
are, however, in the proportions of four to one of
the architectural matters. At the farm of Don
Manuel Salazar, about a mile out from Bella Vista,
the house is built on one of these old mounds; and
quite close to the ruins of the ancient city is a place

called Las Palmas, at which some Italians are located, and where they produce excellent grapes, from which red wine is manufactured.

Amongst the ruins here it is impossible to make out anything but fragments of walls. These are thick and close, over a space of a few square miles, and are enclosed within a triple wall—so destroyed in many places that it is impossible to follow its outline. In Don Ambrosio Cerdan's[*] little book, from which I shall have to quote more hereafter, mention is frequently made of "La ciudad, o Huatica,"—the city, or Huatica. Whence it may be supposed that the original water corporation may have had its head-quarters here. The triple wall whereof I have already spoken was pointed out to me by Mr. Steer, who tried to trace it for some distance, but found it very much broken down,—even the foundations in places, probably rooted up to make way for vine plantations. These walls were respectively one yard, two yards, and three yards in thickness, being, in some parts of their relics, from fifteen to twenty feet high.

To the east of these ruins is the enormous mound called the Huaca of Pando; and to the west, with the distance of about half a mile intervening, are the great ruins of fortress which the natives entitle the Huaca de la Campana (the huaca

[*] "Tratado General sobre las Aguas que fertilizan los Valles de Lima," por Don Ambrosio Cerdan de Landa, Simon Pontero Oidor de la Antigua Audiencia de este Capital. Lima, 1828.

of the bell). From Mr. Cerdan's book I believe this to have been the great fortress of Arambolu, presided over by the Yunca Chief, Huachiçi.

The huacas of Pando consist of a series of large and small mounds, and—extending over a stretch of ground incalculable without being measured—form a colossal accumulation. The principal large ones are three in number; that holding the Spanish name of La Concha (the shell), with

VIEW FROM EAST SIDE OF CENTRAL HUACA OF PANDO.

a wooden cross on it, and not far from where the train passes nearly every hour between Callao and Lima, is apparently separated from the others by a modern wall running through. But as there are many small cultivated farms about, this may have been a recent division; the distance from it to what I call the central mound of the Pando group being only about 100 yards.

My first visit to this so impressed me with its importance and magnitude that I made a second in company with Mr. Steer, who tracked and took measurements of it. It was calculated 103 to 110 feet in height. At the western side, looking towards Callao, there is a square plateau with an elevation of about 22 to 24 feet, which measured 95 to 96 yards each way—that is, from north to south, and from east to west. At the summit it was tracked 276 to 278 yards long, and 95 to 96 yards across. On the top there are eight gradations of declivity, each from one to two yards lower than its neighbour, counting from west to east, or in the direction lengthways. Tracking these in the length of the mound, Mr. Steer found them to measure as nearly as possible,—

1st plateau	96 to 97 yards.
2nd „	„ „ 25 „ to 26
3rd „	23 „ 24 „
4th „	11 „ 12 „
5th „	„ „ 24 „ „ 25
6th „	23 „ 24 „ „ „
7th „	35 „ 36 „
8th „	„ „ 36 „ „ 37
	Total of 278 yards.

The broken structure of adobes, with the scattered earth, made the tracking process of measurement impracticable to an exact foot or two.

This was measured over twice, in order to avoid errors. Returning back, or rather descending, we found the square plateau first mentioned, at the base, to consist of two divisions, one six feet lower than the other, but each measuring a perfect square of 47 to 48 yards—the two joined forming, as I mentioned at first, a square of 96 yards. Besides this, and a little forward on the western side, was another square of 47 to 48 yards.

On the top, returning again, we still find the same symmetry of measurement in the multiples of 12.[1] Tracking it in its breadth from north to south, three levels were found in this measurement. The first lower down could be made out as 17 to 18 yards wide; the second or highest summit, 59 to 60 yards across; and the third descent again, 23 to 24 yards. In all these measurements the difficulty increased more and more of footing it correctly. And the same would exist if measuring it by rule, as much on account of the disintegration of its elements from great antiquity, as to what is plainly evident on its western face, of how it has suffered from earth-

[1] Further investigations amongst the prehistoric monuments may bring to light, that amongst these people was possibly made the first Zodiac, or lunar calendar in Peru. In Mr. Bollaert's "Antiquities," &c., p. 146, is an illustration with an account of "golden breast-plate or sun," sketched by Mr. Markham when in Lima, and which, although in the possession of General Echenique of that city, was accredited as found at Cuzco. This Mr. Bollaert supposes to be a lunar calendar or zodiac—the only example he knows of. He describes the twelve months of the Inca Zodiac, as represented on that plate. The persistence of the multiples of twelve, in the measurements of nearly all the ruins in the Huatica valley is a very curious fact.

quakes. The mound is of the truncated pyramidal form, and was calculated by Mr. Steer, allowing 100 feet greater breadth at its base, to contain a mass of 14,641,820 cubic feet of material.

One of not the least extraordinary things connected with this great work is the fact of its chief

SKETCH TAKEN OF PARTS ON TOP OF CENTRAL HUACA OF PANDO.

architectural composition being made up of sundried bricks, or adobes—each of these being six inches long, four inches wide, and two inches and a half thick. More wonderful still is it that many of these adobes have the marks of fingers on them, —leading us to believe that they were the labour of human hands.

But this, as I have already said, does not constitute more than one-third of the Pando huaca. Walking down past the southern corner, where the

adobes are tumbled into a conglomerate mass by
some earthquake, we see skulls, with bones of
arms and legs, cropping up in many places. The
same adobe work is visible throughout, and the
whole length of these structures, although made in
an ovoid form, may be calculated, in Mr. Steer's
opinion as well as my own, to range between seven
to eight hundred yards of length. The remainder
are all lower than the central one, except that of
Concha, which, although quite as high, is only
about half the length of the previously named.

Before passing through the ruins of the old
town, and looking back at these colossal mounds, I
cannot help wondering what Senor Don Mariano
Eduardo Rivero means by a note,* wherein he talks

SKETCH OF PORTION OF HUACA OF PANDO, SHOWING EFFECTS OF
EARTHQUAKE.

* "Peruvian Antiquities," p. 168.

of "a large number of huacas of different sizes, some being more than *fifty yards in length*, and about *fifteen in height*, from Limatambo to Marengo."

Now, Limatambo is a small farm on the railroad from Lima to Chorillos, about a few miles outside of the capital, and Marengo is the very next farm to the so-called Huaca de Campana, this grand old fortress of Arambolu, which is here within a few hundred yards of us, and certainly not more than four miles outside of Lima. Therefore this author's observation was not very extensive, or he would not have written of these grand works only as measuring " more than fifty yards in length and about fifteen in height." Yet Senor Rivero, by the title-page of his book, was "Director of the National Museum of Lima," as well as "Corresponding Member of various Scientific Societies in Europe and America."

The legend about the name of the Huaca de la Campana (or Huaca of the Bell) is almost too ridiculous to repeat here. But I " tell the tale as 'twas told to me" by Mr. Campbell, a Scotch resident at the chacra, or farm, of Desemparados, not far from the town of Magdalena.[1] This is, that in times gone by, the Devil (of whose interest in Peruvian affairs we have already had several incidents[2])

---

[1] I cannot pass by the opportunity of thanking Mr. Campbell for his kind help, and hospitality, given to me on several occasions of my visits to the Huatica valley.

[2] *Vide* chap. ix. p. 149.

managed to get hold of a bell, that by some magical means had been brought to the top of this old fort. Some of the clergy, desirous of getting it away, had dug round it for the purpose; but the more they dug, the deeper went down the bell, until probably it sunk, in the words of Milton, to that deeper depth which, "deeper than the deepest depths," is found below.

On my last visit here, with Mr. Steer, I sounded the hole, in which the bell is reputed to have been, with a piece of cord, having a stone attached, and found it to be forty-two feet deep. It is about the compass of an ordinary well. The Capitaz of Senor Osma, who was with us, at once took the ring out of the bell, by telling me that he knew of the hole in question being dug by the father of Senor Osma, and some other gentleman, in quest of treasure. The place where this opening is cut passes through adobones,¹ or large square masses of mud brick—generally from a yard to a yard and a half in length, and of equal thickness. These I observe everywhere as a characteristic feature of the architecture, to distinguish the fortresses from the burial-mounds.

The fortress, mayhap the castle of Arambolu, or Marongo, is a huge structure, calculated by Mr. Steer to be eighty feet high, and found by tracking to be from 148 to 150 yards in measure-

¹ Adobones are large mud bricks—some from one to two yards in thickness, length, and breadth.

ment—in length as in breadth—thus constituting a
perfect square. Some of the adobe walls, a yard
and a half in thickness, are still quite perfect. That
this was not likely to have been a burial-mound
may be presumed from its formation. Great large
square rooms show their outlines on the top, but
all filled up with earth. Who brought this earth
here, and with what object was the filling up

RUINS OF PRINCIPAL HUATICA FORTRESS (ARAMBOLU).

accomplished? for the work of obliterating all
space in these rooms with loose earth, must have
been almost as great as the construction of the
building itself.

About two miles south of the last-named large
fort, and in a parallel line with it as regards the
sea, we find another similar structure, probably a
little more spacious, and with a greater number of
apartments, or divisions by walls, on the top of

which we can walk now, as it is likewise all filled up with clay. This is called San Miguel. But from

SKETCH OF ARANMOLL' FORTRESS, TAKEN ON THE TOP.

Senor Don Ambrosio Cerdan's pamphlet, already noticed, I believe these to be the ruins of the old

RUINS OF SMALL FORTRESS.

fortress of Huatillco. It is nearly 170 yards in length by 168 to 170 in breadth, and is one enormous structure of nearly 90 feet high. Indeed, I agree with Mr. Steer, that if the *débris* of broken adobones at the base could be cleared away, it might be as perfect a quadrilateral as any of the others. That it was as important as Arambolu may be assumed from the fact of the ruins of small forts quite close to it, and those of a little temple, with niches in the walls for idols, about three hundred yards off.

The whole of these ruins, big fortress, small forts, and temple, were enclosed by high walls of adobones, but all of wedge-shape form, with the sharp edge upwards. Mr. Steer calculated the

RUINS OF OLD TEMPLE.

cubic measurement of the fortress of Arambolu at

20,220,840 cubic feet, and that of Huatillco at 25,650,800 feet. These two buildings were constructed in the same style—having traces of terraces, parapets, and bastions, with a large number of rooms and squares—all now filled up with earth.

From the relative positions of the relics described in this chapter, I come to the conclusion, that the fortresses of Arambolu and Huatilleo were to protect from invaders the city of Huatica, with the burial-mound of Pando behind. Because the first-mentioned buildings are nearer to the sea, and more to the south, from whence the enemy might be expected. The fortress of San Miguel, or Huatilleo, may be supposed, however, to have a more direct bearing in reference to the old temple of the god Rimac, as it stands in almost a line direct between the latter and the Pacific Ocean.

CHAPTER XIV.

Fortresses near Senor Osma's quinta.—Fortress of Garmendi.—Village of Magdalena.—Ruins of temple in four groups.—All filled up with clay.—Ruins of temple of Rimac.—Immense extent of enclosure.—Turkey buzzards amongst the relics.—Country residence of Viceroy here.—Railroad from Lima to Magdalena.—Iconoclastic barbarity.—Bad roads.—Warmcochco Castle.—Chacra of Conde de San Isidro.—Painting of San Isidro.—Winged Seraph at the plough.—Burial-mound of Pan de Azucar.—Partial exploration of it.—Articles found.—Senor Raimondy's opinion.—Measurement of this huaca.—Burial-mound of Juliana (Ocharán).—Enormous structure.—Multiples of twelve.—Enclosure of half a million square yards, or 117 acres.—Mr. Steer's calculations.—Adobes building the mound.—Cave of hermit who was burned by the Inquisition in 1673.—Mira Flores.—Chorillos.—The friar's leap.—The hereditary asses.—Central part of Chorillos.

About half a mile distant from the Arambolu fortress, along one of the roads from Bella Vista to Magdalena village, we find the ruins of what Mr. Campbell agrees with me, in believing to be the remnants of the old temple, dedicated to the god Rimac. This supposition is not founded on any remarkable architectural features, as on the fact of its being an immense large square—composed of four huge masses of ruins—one on either side of the square, and another quadrilateral space in the centre. I believe this to be erroneously considered, as Mr. Campbell tells me it is generally supposed, the place where the hermit, Mateo Salado, dwelt for some time. He was burnt by the Inquisition at Lima—in 1673, or just 200 years ago.

RUINS OF A FORTRESS, OR CASTLE, ON RIGHT SIDE OF SENOR OSMA'S FARM.

On many of the old ruins we often find half a dozen turkey buzzards—"the scavengers of nature," as Swainson calls them—which render such material service to Calláo and Lima. Here they look rather indolent, as it appears probable they have come out to whet their appetites in the pure air of this valley for the offal feasts in the streets. Our road passes by the farm of Senor Osma, and in this half-mile of progress there are no less than from six to eight remnants of buildings. Of these Senor Zaballos took two sketches for me.

There was an old fortress of Garmendi in this

CHAP. XIV.]   FORTRESS OF GARMENDI.   289

valley, which may have been that of San Miguel, for much of our exploration can be no more than conjecture. After leaving behind the farm of Senor Osma, we come to a bifurcation of the road—that to the right leading down to the village of Magdalena, and by the chacra of some gentleman from Lima, whose name I forget; that to the

RUINS OF CASTLE ON LEFT SIDE OF SENOR OSMA'S FARM.

left skirts the ruins which we are about to examine. Branching off by Ascona, (another farm,) this latter comes out by the race-course, and the penitentiary after a ride of three miles to the city of Lima. On this last-named road we take a turn round the corner of the old wall, enclosing the temple, to have a sketch of part of those which remain.

Mr. Steer's measurements of them are as follow :—The most southern of the four masses—

that represented in the illustration,—he ascertained to be 70 feet high and 153 yards square at the top—the cubic contents calculated at

PART OF RUINS OF DOUBLE WALL AT TEMPLE OF RIMAC.

14,536,989 feet of material. This is only one, though apparently the largest of those within the enclosure of the big walls. The ruins, tracked by him, measured 560 yards in one direction, and 424 yards in the other—thus constituting a quadrilateral enclosure of 237,440 square yards, or about 49 square acres.

On the top of this, as on the fortresses of Arambolu, and San Miguel, were also discernible the outlines of large square rooms, filled up, as all the others, even to the topmost height of 70 feet, with earth or clay.

Hence our road lies through the little village of

Magdalena, which has nothing about it to justify Senor Rivero's suspicion of its being erected on the site of the old Huatica city. It is a town with a few hundred inhabitants—all of the *festina lente* class—a chapel, with the Curé's house alongside—an aqueduct coming from the Rimac and separating the square from the chapel; one comfortable-looking little house, reported as formerly occupied by a Viceroy; and an extensive view from a look-out (Mirador) on the top of the same. Between it and the farm of Mr. Campbell, only about 1,000 yards off, is a considerable-sized mound as regards extent, from which bricks have been made, and wherein bodies were found buried. On Mr. Campbell's own farm there are no less than thirteen of such heaps, all of which, when explored, turned out human remains.

From this we go across the line of the railway now being constructed between Lima and Magdalena, with the object of making a new sea bathing-place for the former. The valley through which this railway has to pass is certainly one of the prettiest, and most picturesque—with all the charms of fresh air, and rural scenery. The new town, or "Pueblo Nuevo," a title which grates upon my ear in the midst of these grand old Indian names, is situated close to the sea, as that of Chorillos is. There is, however, a precipitous bank of 60 to 70 feet high to be cut away to make a descent to the shore, and the locale on which it is situated is right in front of the Pacific, instead

VIEW OF ONE QUARTER OF SUPPOSED TEMPLE OF RIMAC.

of being sheltered by a protecting rock as Chorillos is. The line passes through several burial-mounds, and I have been told, on good authority, the working-men at this place—the navvies—have smashed up into small bits several precious mummies that were taken out in their integrity. Such iconoclastic barbarity ought not to be permitted.

The roads about here are certainly badly in want of a Macadamite reformer. Wherever water manages to lodge itself, by breaking out of an aqueduct, there it is allowed to remain; and as nearly all the roads outside of Lima, as well as Callao, are knee-deep in fine dust, the consequences to travellers may be imagined.

We are on horseback, however, and manage to get along gaily, after a good breakfast from our hospitable friend, Mr. Campbell. Turning a corner, by General Echenique's house, we travel along in the centre of ruins. One is pointed out to me by

REMAINS OF POST TO THE LEFT OF RIMAC TEMPLE.

Mr. Campbell as what is called Warmcochee Castle, from which there is a mile of a straight road. Then, turning down to the right, we find ourselves amongst another collection of old fortresses, castles, towers, palaces—or whatever they may be—and go in for a while to the stately-looking farm-house of Senor Paz Soldan. This is called the Chacra of Conde de San Isidro, after its former Spanish owner. It consists of a large house, with a lofty square tower, a great extent of out-houses, a yard, and a spacious garden, with a considerable-sized orchard of olive-trees on its southern sido. In the principal sala is a painting of San Isidro, represented in a "My-name-is-Norval!" style of attitude, and a roll of paper in one hand. He is dressed in a green frock-coat, fastened round the waist by a strap, and, if I were not told otherwise, would take him for a French post-boy. On the right side is a pair of oxen ploughing,—driven by a winged seraph, having a garter on one leg, and the other naked. This picture did not at all chime in with the wingless Cholos whom I saw, not driving, but seemingly drawn along by some bullocks that were ploughing in a neighbouring field. But San Isidro was the patron saint of agriculture.

SUGAR LOAF HUACA (SAN ISIDRO).

In front of Senor Soldan's house, that is to say between it and the Ocean, and at the distance of about a quarter of a mile (as we have a détour to make), is one of the real huacas, or burial-mounds, called the Pan do Azucar (or sugar-loaf), from its shape. I had previously been informed by Senor Raimondy of his having made considerable explorations of this mound, and finding nothing in it but bodies of ordinary fishermen, relics of nets, and some inferior specimens of pottery. He likewise told me that it was all constructed of layers of loose earth over layers of bodies—whence he inferred that all the huacas, or mounds, in the Huatica valley were of a similar nature. On my first visit, Senor Soldan, junior, was kind enough to furnish me with a man, as well as the loan of pickaxe and shovel. Neither of these proving of any use, I made a second trip, with Mr. Steer and Mr. George Wilson of Callao. We brought with us one of the mule-cars, kindly lent by Mr. Sterling, of the Lima Railway Company, two shovels and pickaxes, with some sacks, and had a grand day's exploration. Senor Zabulos, too, was amongst our company, to take sketches.

This huaca, measured by Mr. Steer, proved to be 66 feet high at its central point. Its broadest measurement was 80 yards at the base, and its longest 130 to 131 yards in extent. It was a mound very difficult of calculation on account of being so irregular in formation. But Mr. Steer, allowing an average height of 30 feet, estimated it to contain 3,736,800 cubic feet.

Numbers of skulls, parts of legs, and other fragments of humanity, much of which I believe to have been the result of Senor Raimondy's excavations, lay scattered about. I did not, however, like to take these. So Mr. Steer with pickaxe, and Mr. George Wilson with shovel, commenced to excavate. We did not find what Senor Raimondy described—a layer of loose clay over a layer of bodies. For in several places we came to enclosures made with adobones. Although the generality of these were done in a rough, shapeless manner, as if the work had been one of great urgency.

Amongst the things turned out, and which I sent with about forty skulls to the Anthropological

HUACA OF JULIANA (OCHARAN), FROM EASTERN SIDE, TAKEN AT A MILE DISTANCE.

Institute, were a few bits of red and yellow dyed thread, being relics of cloth; a piece of string made of woman's hair, plaited, and about the size of what is generally used for a watch-guard; some pieces of very thick cotton cloth, bits of fish-nets, portions of slings, and two specimens of crockery-ware of excellent material. The place appears to me to be one mass of human bodies; but the man who came with us from Mr. Soldan's house tells me that in the time of Senor Raimondy's exploration, several specimens of pottery, together with many of silver, were taken out of it. I may add that this mound has got a broken wooden cross on the top, which is not included in the sketch: for in such a spot, and with the carelessness of the people to its influences, I believe the holy symbol to be not far from desecration.

About a mile farther on, in the direction of Mira Flores, is, however, the largest of the burial-mounds in the Huatica valley. The sketch may not be recognized by those who pass there daily between Lima and Chorillos, for in its actuality there is a small wooden house, constructed to shelter the watchers who guard the vineyards about. As this anomalous structure in such a place always reminded me of the idea of a fly on the back of an elephant, I asked Senor Zabalos to omit it in the drawing.

An old man here told me this was the burying-ground of Ocharín—a district in which the Chief Caçique, named Pacallár, was the governing power long before the time of Cuys Mancu. How this Solomon came by his knowledge I cannot tell; but on looking over the small map of the district, published by the Lima, Calláo, and Chorillos Railway Company, I see these very names noted down, as connected with locales between Mira Flores and Chorillos.

This mound presents as it is approached, the appearance of an imposing and enormous structure. To the eastward are three large squares of rubble stone, probably the burial-places of some of the *plebs*. The direction of the structure in its length runs from north to south, and the declivities of the terraces on the top go from nearly the centre;—the greater number being on the northern side. It is 95 feet of elevation in the highest part. It has an average width of 55 yards on the summit, and a total length of 428 yards. By compass bearings, its track is from S.W. to N.E., and its terraces or esplanades at top measure as follow:—

1st grade	.	90 yards long by	52 broad.
2nd [1] „	.	130 „ „	60 „
3rd „	.	38 „ „	52 „
4th „	.	45 „ „	54 „
5th „	.	40 „ „	59 „
6th „	.	85 „ „	86 „

Sum total 428 yards, multiplied by 3

giving 1,284 feet, which may be observed as another multiple of 12.

But the most wonderful part of this mound

[1] This is the highest, as the measurements are reckoned from south-east to north-west.

CHAP. XIV.] IMMENSE WALL OF OCHARÁN. 299

SKETCH OF TOP OF HUACA OF JULIANA (OR OCHARÁN).

SOUTH END OF HUACA WITH HERMIT'S CAVE (MATEO SALADOS).

is, that it has been enclosed by a double wall somewhat similar to that of the Rimac temple, although not quite so thick. This wall, tracked by Mr. Steer, measured 816 yards in length, by 700 yards across, as far as the vestiges can be traced, thus giving an area of enclosure of 571,200 square yards, or 117 acres. May I not ask here, what are the great squares mentioned by Mr. Markham [1] at the old Chimoo town, near Trujillo, of 276 yards one way, and 160 the other, when compared to this?

Within the enclosure are the square places of rubble stone, already mentioned, which are about eight feet high, and not included in Mr. Steer's calculations. From the top of this mound I brought some sun-dried adobes, larger than those at Pando.

Mr. Steer further calculated the contents of the mound to be 12,711,600 cubic feet. This is made on the allowance of 60 feet average to the height. But it appears to me that, the whole building being of the somewhat truncated pyramidal shape of Pando, the calculation is under-estimated.[2]

[1] "Journal of the Royal Geographical Society," vol. xli. 1871, p. 322.

[2] At the southern end of this huaca is the cave, on previous page, into which I crawled to find its extent. It goes in to a length of twelve feet, is about three feet across, and the same in height. I believe this to have been the dwelling of the Frenchman, of whom Rivero speaks, "Mateo Salado, who passed for a hermit, until he was burned in 1573 by the horrible tribunal of the Inquisition." (Op. cit. p. 168.) Nowhere else in this valley is there evidence of such a thing.

The Huaca of Ocharín was used as a vantage ground by the artillery of General Echenique in the war of 1854, when General Castillo fought him here—the army of the latter being stationed near Mira Flores. The fight took place on the 4th of January in the year just mentioned, and next day General Castillo entered Lima triumphant. Echenique's squadron was stationed at sea in front of this position, and, I am informed, fired right into Mira Flores. But of this I confess myself doubtful, as they would have to shoot over a sea-bank eighty feet high, and the place aimed at behind was invisible to the fleet.

Between Ocharín and the sea are from fifteen to twenty masses of ruins, like those already described. Whilst from the top of the main structure we have a view of Lima and the surroundings, with the little village of Mira Flores about a mile distant. Towards the west, the Pacific Ocean stretches out with its great glassy sheet, and the southern view is bounded by the bathing place of Chorillos—the Brighton of Lima,—backed by a bluff high rock called the Morro. This is overtopped by a cross, and from behind it is reputed to have jumped into the sea one of the friars of old in times gone by. Consequently, it has the name of Salto del Fraile, or Friar's Leap.

Many illustrations of Chorillos are given in Dr. Manuel Fuente's handsome work on Lima.[1] The

[1] "Lima; or, Sketches of the Capital of Peru: Historical,

chiefest features of it are its propinquity to Lima,—being reachable by a nine miles' trip on a railway, as well as its airy Malecon, or quay, constructed by General Castillo, to whom Chorillos owes most of its present success. Some of the so-called ranchos (or huts) here, especially that of General Pezet, in front of the railway station, resemble palaces more than houses for a bathing-place. The original Indians of Chorillos were fishermen; and, before the railway, the women used to carry their fish to Lima on a mule's or ass's back. They were likewise the general messengers of the gentry temporarily located here. On St. Peter's Day there is always a grand ceremony and a procession in this town, terminating in a wooden statue of the saint being brought out to sea in a canoe, to inaugurate the fishing season. From the luck of the catch on this occasion is augured the good or bad condition of the approaching fishing time.

Amongst the legends of Chorillos is one connected with Palm Sunday. "The history of Las Burras del Senor" (the Lord's she-asses), says Dr. Fuente,[5] "is well known. The first ass employed for the procession, many long years ago, naturally became an object of veneration for

Statistical, Administrative, Commercial, and Moral." By Manuel a Fuentes, Advocate of the Peruvian Tribunals and Member of several learned societies. London: Trübner and Co., 60, Paternoster Row, 1866.

[5] Op. cit. p. 107.

MALECOT (OR PROMENADE) AT CRONSTADT.

the Indians, who not only allowed it to remain at liberty and unworked, but also fed it well. Rest and abundant food had made the animal very fat. It had the free range of the village and the neighbouring valleys; but on Palm Sunday it spontaneously went to the church, accompanied by its young one. The race of this sagacious ass is not extinct. Its descendants still perform the same services, and enjoy the same privileges and attentions as their predecessors. It is said that down to the present time there has been no instance of the ass having failed in its attendance, or of its having come without a foal."

The central part of Chorillos would, doubtless, be more agreeable as a sea residence if the streets were a little wider. Here there is a much better regulation of hygiene than either in Callão or Lima. For the streets are not only well swept, but all the sweepings are burned.

His Excellency Senor Don Manuel Pardo, the existing President of the Republic, occupies in summer time one of the prettiest houses—I cannot call it a rancho—in Chorillos.

CHAPTER XV.

Lima.—The "City of the Kings."—Number of authors who have described it.—Foundation by Francisco Pizarro, the conqueror.—Its former wealth.—Streets paved with blocks of silver.—Confounding calculations.—Knocking down of the old walls.—Boulevards made by Mr. Henry Meiggs.—Want of fireplaces in Peruvian houses.—Principal plaza and cathedral of Lima.—Body of Pizarro in the vaults.—Doubts of its genuineness.—Place of assassination of Pizarro.—Palace of the Executive.—Plaza de la Indopendencia.—Bolivar's statue.—Chambers of senators and deputies.—House of the Inquisition.—University of San Marcos.—Foundation in A.D. 1576.—Mint in Lima.—Large number of chapels.—English kings doing duty for Incas.—Penitentiary.—Public buildings of Lima.—Its deficient hygiene.—Dr. Huxley's opinions of the immorality of Lima.—Author's contradiction of it.—Saya y Manta.—Literary ladies in Lima.

Although Lima is entitled by some of its admirers "the Paris of South America," I am afraid there are not many travellers, who, at the first visit will endorse the simile. By others it is said to be "the heaven of women, purgatory of men, and hell of asses."

Under the name of "City of the Kings" (Ciudad de los Reyes), the Peruvian capital was traced out on the 6th of January—the Epiphany—in A.D. 1535; but the actual foundation did not take place till the 18th of the same month, when it was done with all Spanish pomp and form by the conqueror, Senor Don Francisco Pizarro. In all the histories, or descriptions of Peru that I have read, there is not a word said about Pizarro's having received any opposition from the natives in the valley of the Rimac, nor even any mention of this place in the pages of Garcilasso de la Vega, from the time of its conquest by Pachacutec, the Inca, till Pizarro came unopposed to settle down in it. For which reasons, it seems to me, the antiquity of these places described in the valley of Huatica may be allowed to be of a far more remote age than they are usually considered.

Lima has been well described, and by many writers—by the brothers Ulloa, by Frozier, by Stevenson, Markham, Bollaert, Paz Soldan, Dr. Baxley, and by a score of others. But the City of Kings has had so much of transition about it that what was written of it, even so late as ten years ago, cannot hold good to-day. Moreover, every traveller has his special peculiarities of noticing what strikes his own faculty of perception, so that I may possibly hit upon one or two features of Peruvian characteristics in the capital, that have not been noticed by previous writers.

During the colonial period Lima had forty-one Viceroys—from Pizarro to Pezulla. Of its wealth and magnificence in some of these times Frezier[1] tells us that two days after his arrival in the

[1] "Relation of a Voyage from the Sea of the South to the Coasts of Chily and of Peron, done during the years 1712, 1713

capital he witnessed the celebration of the Festival of San Francisco de Assiz, to which he devotes several pages in describing all its ceremonies. Those were flourishing days for the convents, no doubt, as one of them is said to have accumulated 350,000 dollars in one year. That wealth was on almost as magnificent a scale, as the neighbouring Andes are in their towering majesty of rock, may be inferred from the following, which I translate:—
" As in the cities of Europe carriages are reckoned to calculate magnificence, at Lima they have 4,000 caleches, the ordinary carriages of the country, drawn by mules. But to give an idea of the city, it is sufficient to relate that the merchants showed riches at the end of the year 1683, at the entry of the Duke de Palata, when he came to take possession as Viceroy. They paved the extent of the cuadras (150 yards long) of the Merced and Mercaderas (by which he had to enter the Royal Square—the Plaza Principal—where the palace is) with ingots of silver, which weighed on an average 200 marcs—were twelve to fifteen inches long, four to five inches wide, and two to three inches thick. This amounted to the worth of 80,000,000 (eighty million) crowns, or about 32,000,000 (thirty-two million) pounds of our money on the basis that it stands at present."

Without being hypercritical, I may here observe

and 1714." Published at Paris in 1716, by Monsieur Frezier, Ordinary Engineer of the King.

that Mr. Frezier's arithmetic puzzles me. I have copied these figures as they are in his book, one 8 and seven 0's (expressing 80,000,000) of crowns with 32 and seven 0's (representing 32,000,000) of pounds of our money. And whether the pound in this case, as conveyed by the word "livre," means a French synonym of the 20 franc, or of an English pound sterling, neither can supply a sum of 32,000,000 by any kind of calculation that I am aware of from 80,000,000 of crowns, which I have always supposed to be 5s. each. But this was in the days before Gough and Vostor.

Stevenson says[1]:—"When the Viceroy, Marquis de la Palata, entered Lima in 1682, the streets through which the procession passed were *all* paved with bars of silver." The word *all* is put in italics by me to do it honour, as it seems only in the same ordinary type as the rest in its original. Indeed, I doubt whether it should not be put ALL; for from the entrance-gate of the Callão road to the Plaza the number of streets (of course, meaning squares) is not less than from twelve to fifteen, and these being ALL paved with silver, it was a great shame for Frezier to have said there were only two.

The city of Lima was surrounded by a wall, Paz Soldan tells us, in 1685, by order of the Viceroy, Duke of Palata, just mentioned. They were afterwards repaired by the Viceroy Abascal.

[1] Op. cit., vol. I. p. 324.

during the time of the struggle for independence. Wonderfully strong, they were about five yards high, and four yards thick, with thirty-four bastions and twelve gates.

These were, however, of recent years, gradually becoming useless, the walls tottering and the gates broken up. But in the present year (1873) an effectual *coup de grace* has been given to their inutility, by the fact of the greater portion of them having been bought, (to be turned into practical usefulness), by Mr. Henry Meiggs. To effect this a considerable length in the neighbourhood of the Exhibition Palace, between which and the walls in question the Chorillos Railway runs, have been pulled down. A boulevard of more than a mile long has been planted with trees, extending from the front of the palace to the gate of La Piedra Liza,—that by which the traveller makes his exit for the road to the ruins of Pacha-Cámac. On each side of this boulevard the ground is levelled for the building of houses, and the whole arrangement will admit of an increased quantity of fresh air from the Pacific into Lima.

Much of the first impressions of a visitor to this city must depend on the period of the year at which he arrives. If he comes when the Garuas' prevail—from May till November—the streets appear the epitome of discomfort, and the insides of

---

' *Garuas* means very small rain, which is more like a heavy dew than even a Scotch mist.

CATHEDRAL OF LIMA.

houses scarcely less so. For in Peruvian dwellings there are no fire-places, and the sense of their absence is doubly palpable when one is obliged to feel his feet moistened from slipping on the muddy streets, as to have his clothes saturated with damp.

The Plaza Principal, or principal square is, of course, the first attraction for the new comer. In this he will see one of the stateliest cathedrals in South America, founded by Pizarro, but requiring, after its foundation, ninety years to complete the building, owing to earthquakes and political imbroglios. It cost beyond 100,000*l*. The original building was nearly totally destroyed in the earthquake of 1746, but was rebuilt by that excellent man, the Viceroy, Conde de Superunda. Descriptive details of its architecture are given by Dr. Fuentes, which are unnecessary for me to repeat.[1]

During my residence in Lima I went on two different occasions into the crypt under the choir for the purpose of seeing what is there shown as the remains of the conqueror, Francisco Pizarro. I had previously been told by Senor Raimondy, that a finger had been taken off one of the hands. Dr. Fuente says that[2] "in this pantheon is preserved the head of Francisco Pizarro, with the remains of his daughter Francisca, who bequeathed considerable property to pay for the celebration of daily mass at the high altar. The cost of ornaments and the other

[1] Op. cit., part ii. p. 18.   [2] Op. cit., p. 24.

expenses occasioned by this mass are paid with the interest of 1,000 gold piastres left for the purpose." The negro sacristan who brought us down, and held a lighted candle, showed me a body of a well-proportioned man, not only with one finger off, but with all the metacarpal bones up to the wrist taken away. He was in a niche, and over him was an old silk cloak, from which I was permitted to slice off a bit as a relic. I very soon threw it away, however, on being told by the Rev. Mr. Strong-i'-th'-arm, an English Roman Catholic clergyman attached to the cathedral for many years, that he believed a great many skeletons, and no inconsiderable number of silk cloaks, had been doing duty for the memory of the great Pizarro, since the Conqueror was accredited to have been deposited here.

For there is in reality no vouchable proof that his remains were ever brought to this cathedral. All that history tells us is, that on the 26th of June, 1541, or only six years after the foundation of the city, he was assassinated at his own residence—it never could have been a palace as it is entitled by some writers—in a narrow alley leading from the western side of the plaza down to the Calle de Plateros (street of the silversmiths) in the adjoining square. These assassins were the followers of his rival, Almagro, and, to the number of eighteen or twenty, cut him down on the stairs of the house. I went to have a look at it one morning; and it certainly appears a very out-of-the-way place for the conqueror of Peru to reside in. The alley is now called the Callejon de Petateros—the mat-makers' lane. Besides mat-makers, there are one or two fourth-rate Italian eating-houses in it.

FRONT OF PIZARRO'S PALACE.

Facing the entrance from the principal square to the mat-makers' alley is the front gate of Pizarro's palace, now used as offices for the Government Executive, as the Ministry for Foreign Affairs, the same for Treasury, War, and Marine Department, as well as Ministry of the Interior, with official apartments for the President himself. The last President, his Excellency Senor Don Jose Balta, together with his family, resided here; but the present Executive, Senor Don Manuel Pardo, prefers to remain with his family in his own private house some five squares off, or at Chorillos in the bathing season,—coming hither every day to perform his functions as Citizen President. Here, or at his own private house, he is always accessible to the humblest person in the Republic.

This palace has been very appropriately described by Senor Paz Soldan,* as "a confused, intricate, and heterogeneous agglomeration of saloons, disproportionate in their dimensions, drawing-rooms and closets of different forms of construction that constitute a labyrinth." The palace occupies a whole square, including the police barracks outside and a few public offices in the same position.

It requires a large appreciation of Republican liberty to persuade oneself that the palace of the head of the Government could be occupied, as this is at its base in the side facing the plaza, as well as that up the Calle del Palazio, or Palace Street, with little huckster shops, in which are seen gridirons for sale, and old hatters' stores adjoining. "The divinity that doth hedge a king" is certainly sadly wanting in the case of the surroundings of a Peruvian President, as the old palace of Pizarro plainly testifies.

In the middle of the plaza is a bronze fountain, that pours its waters out over a pretty collection of flowers, enclosed within iron railing. From this plaza going to the northward, we might cross the river Rimac over the handsome bridge, and away

* "Geografia del Peru," p. 292.

to the Alameda, or to the Ancon railway station. But I prefer asking my readers to accompany me three squares directly east from Pizarro's palace, along the Calle Arzobispo, or Archbishop Street, to the Plaza de la Independencia, as it is called now, with a statue in its centre, of Bolivar,—one of the great heroes of South American Independence.

This is from a model, the work of the sculptor Adam Tadolini, and was made at Miller's art foundry in Munich. It is of bronze, and has on one side the inscription—

> "To Simon Bolivar,
> The Liberator.
> The Peruvian Nation,
> In the year MDCCCLVIII."

Laterally, at its base, are cut designs of the battles of Ayacucho and Junin. Both of these were fought by Bolivar in 1824, and were amongst the principal incidents conducing to the realization of throwing off the Spanish yoke.

In this square we find likewise the Royal and Pontifical University of San Marcos, founded by Royal Decree in A.D. 1551. As it was finished in 1576, it stands to-day—nearly three hundred years old,—with the exception of some repairs that had to be made after the destructive earthquake of 1746. In this building is the hall now used for sittings of the Chamber of Deputies, the walls of which constitute a mass of most elaborate carved wood-work. This hall was formerly the chapel of the University. The building likewise contains, in present use, the secretary's offices and archives of the Congress—another large saloon given over to the Medical Society—and one for the University's proceedings, which last is used also as a place of meeting for the College of Advocates. "In this hall," says Doctor Fuente,' "there are ninety-two low seats, and seventy-three higher, besides two galleries,—one of them for the canons, the other for the ladies. Its architecture, though old, is substantial and handsome; the upper part of the walls is entirely covered with portraits of former professors and rectors, amongst whom are some persons of distinguished literary merit."

There is, however, another building in this square, about which neither Mr. Paz Soldan nor Dr. Fuentes writes a word, and that is the house with the convex roof in front of the statue of Bolivar, seen in the sketch. Perhaps the memory of it ought to be let perish, or probably I would have said nothing about it if it had been, as it ought to be, at any sacrifice, levelled to the ground. This is the present Senate House, and was formerly the terrible Inquisition tribunal. I visited it one day, and was conducted through the greater portion by the care-taker—the members not being then sitting. The room, in which the terrible Inquisition business was carried on, is now where the representatives congregate. My guide

' Op. cit., p. 46.

PLAZA DE INDEPENDENCIA, WITH STATUE OF BOLIVAR AND CHAMBER OF INQUISITION.

pointed out to me the spot in which the accused were to be put kneeling during their trials. The roof is of most exquisite carving, in the same style as is done in the former refectory of the Jesuits, behind the church of St. Peter, and interior to the National Library. The man could not show me the place where it was said there was machinery for moving the head of a crucified Christ, which was made to confront the accused, and to approve of the sentence by bowing. But I saw and felt enough, during my short visit there, to make me impressed with the conviction, that it was a great mistake of the National Government not to have demolished this building, when they changed the name of Plaza de la Inquisicion, into Plaza de la Independencia.

Besides that of Bolivar there was formerly in the Alameda, at the other side of the river, a statue to Christopher Columbus, which has, recently, been transferred to the open space between the Exhibition Palace and Meiggs' boulevards—in fact, the proper place for it to be, before the eyes of the world, instead of keeping it hidden up as it was before.

There is also a mint in Lima, chiefly under the direction of English engineers. By this we can pass out to the Botanical Gardens, which I am sorry to record are not well attended to.

Lima has from sixty to seventy chapels, to write a description of which would need some volumes, and would, moreover, be a work of supererogation, as it has been often done before.

The chapel of San Pedro, formerly the Colegio Maximo of the Jesuits, was, at the time of Stevenson's visit to Lima, (in the first decade of the present century,) an Oratorio of San Felipe Neri. This is the only description he gives of it, although furnishing elaborate details of many of the other chapels, as of the Cathedral, Saint Lazaro, Santo Domingo, Santa Rosa, and La Merced.

San Pedro had for me many attractions during my twelve months' stay at the Hotel de Maury, only two squares off. These I cannot account for, but I found myself frequently wandering about its precincts. The railings, that are represented as facing it, in Senor Paz Soldan's Geographical Atlas, no longer exist. On a stone near the front of the main entrance door, and about ten feet high, is engraved A.D. 1656,—the date of its construction. The architecture inside at once shows, to the visitor, the beautiful style which characterizes Jesuit buildings all over South America. It occupies a whole square Cuadra* of ground, and the gate entrance to what was formerly the cloisters from the Calle San Pedro brings you into a patio—silent as the catacombs, and deserted as the Sahara. In front is some attempt at remodelling the cloisters, but the brick and mortar seem to have been put up many years ago, although the decayed scaffolding still clings about. Turn to the right, and knock

* Square Cuadra represents a square of 150 yards each way.

gently at the middle door. It will be opened by a venerable old gentleman, very thin, meagre, and feeble-looking, who salutes you courteously, taking off a little skull-cap he wears, and—if you have an introduction to him—who will invite you inside. Here you find yourself in the National Library of Peru, and asked to take a seat by the only occupant of the place with yourself. The old gentleman who let you in, is no other than the celebrated Doctor T. de Paula Gonzalez Vigil, once a Roman Catholic clergyman, till he was excommunicated by the Pope for some of his writings. He is, however, the librarian here; and if you come any time of the day from sun-dawn to sun-down, Dr. Vigil is never absent.

Between this library and the front street is a reading-room, where half a dozen to a dozen newspaper readers are seated. But the library itself consists only of a few thousand books—the greater part of them being religious vellum-bound volumes, and such as only an antiquarian of a theological turn of mind would think of consulting. In the small room here was exhibited, at the period of my first visit, the celebrated painting of the "Funeral of Atahualpa." From this it was taken to the Exhibition Palace. At the opposite end of the library a small door leads into what was the refectory in the time the Jesuits held it, and where there is a ceiling of carved cedar-wood. This is a wonderful work—nearly sixty feet long (the whole length of the room), and well worth the visit of all art-admirers. Returning from the library into the Patio, and walking across it, I see an entablature of copper in the wall, from which I transcribe the following inscription:—" Reynando la Mag. de Philippo iii. N.s. ano de 1617, El Exmo Senor D. Francisco Borja, Principe de Esquillacho, Virrey des estos Reynos mando rredificar este Marmol,* que es la memoria del castigo, que se dio a Francisco de Carabajal. Maes sedo Campo de Gonçolo Pizarro en cuya compania fue alevo y traydoras Virrey y senoral national cuyas cassas se derryvaron y sembraron de Satano de 1548, y este es su solar despues Reynando la Mag. Philippo iii. N.s. El Exmo Senor D. Pedro Toledo y Leyva, Marques de Manchera, Virrey de estos Reynos, Gentilhombre de su Camara y de su consejo de Guerra, estando este Marmol otra vez perdido lo mando renovar ano de 1645." The translation of this old Spanish amounts to a record, that during the reign of his Majesty Philip III., and in the year 1617, Prince Borja, at the time Viceroy out here, sent to renew this marble, which is in memory of the punishment that was given to Don Francisco Carabajal for something in which Satan was again a *particeps*

---

* "Este Marmol" is on the inscription, although the plate is of copper. It would appear to have been done by an illiterate person, but that we must remember the spelling of the Spanish is of the seventeenth century.

criminis in 1548. Once more it was replaced, when the Marquis de Manchera was Viceroy, in 1645; and the tablet from which I copy is, I believe, the identical one last mentioned.

The punishment of Carabajal is thus related by Prescott:[1]—" He was carried to execution on a hurdle, or rather in a basket, drawn by two mules. His arms were pinioned, and as they forced his bulky body into this miserable conveyance he exclaimed, 'Cradles for infants, and a cradle for the old man too, it seems.' Notwithstanding the disinclination he had manifested to a confessor, he was attended by several ecclesiastics on his way to the gallows; and one of them repeatedly urged him to give some token of penitence at this solemn hour, if it were only by repeating the *Pater Noster* and *Ave Maria*. Carabajal, to rid himself of the ghostly [why ghostly?] father's importunity, replied by coolly repeating the words *Pater Noster* and *Ave Maria*. He then remained obstinately silent. He died as he had lived, with a jest, or rather a scoff on his lips."

Turning to the left, beneath the same arcade, I come to a door that was once green, but is now an indescribable colour, from the must of ages. This tells, with a label on the outside, that it is "El Museo Nacional," the National Museum. But there is a padlock on it as large, probably, as any in Newgate, and the porter at the *porte-cochère* does

[1] "History of the Conquest of Peru," p. 418, book v. chap. iv.

not know anything about the key. I made a pilgrimage to the door of this museum scores of times during my residence in Lima, but the lock was always there. Even Dr. Vigil, at the opposite side of the Patio, knew nothing about it, for it was not in his department. After the creation of the Society of Fine Arts, referred to elsewhere, I was one of the committee asked to inspect it, with a view to the removal of its contents to the Exhibition Palace, for the formation of a new museum. But my imagination of these was sadly disappointed. On its walls are hanging portraits of all the Viceroys who formerly governed in Lima. Outside of these the collection of other objects was confined to a few hundred birds, some animal monstrosities of double-headed calves, *et voila tout*. The dozen or two specimens of prehistoric crockery-ware, that it had contained, were already sent to the Exhibition Palace, and the whole was not worth the cost of being removed. I could not help reflecting on this as a cogent illustration of the absence of national taste, to say nothing of national pride, in the city of Lima,—where the large Exhibition Palace could be filled with archæological proofs of the ancient glories of Peru, without going farther than six to eight miles outside the city walls.

At the Museum of the Faculty of Medicine there are not more than from twenty-two to twenty-four skulls of Indians, most of them being abnormal, and the majority picked up by Senor Raimondy in

BRIDGE OF LIMA.

his travels. A few wooden idols complete the contents there. Senor Don Miccno Espantoso has the rarest specimens of pottery-ware that are to be found in Lima, as well as cloth, and ornamental art work, with gold and silver cups, and idols. These are valuable because the owner knows from whence they all came. It is not so, however, with a very large collection left by the late Senor Ferreyras, as the locale whence any of them was obtained is not known. Another lot is in the possession of Senor Cundamarin, formerly Postmaster-General in Lima. A doctor, whose name I forget, and who lives in the Plaza de Bolivar, has some few more. With these I believe I have exhausted the catalogue of holders of the ancient treasures of Peru.

The persistence of the Inca delusion is still carried out in Peru, after a fashion that may be said to border on caricature. Here at Lima, and not far from the principal plaza, I see outside of a photographer's establishment a large cardboard, about a yard square in size, framed and glazed. On it I observe a couple of dozen of figures, of *carte de visite* size, and these are marked underneath "The Incas of Peru." They have all a family likeness in the hats, the large-lobed ears, and the half-pike, half-halberd-looking symbol of authority clutched in the hand. I had passed them by many times, and, after several casual glances, was impressed with the idea, that I had, some time or another, seen them before I came to Peru. When one day scrutinizing more minutely, I at once recognized the models of the vignettes of our ancient English kings—the Williams, Richards, Edwards, and Henrys—that were put at the headings of the chapters descriptive of their reigns in Goldsmith's "History of England." Take off the big ears—which, by the way, the coast tribes cultivated long before the Inca period—dock off a feather or two here and there, and you have the Anglo-Saxon monarchs of our school-boy days doing duty at the present time for the Incas of Peru—the first of whom dates only as far back as the time of William the Conqueror.

Of the hospitals in Lima I cannot speak too

PENITENTIARY OF LIMA.

highly; and without desiring to make any disparagement, feel bound to particularize those of San

Andres and the French hospital,—both cared for in all their excellent *régime* by Sisters of Charity.

The Lima Penitentiary, although unobtrusive in its general features, is one of those institutions which reflect credit, not only on its founder, but on the executive of its administration. The whole foundation and carrying out of this admirable prison is due to the great powers, as well as acute observation, of Senor Don Mariano Felipe Paz Soldan, who, in 1853, commissioned by the Peruvian Government, visited Europe and the United States to make observations on, and take notes of, similar establishments abroad. It would be a difficult matter to convey to any one who had not visited it, a correct idea of the perfect security of this place of confinement. In the centre of the building is a large circular watching-place, from whence radiate outwards, like a star-fish, the several corridors, in which the warders can always see that the prisoners are at their posts. These corridors are two stories high, and the building in its original plan was intended for a thousand cells. But this has been only two-thirds finished. The prisoners are all obliged to work in some useful trade, as carpenters, tailors, cabinet makers, tinkers, and so forth; while the sale of their manufactured work makes no unimportant item in the general daily expenses of the building. The wall enclosing it is thirty-five feet high, and the only entrance by the principal door abuts on the street, facing the Chorillos Railway. Its southern wall is at the other side of the road, opposite to the grand entrance of the Exhibition Palace.

Besides those described, Lima has several other public buildings. Amongst them are eight National colleges; one for the study of jurisprudence; an ecclesiastical seminary; a college for the study of medicine and the accessory sciences; one for secondary instruction; a normal school; a naval and military institute; a college for obstetrics; a school of arts and trades; and an industrial municipal school—the last-mentioned inaugurated by his Excellency Senor Don Manuel Pardo, at the end of last year, before a brilliant assembly of the *élite* of Lima. Moreover, we find an orphan school, lunatic asylum, general cemetery, two theatres, in one of which, "Odeon," the celebrated Italian tragic actor, Ernest Rossi, delighted the Limaneso last year by his Shakespearian performances. Likewise a pit for cockfights (private property), and a bull-fight circus, belonging to the board for relieving the poor,—said to be the largest bull-fight circus in the world. Such is fame!

I cannot help expressing an opinion about what I conceive the imperfect hygienic condition of Lima, although it is in many respects superior to that of Calláo. Formerly those abominable acequias, or aqueducts, running in the centre of the streets, were open, and furnished browsing grounds for the turkey buzzards. Now much of the offensiveness is removed by their being covered over, and converted into sewer-pipes through the town. This is, however, not a system of drainage, in any sense of the word, adapted to such a climate as that of Lima. For at several corners of streets is to be found a kind of trap-door, opened every night at ten o'clock to have the excreta of the inhabitants put therein. No doubt such an arrangement would be comparatively unobjectionable, if there were a perpetual current of water running through, instead of as it is now, most irregularly intermittent. My readers will understand my objection when I remark, that the trap-doors are opened every night to receive the ejecta, whilst it sometimes happens that the water, which is always a puny stream, is not turned on once a week.

Much has been said, and with very good reason, of the beauty of the ladies of Lima. During my two years' residence out there I have seen many of them exceeding, in every grace of womanhood, even the angelic designs in Dr. Fuente's work. But as I know a good deal has been written condemnatory of their moral character,—for which depreciation I believe exists little foundation,—I consider it my duty to protest against such unmanliness.

The author of the latest work that I have seen published about Peru,¹ after a good deal of namby-

¹ "What I saw on the West Coast of South and North

pamby writing of an offensive character, as well as insulting to the religious ceremonies of the Catholic Church in Lima, talks of the beautifully graceful garb of the Lima ladies in olden times, the *Saya y Manta*, as a thing only invented for immorality. He describes the *tapada*, its successor, as a garb of equal, if not greater, foulness in design, and as

SAYA Y MANTA (ANCIENT COSTUME OF LIMA LADIES).

"a device of Paris civilization." He quotes at some length from "*À travers l'Amérique du Sud, par F.*

America, and at the Hawaiian Islands." By H. Willis Baxley, M.D. New York: D. Appleton and Co., 443 and 445, Broadway, 1865.

SWEEPING GENERALIZATION.

Dabadie, Paris, 1859 "—a Frenchman and reputed Roman Catholic—to prove that all the women are bad, but that their badness is inevitable, as of cause and effect from the viciousness of the men—priests and nuns alike included.'

TAPADA (LATER COSTUME OF LIMA LADIES).

What the opportunities of Monsieur Dabadie, or Dr. Baxley may have been, to learn the minutiæ of this state of affairs I cannot say. From the text of Dr. Baxley's work, I should imagine he was not a sufficiently long time in this part of Peru to

"Chastity is more common, and infidelity more uncommon, amongst the Peruvians than in most countries of the old world." (Stevenson, Op. cit., vol. i. p. 390).

permit experience for such a sweeping generalization. I have often heard the changes rung upon the same topic, in reference to Paraguay, the Banda Oriental, and the Argentine Republic, with all of which I am acquainted for fifteen years. And I have no hesitation in saying, from my experience of South America, that not only regarding Peru, but elsewhere within my knowledge, they are perfectly foundationless, and equally untrue.

Without attempting the *tu quoquo* style of argument, I am inclined to believe that any man coming from the United States or Great Britain, and who may know—as who does not?—the condition of the social evil in the large towns, ought not to forget the sublime reminder of Our Saviour, "He that is without sin amongst you, let him first cast a stone." Such a sentiment as is conveyed in the words of Eliza Cook might be no harm for men like Dr. Baxley to study and reflect upon:—

> "Great teaching from a greater Teacher—fit
> To breathe alike to infancy and age.
> No garbled mystery encircles it;
> And noblest hearts have deepest read the page.
> Carve it upon the heart, and temple-arch:
> Let our fierce judges read it as they go:
> Make it the key-note of life's pompous march,
> And trampling steps will be more soft and slow;
> For God's own voice says from the eternal throne,
> Let him that is without sin first cast the stone."

The ladies of Lima, in addition to their unimpeachable *morale*, can count amongst their numbers many of high literary celebrity. When Mr. Markham wrote about Peru, more than twelve years ago, he enumerated, with the press of its capital, the "Revista de Lima,"—"a bi-monthly periodical containing archæological, biographical, historical and financial articles and reviews, generally very ably written in an enlightened and liberal spirit, and by men who evidently take an earnest view of life."[*] This publication did not exist during the greater portion of my residence there, having been doubtless swept away by the vicissitudes of the several revolutions, which intervened between 1860 and 1872. But on the 1st of April, 1873, appeared again the first number of the "Revista de Lima" —not solely directed to literary, but including scientific, and historical, subjects. Amongst its contributors are two Peruvian ladies — the Senoritas Carolina Freire de James, and Juana Manuela Gorsiti. The first-named gives an article on "The Altar Fireside," ("El Hogar,") and a moral essay on charity, with the quotation of "*bis dat qui cito dat*," rendered into Spanish;[†] whilst the second is the authoress of an allegory under the title of "A Drama in Fifteen Minutes."[‡]

During the month of June last, there appeared in the *Nacional*, newspaper of Lima, a series of

[*] Op. cit., p. 310.
[†] "Quien da pronto, da dos veces."
[‡] "Un Drama en quince minutos."

treatises, under the title of "*Conferencias Femininas,*" or "Feminine Discourses," from the pen of a lady, a native of Lima. They were published with the *nom de guerre* of Maria de la Luz, and although I have the pleasure of knowing who the lady is, and that she belongs to one of the first families in Peru, I regret that I do not feel authorized to give the name. The last article of hers that I saw, "On Ethics and Theology," is characterized by lofty thought, eloquent teaching, and epigrammatic reasoning. It also possesses the charm of being peculiarly feminine, for it relates to the sound culture of the female mind in connexion with the domestic virtues, as opposed to the bigotry and intolerance of "feminine inclinations, marked by fits of frantic devotion, alternated with indifferentism and frivolity." All honour should be given to such womanly teaching!

CHAPTER XVI.

Exhibition Palace at Lima.—Originated and inaugurated in President Balta's time of office.—Delays in opening.—Doctor Fuentes its presiding genius.—Situation of the Palace.—Description of contents and of adjacent grounds.—Lack of archæological subjects exhibited.—Mummies at Exhibition.—Magnificent painting by Peruvian artist, Monteros, of the waking of Atahualpa.—Death of the artist of yellow fever in 1868.—Luis Molina's statues of Indian man and woman.—Excellence of execution.—Mosaic tables from Ecuador.—Wonderful clock by Major Don Pedro Ruiz.—Condors in the garden.—Huacas or burial-mounds outside the walls.—Obscure antiquity side by side with modern civilization.—View of Callao from top of Palace.—Absence of President Balta from opening ceremony.—Political storms foreshadowed.

THE National Exhibition Palace at Lima, which was opened on Monday, 1st July, 1872, was sanctioned by vote of Congress in the month of September, 1869, and the building was commenced on the 1st of January, 1870. It was originally expected to have been finished, and the inauguration to take place, on the 1st of July, 1872. But in all South American countries, it may be scarcely necessary to observe, delays such as that just mentioned seem to be a *sine quâ non* of every undertaking.

The originator, as well as planner, of the design of this palace is Doctor Don Manuel a Fuentes, already well known in connexion with his elegantly illus-

trated " Guide to Lima." Its architect was Senor
Don Antonio Leonardo, an Italian; and the total
space allotted to the gardens, palace, machine
show-rooms, theatre, coffee-houses, concert-room,
animal cages, and *parterres* comprises an area of
192,000 metres, or about forty-eight square acres.

PRINCIPAL ENTRANCE TO LIMA EXHIBITION PALACE.

Situated in the suburbs at the southern side of
the Penitentiary, the Exhibition Palace of Lima
is one of the most stately and graceful buildings
in the capital of Peru. It stands at the distance
of about a mile from the principal square, or plaza,
where we see the palace of Pizarro. In front of
the Exhibition house, and within the enclosure, is a
space of 225 metres long by 172½ metres wide. To

it there are three entrances—the principal one, opposite the Penitentiary wall, being used on State occasions. Next to the Chorillos railway are the two entrances for the public, and quite close to where tickets are issued in an adjacent small building. These gates are called the "Santa Maria" and the "Vivanco"—the first in honour of the Minister of the Interior of that name under President Balta, who held office at the time of opening, and the second after General Vivanco, who was President of the Executive Commission, or Board of Directors, entrusted with carrying out the work.

Entering the grand gate you pass by a theatre on the right, with a refreshment-room to the left of the avenue. . Farther on is a conservatory for hot-house plants, with a little Turkish gloriette, in which a cigar can be enjoyed. By a fountain built with the surrounding of large stones— forming a mound on which is a colossal figure, resembling Hercules slaying the Lernæan Hydra— between rows of gas-lamps, and, on the day of opening, amongst a forest of Peruvian banners, thicker than were "leaves in Vallombrosa,"—a walk of 130 metres from the main entrance brings the visitor to the vestibule of the palace. Each front door has a marble Cerberus on its side.

To the right, as you enter, is a room about four yards square, in which, on two tables and in a glass case, are arranged all that was worth bringing from the National Museum of Peruvian antiquities. Mariano Felipe Paz Soldan[1] says the Museum had, when he published his book ten years ago, 5,330 objects of Zoology, antiquities, and so forth. Here we do not see half of the 330, leaving out the 5,000. They consist of mummies in a glass case, some of those which furnish illustrations to Dr. Tschudc's and Senor Rivero's book,[2] and that were obtained at Cajatambo at the other side of the Andes. On one of the walls is painted a great oval face of a deep red colour, backed with yellow and fringed with blue, supposed to be the artist's idea of a presiding Sun. For all these things are credited to the Inca sun-worshippers—although probably many a time the real sun shone over them before ever there was an Inca in the land. One of these mummies is said to have been found at Ayacucho. They are all in the usual squatting posture, and one with a rope round its neck is said to have been executed. In two the hair and teeth are well preserved, the tresses of one—a lady—being as nicely plaited as when she went to her last dinner, route, or dancing party.

Amongst these things exhibited are several water-crofts of prehistoric crockery-ware—cloth of exquisite dye—feather hats, bows and arrows, stone hatchets, and canoe paddles. Here also we

[1] "Geografia del Peru," p. 308, published in 1862.
[2] "Antiquedades Peruanas," published at Vienna in 1851.

EXHIBITION PALACE AT LIMA.

[Vol. I. p. 31.

find the terra-cotta mask, which I have already mentioned as found at Chancay.[1]

Before going up the grand staircase, by which one can mount either to the left or to the right, I am magnetically arrested to gaze on the magnificent large picture by the Peruvian artist, Monteros, representing the funeral rites, or obsequies, of Atahualpa, the last of the Incas. It is the scene which is thus described by Prescott:[2]—"The body of the Inca remained on the place of execution through the night. On the following morning it was removed to the church of San Francisco, where his funeral obsequies were performed with great solemnity. Pizarro and the principal cavaliers went into mourning,[3] and the troops listened, with devout attention, to the service of the dead from the lips of Father Valverde. The ceremony was interrupted by the sound of loud cries, and wailing as of many voices at the doors of the church. These were suddenly thrown open, and a number of Indian women, the wives and sisters of the deceased, rushing up to the great aisle, surrounded the corpse. This was not the way, they cried, to celebrate the rites of an Inca, and they declared their intention to sacrifice themselves on his

---

[1] *Vide* chap. viii., p. 128.
[2] "History of the Conquest of Peru," p. 212.
[3] Crocodile fashion may be supposed, for the man they had murdered.—T. J. H.

tomb, and bear him company to the land of spirits. The audience, outraged by this frantic behaviour, told the intruders that Atahualpa had died in the faith of a Christian, and that the God of the Christians abhorred such sacrifices. They then caused the women to be excluded from the church, and several, retiring to their own quarters, laid violent hands on themselves in the vain hope of accompanying their beloved lord to the bright mansions of the Sun."

It is the incident of forcing the women out of the church by the soldiers that is depicted by the artist.* There is only one painting that I have ever seen that has had the same absorbing enthralling effect upon me as this of Atahualpa, and that is the exquisite portrait of Kemble by Sir Joshua Reynolds, which I used to sit and admire, for hours upon hours, in the National Gallery more than twenty years ago.

This picture by Monteros was executed during his stay at Florence some years past; and the National Congress of Peru presented him with 20,000 soles, or about 4,000*l.* for it in the year 1867. He unfortunately died at Callao during the yellow fever epidemic of 1868.

What pleased me most in this Exhibition was the number of works of art by native artists. Even the excellent carpentry of the prisoners

* The frontispiece to second volume is taken from a photograph of this picture.

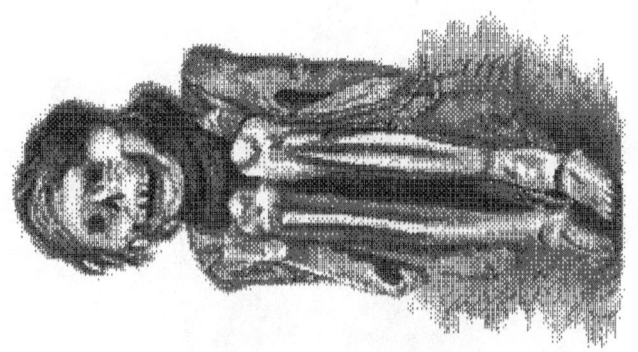
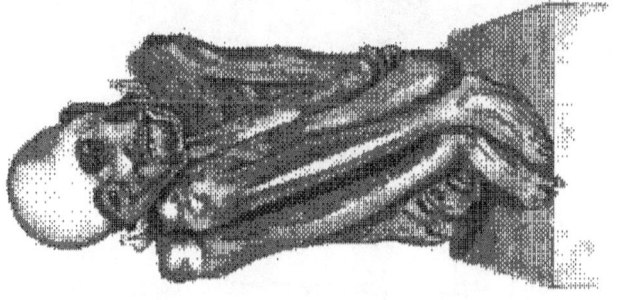

MUMMIES AT THE LIMA EXHIBITION.

CHAP. XVI.]   SELF-EDUCATED ARTIST.   337

in the Penitentiary was a thing of which, if I were a Peruvian, I should be proud.

Passing by the English exhibitions, the like of which can be seen any day in London, Liverpool, Sheffield, Birmingham, or Manchester, I come to a piece of Mosaic work, representing a large square of different classes of wood from Tumbez, by a native artist, Henry Ximenes. In one of the rooms here

GYPSUM STATUE OF INDIAN WOMAN.

we find some exquisitely chiselled figures by an Indian artist of Peru, self-educated, named Luis

Medina,[1] a native of Huamanga in the valley of Ayacucho. They consist of the descent of our Saviour from the cross, in which the artistic arrangement of the grouping is impressive in the extreme. This is small, but it is done in marble from the valley of Medina's birth-place. Of the same material, and in this room, by the same hand is a holy-water pot. In another room we find more of Medina's work in a bust of Coronel Santa Maria, a sleeping Venus of life-size, and two statues,—one of an Indian woman, and the other of an Indian man. These last-named are of gypsum, or sulphate of lime, but for life-like expression, for natural pose—as even the very veins are represented on the leg of the man—these figures are unrivalled.

In one of the corners of the upper story was the model of a mountaineer in clothing made of coarse matting, which they say is the pattern of dress worn by the Indians of old times in crossing the Cordillera. It has a helmet of the same material as the under-dress, in which are holes for the eyes, and an aperture for the mouth to breathe through. Near to this, on the end wall, we pass by an allegorical painting of Peru, representing an Indian of bushy beard, with his hand on the globe, and a hatchet at his feet. He has one arm a-kimbo, and close by is a pillar, on which Liberty is seated. On this pillar are painted the names of

[1] I am glad to mention that Medina got a silver medal and 500 soles, or about 100*l*.

Buenos Ayres, Chile, Colombia, Mexico, Bolivia, and Peru. Over the whole is a streamlet, on which are inscribed—in Spanish of course—the words, "Peru, sovereign and free, the friend of all nations, whilst independent of them!"

GYPSUM STATUE OF INDIAN MAN.

The machinery is too extensive to record here. Amongst it may, however, be noticed a die-stamping machine, from the School of Arts in Lima, done by a student of three years, Don Jacinto Martciorena.

The neighbouring Republics of Chile to the south, and Ecuador to the north, have sent their contributions likewise. Amongst those of the former is a large collection of agricultural products, as well as a steam-engine made by the boys of the Escuela de Artes (School of Arts) in Santiago. From Guayaquil, the chief seaport of Ecuador, are two circular tables, one made of thirty-six different classes of wood, done in Mosaic pattern, to the number of 3,000 pieces. Another of the same kind has 5,000 bits in its composition. The name of the maker is Eurique Jergens, and he has occupied three years in the manufacture of each.

Passing out into the garden, one cannot help feeling puzzled, amongst such an *embarras des richesses*, to discriminate as to what had best be noticed. But Peruvian art claims the first place. Quite close to the refreshment-room is a house, having a convex roof, which is the locale of a clock. This timepiece is the work of a native Peruvian, Major Don Pedro Ruiz. He spent six years in its manufacture. Besides the dial for indicating the hours are six others to show the days of the week, the months, phases of the moon, historical data, equinoxes, years, and centuries. It likewise marks the leap-year. It presents historical pictures by its revolutions. There are thirteen bodies of wheels, requiring to be wound up at different intervals; those of the hours every twelve days; those of the years and centuries need to be wound up only once in thirty-two years. Attached to the clock by its machinery is a barrel-organ, which, regulated by a spring, plays only two airs, the Peruvian National Hymn, and the more popular air, the "Dos de Mayo," or 2nd of May.

The tower, which contains this clock, is of an arched form at the top, being about sixty feet high at its loftiest point, with a breadth of fifty feet. There is a bell on each extern side; that on the right to strike the quarters; that on the left to chime the half-hours. On the front, near the top, are painted the Peruvian arms, under which are two dials. One of these has printed on it "The Congress of 1868," and "His Excellency Don Jose Balta protected this work." The other presents "Begun in 1866, and concluded in 1872, by Pedro Ruiz."

I have been particular in describing this work, because, for a man with such limited means at his disposal to cultivate the art of clockmaking, as must necessarily be in the way of a major in any South American army, it reflects the highest credit on his native genius.

Amongst the birds in the Exhibition gardens are a few Condors, which seem, in cages, to be out of their element, from what Mrs. Hemans describes,—

"Their high Peruvian solitudes among."

More anomalous still is what greets my eyes, as,

returning to the building, I see from the topmost roof the shipping in the Bay of Callao, and, not more than a stone's throw from the outer wall, the ruins of some huacas, or burial-mounds. A writer in "Chambers' Journal"[*] observes truly of such an anachronism as we have here, "There is more mystic solemnity attached to the absolutely obscure antiquity of these records of the past in the New World than to even the most venerable records of the Old. The latter have an unbroken sequence of traditions and history. They are links in the great process of time, and events. We understand, or think we understand them. But these New World mysteries puzzle us, existing, in their unfathomable antiquity, side by side with all that is modern and most full of change—evidences of extinct races, which lived unconscious of the existence of half the planet, as half the planet was of them."

Although we have all that here side by side, we can say to-day amidst the Palace grounds—*tout cela est changé*. Whilst the Peruvian nation is not only no longer unconscious of half the world, or half the world of it, but is rapidly shaking off the hereditary bondage of exclusiveness, and by its railways, its telegraphs, and its Exhibition Palace, is taking its proper place on the map of the world.

[*] "Chambers' Edinburgh Journal," part xcvi., December 30, 1871, p. 765.

Amongst any other people than one of the passive, unexcitable nations of South America, the absence of his Excellency President Balta would have given rise to a sad discouragement at the opening of the Exhibition. For he was known to be at his palace, only half a dozen squares off, and yet he sent Minister Santa Maria to represent him in the official programme of the inauguration. Many of those retrospective prophets, whom one meets every day, have since that time said, how *they* knew he was in fear of the moral thunder-cloud, that was gathering over his head, and which burst with such unexampled fury in less than a month after this event on the capital of Peru.

END OF VOL. I.

www.ingramcontent.com/pod-product-compliance
Lightning Source LLC
Chambersburg PA
CBHW032020220426
43664CB00006B/309